JUST CAN'T

GET ENOUGH

THE STEVE COOPER YEARS

CHRISTIAN BROWN

First edition

Publisher name: CB Publishing 2024

PICTURE CREDITS

Cover photo – Ritchie Sumpter

All other images are from the author

Ebook ISBN: 978-1-0685569-0-6

Paperback ISBN: 978-1-0685569-1-3

Hardback ISBN: 978-1-0685569-2-0

For Dad and for those who dare to dream

TABLE OF CONTENTS

"There's the easy way, the hard way and the Forest way"
Lee Clarke, Red Side of the Trent

PROLOGUE

I'm sure that everyone remembers the first time they were taken to watch a game as a kid. Well, at least in some capacity. I certainly remember bits of my first game. Saturday May 1, 1999 was the first time that I, aged just five, stepped into The City Ground for the first time, walking up the steps and being exposed to a luscious green pitch with some white markings and four stands I still refer to as home to this day. We'd not long been officially relegated from the Premiership (as it was known then), but we defeated Sheffield Wednesday 2-0 thanks to goals from Alan Rogers and Hugo Porfirio.

It was certainly an eventful first game for me to go, as Mark Crossley also saved a penalty that day – to which I was completely unaware, as everyone around me stood up to celebrate and I'd not yet mastered the art of standing on your seat. All I know is that I absolutely adored that experience and legend has it, five-year-old me turned to my Dad after entering the ground and said, with the graceful cheek and innocence children have, "Man United? Never!" Considering United wrapped up the treble a few weeks after, it maybe wasn't the wisest choice of allegiance...

Regardless, everyone who grows up interested in football wants to play for their team and dreams of putting pen to paper on a contract for them, but little do they know that they mentally sign a contract for life with the club that they love at the very moment they see that pitch in all its glory. An unbreakable pact of devotion and loyalty, stronger than any marriage, relationship or arrangement, is forged the second you reach that top step as a wide-eyed child. Once you're in, you're in. There's no turning back and you stick with that club through happiness and sorrow for the rest of your life, through success and pain and through thick and thin. In Forest's case, it has certainly been a case of thin, thinner and thinner still.

You see, supporting Nottingham Forest has been...challenging, to put it mildly, for anyone born in or after 1993. Obviously not as challenging as following clubs who have gone to the wall, but it's all relative. Maybe Brian Clough, unable to walk on water any longer, had used up the last of whatever magic he convinced the footballing gods to sprinkle over Trentside as he emotionally bid farewell following relegation in the inaugural Premier League campaign that year. Maybe the resurgence led by Frank Clark for the following two years was just an Indian summer of sorts, while Dave Bassett's promotion winning side offered a mere flashback of days gone by.

In any case, since relegation in 1999, there hasn't been a lot to be enthused by. There were moments, granted. Paul Hart's side in 2002/03 is the first Forest team I properly fell in love with and to this day, Andy Reid remains my favourite Forest footballer. Billy Davies' first spell was great too, with Forest going a whole calendar year unbeaten at home in the league and securing that achievement by battering rivals Derby County 5-2 on a magical night under the lights at The City Ground. Other than that though, it's been slim pickings to put it mildly.

Whether it be administration threats (on more than one occasion), play-off heartbreak (also on more than one occasion), or the indignity of relegation to a tier the club hadn't been in for 54 years (thankfully only once), it's certainly been a character building time and two decades is a long time to be away from the bright lights of the top flight. Of course, no-one has a divine right to be there, but there are some who believe that a club like Forest, with those glistening two stars above their badge to commemorate winning the European Cup twice, should be there mixing it up with the elite. As fans, we certainly do.

In the club's quest to do so, however, you could be forgiven for referring to Forest as False Dawn FC. See, it's never been boring supporting Forest, but every time it seemed we had our house in order, every time it felt we were ready, every time we believed we had a team that could compete, someone would somehow find a way to smash the self-destruct button – sometimes repeatedly – and dash our hopes and dreams for that year in the process. It was an art form that we'd seem to have perfected.

However, that all changed on the 21st night of September in 2021. Maybe Earth, Wind and Fire were onto something with that lyric after all, as it was on that day that Steve Cooper was announced as Nottingham Forest's head coach. Little did we as fans know at that point that the Welshman would find a way to bring the good times back. Maybe he dug up a box of hidden fairy dust left in Clough's former office, or maybe, as Coops bedded himself into the fabric of the club, community and city, he found a way to conjure it up himself.

For a club that is built on the premise of miracles, he discovered a way to generate two. The magic carpet ride we were taken on from September 21, 2021 to December 19, 2023 can never be forgotten and is something that all Forest fans will forever be grateful for, but especially by a certain generation of fans. Specifically, my generation of Forest fans. The children of the disastrous Fawaz Al-Hasawi era, the youth that kept coming to games even though we lurched from one chaotic year to another, the kids that were dragged by their parents to spend their weekends watching Forest play Carlisle United, Cheltenham Town or Walsall in League One.

Those that came before at least had the glory days to look back on to comfort themselves; they could warmly reminisce about those nights in Munich and Madrid, or winning the league at Coventry. They could think back to Brian Rice chipping the keeper at Highbury to beat Arsenal, or when Forest battered United 4-0 at Old Trafford en route to the title. Or the days lifting trophy after trophy after trophy at the old Wembley, when trips to the Home of Football became as regular for the people of Nottingham as the annual Goose Fair. Or the Bryan Roy and Stan Collymore link-up that ravaged just about all who came before them as Forest finished third in the Premiership in 1995. Or even how good Kevin Campbell and Pierre van Hooijdonk were as a pair as Forest ran away with the second tier in the 1997/98 season.

And they could do so with big, white Colgate smiles as they remembered better days, days where the club weren't being consigned to defeat by the likes of Paul Peschisolido, Rudy Gestede, Stephen Dobbie or Jordan Rhodes. We couldn't. We hadn't experienced those days, barring the odd third round cup game. Sure, we'd all seen the grainy VHS tapes of Forest lifting lots of silverware and of course there's a huge sense of pride in that, but it doesn't quite make up for seeing weak minded players, light years away from the quality of those successful teams, who played as if it was alright to lose so long as they'd ran around a bit.

In fairness to the older fans, that last part was just as infuriating for them as it was for the rest of us, but at least they had warm and fuzzy memories to hold onto for those miserable defeats. I also feel it's important to stress that no-one gets into football for glory as no matter how hard the elite try and ringfence it, it's a cyclical sport. It's incredibly rare for one team to keep winning for decades on end and even glory hunters who support teams like Manchester United or Liverpool, without knowing where either Manchester or Liverpool is on a map, do so knowing they aren't guaranteed to win a trophy every year.

But, as fans, you just want a taste of it. You just want your team to be competitive, to give their all, to mix it up with the best and to go as far as possible. For years, it felt like Forest were simply incapable of doing that. And to be honest, I reckon even some of the older guard probably thought we might never be able to do so again...until Cooper arrived. And that is why I wanted to write this book. I wanted to relive the best time supporting my club (so far). I wanted to put down in words what happened, as it's so meaningful to me and fans of all ages. The younger ones who this was all new for and the older ones who got to relive their youth as Forest landed punches against top flight sides one more time.

You see, the transformational impact Cooper had on this football club cannot be understated. It wasn't just a case of winning football matches, ending hoodoos or going deep in the cups. It was so much more than that. The connection that Steve had with the fans was so unique in today's game. It felt at times like we would go into battle for him if he'd asked us to. And we did, in other ways – namely by making The City Ground one of the most intimidating places to go to in the entire country. You only have to look at Forest's home record under Cooper to see how important that connection was.

The secret for that? He made fans feel valued. So often in modern football, fans are treated as customers – viewed by businesspeople with no football background whatsoever as numbers on a piece of paper that go to games and leave clutching bags of merchandise. It gets worse the higher up the leagues you go and you only need to look at some of the Premier League teams in London to see how far the game can go from its working class roots. But with Cooper, it all felt so different. It's a cliché, but he made us feel like a 12th player and it's something we revelled in.

This never wavered, even when there were bad times. How many clubs can say they'd be singing their manager's name non-stop at 3-0, 4-0, 5-0 or 6-0 down? If that isn't testament to a man who became a much loved adopted son of Nottingham, then what is? He was someone who understood us. He understood the club and treated it with the respect it deserved. He understood the city – whether it was visiting community projects or whether it was wearing designer clothes made in Nottingham. He just got it. And ultimately, he had our back and we had his – right until the very end.

It was a truly special journey and it created a bond that will never be broken. No matter what direction Forest go in and no matter how successful managers are at the club, it's difficult to envision a world where that bond is replicated. Naturally, successful managers will be appreciated and should someone take Forest back to where the current Greek ownership wants them to be, they're obviously not going to be unpopular. But given there's an element of 'gun for hire' with managers that Cooper simply didn't have, I remain unconvinced that they could galvanise a fanbase in the way that he did.

I hope I'm wrong, of course. But in the meantime, it's time to take a trip down memory lane and we'll start right to the beginning of the 2021/22 season...

CHAPTER ONE – "WELL, IT'S GROUNDHOG DAY...AGAIN"

The start of the 2021/22 Championship season felt different than other seasons – and I don't mean because of the usual pre-season pondering as to where the team will finish over the next nine months, or who they're going to sign. No, the start of the 2021/22 season was special because for the first time since a particularly damaging 3-0 home defeat to Millwall on March 6 2020, Forest fans were allowed back into stadiums after the Covid-19 pandemic. The pandemic was tough on everyone and for football fans, matchdays was one of the hardest things to go without.

The iFollow era offered some release from the doom and gloom, but it just wasn't the same. It never could be. So much about going to football isn't about the game itself, which sounds very silly, but it's true. Obviously how the 90 minutes transpire is a huge part, but going to games is also about the people you go with. It's about the chat on the way in, bumping into people you weren't expecting to see at the ground and having a drink with your mates before the game. It's about going through your favourite turnstile, seeing stewards who have been working at the ground as long as you've been going, soaking in the atmosphere, flicking through the programme, belting out Mull of Kintyre with 30,000 others and then getting food after the game, which is either celebratory or something to cheer you up depending on how Forest have fared.

All these things make up your matchday experience; it isn't just the 11 players in Garibaldi red who will make or break your weekend. Having that experience stripped away was soul destroying and left a mental toll on so many, so just to be able to be back in the ground again was something hugely positive to cling onto ahead of the upcoming season. That was just as well, because let's face it, the Forest team certainly weren't giving much reason to be positive. The 2020/21 season was a total disaster; one that started with the hangover from hell after the infamous Stoke City implosion and ended with the Reds seemingly miles away from a top six charge down in 17th.

Most of the season was like watching a car crash in slow motion and at numerous points, it felt like relegation could be on the cards. Popular manager Sabri Lamouchi was sacked after losing his first four games of the season, but really, he probably should've been sacked after the aforementioned Stoke debacle. For those unaware, on the final day of the 2019/20 season, Forest sat in sixth place, which is the final play-off spot (more on them shortly). Even despite encountering poor form – Forest were winless in five before the final day – they needed just a point from the last game of the season to secure their place in the play-offs. In fact, the Reds could afford to lose as not only were they three points clear of seventh placed Swansea City, but they also had a better goal difference by +5.

Amazingly, even by Forest standards of getting things disastrously wrong, they managed to screw it up. A 4-1 defeat at home to Stoke, while Swansea ran out 4-1 winners at Reading, meant that in the most improbable of circumstances, Forest missed out on the play-offs. The importance of finishing in the top six of the Championship is huge. The play-offs in the Championship take place between the teams who finished between third and sixth, with third playing sixth, fourth playing fifth and the winners of each tie go to Wembley for a showpiece final. The winner of said final gets promoted to the Premier League, so to throw away a chance of doing that on the final day was gut-wrenching.

The Athletic reported that Forest owner Evangelos Marinakis ummed and ahhed about sacking Lamouchi there and then, but opted to show patience and backing instead, which he did to the tune of 10 new first team players. However, after Lamouchi went 10 games without a win across two seasons, the former France international found himself out of a job within a month of the season starting.

In came Chris Hughton, Forest's 19th permanent managerial appointment since relegation in 1999, to steady the ship and to his credit, that's exactly what he did. It was far from pretty (37 goals in 46 league games) and expectations had to be reset after Lamouchi's start, but in the end, it was at least job done – Forest were safe and could at least kick on the following season. That being said, going from a serious play-off contender to a side flirting with relegation didn't go down well with the Forest fanbase, who were already starting to lose patience with Hughton.

It is very possible that the frustration of not being able to go to games spilled over for fans and maybe caused them to get on Hughton's back faster than normal, which would be very understandable, albeit a tad unfair. As such, having fans back gave Hughton the chance to be formally introduced to the Forest faithful, which could only be a good thing. The new season also gave Hughton the chance to have a bit of a reset and get Forest playing football in the way his previous Newcastle United and Brighton & Hove Albion teams did, so pre-season that year had a bit more excitement than normal. Maybe with a few smart signings, Forest could get back to being a play-off contender again.

Pre-season was largely positive, with Forest beating Port Vale and Northampton Town 2-0, while they drew 2-2 with Crewe Alexandra having been 2-0 up. You can never read too much into pre-season, hence why the 2-0 lead at Crewe being blown wasn't really that big a deal. Instead, fans were more pleased with the fact Forest had scored two a game for three games and that academy graduate Brennan Johnson was taking his opportunity after a brilliant loan spell at Lincoln City in the 20/21 season, which saw him score 13 goals in 49 games.

This was important as Johnson, son of former Forest striker David, hadn't fully won over Hughton. In fact, according to The Athletic, Hughton didn't think that Johnson was ready for a full season in the Championship, which was frankly bizarre given his Lincoln return. Had Forest signed a 20-year-old who'd replicated Johnson's form in League One, it would be seen as a very smart investment, but for some reason, there were doubts from management. In addition to that, enigmatic winger Sammy Ameobi had left the club at the end of the previous season, so there was a clear pathway for Johnson in the first team.

Another cause for optimism though was the arrival of Dane Murphy as CEO. The American had been instrumental in Barnsley's recent turnaround, with the Tykes surviving by the barest of margins in his first year (2019/20 season), only to finish in the play-offs in his second, where they lost in the semis to Swansea. Their recruitment had been very good under his watch, from both a player and manager perspective, so it felt like this was a smart move from Marinakis.

Especially given George Syrianos, who had a more data led approach, had joined the club as Head of Recruitment a few months prior. Syrianos boasted a very impressive CV from his time in the Bundesliga and seemed a real coup for Forest. That being said, it felt like recruitment had taken a bit of a backseat as by that stage, Forest had only signed one first team player and that was a back-up goalkeeper in Ethan Horvath, who was presumably a Murphy recommendation given his American nationality.

This was also a slight concern given the club only had Jordan Gabriel, fresh from a loan spell at Blackpool in League One, at right back. However, the focus wasn't on transfers for very long as friendlies against Aston Villa and Burnley had to be cancelled due to a Covid outbreak in the Forest side, which meant that the Reds effectively had to take a week off. This threw a huge spanner in the works for preparation for their first Championship game of the season, which was away at Coventry City on August 8. The blow was somewhat softened with the arrival of Philip Zinckernagel on loan from Watford, who was capable of playing down both flanks or in the number 10 role, but it raised the fear that Forest might be undercooked going into the game.

When it came though, the feeling of being back in a ground was just wonderful. There were 3,784 Forest fans at The Ricoh Arena that day and just to be able to be there, with no masks or social distancing, felt like we'd taken a step back towards normality. Forest started well and it felt like a new dawn. The Reds looked a lot brighter and a lot more forward thinking than they'd done the previous season and the early signs were good. They got a whole lot better when Loic Mbe Soh broke the lines with a pass to Johnson after 36 minutes, who then proceeded to carry the ball down the right at pace for a good 40 yards before cutting a ball back brilliantly for Lyle Taylor to slot home. Bedlam.

There will never be a time, regardless of what league Forest are in, where the Reds take the lead with the first goal of the game and it isn't celebrated wildly. It's a feeling you wish you could bottle up and if someone finds a way to do so, they'll become very, very rich. It's just pure euphoria and the roar from that away end will be something that stays with me for a long time – the sight of strangers hugging each other, people running down to the bottom of the stand to celebrate, an outpouring of noise...yeah, football was back. When half-time rang out, it was a happy away end. Forest were playing well, deserved their goal and Johnson had stepped up.

Sadly, this wave of positivity didn't last. Within minutes of the second half starting, it was clear that Forest were going to try and see the game out, without offering much in return. This worked for about 20 minutes before the players started to tire rapidly and Coventry gained momentum. This was their first game back in Coventry for two years, after a legal fall out with their owners and they weren't going to let their first game back end in defeat. Once Ben Sheaf rattled the crossbar from distance, their fans started to sense it, with their rendition of 'Twist and Shout' booming from all corners of the ground relentlessly.

As the clock hit the 80 minute mark, Forest were hanging on for dear life and when Callum O'Hare nutmegged Jack Colback out wide and darted inside, there was a sense of inevitability about what was coming next. O'Hare's low driven ball sparked pinball in the Forest box, before the ball eventually fell to Viktor Gyökeres, whose deflected effort looped over goalkeeper Brice Samba. The home crowd erupted and their players smelt blood, but Forest stubbornly held firm...until the 96th minute.

Midfielder Ryan Yates needlessly fouled O'Hare in a dangerous area and the resulting free kick found Dominic Hyam, who forced Samba into a save from a header. As the ball rebounded to Kyle McFadzean, he fired goalbound and Samba initially looked like he'd dealt with it, but it immediately became apparent he'd made a rare error. Instead of parrying away, he'd palmed the ball into the ground and as he'd done so, it had looped over both him and the line almost in slow motion as he desperately tried to claw it out. With pretty much the last kick of the game, Coventry got their fairytale win back home and Forest left with nothing.

Naturally, Hughton blamed the result on tiredness and the situation, which he had every right to do so as on this instance, he was probably right. For now, the pitchforks were kept in the shed by the Forest fans, but the murmurs of discontent were growing. They at least subsided briefly as the club finally addressed the right back position by signing Jordi Osei-Tutu on loan from Arsenal, while a day later, the Reds defeated Bradford City 2-1 in their first home fixture with fans for nearly 18 months, as a João Carvalho double saw them progress to the next round of the Carabao Cup.

A first league match with fans inside The City Ground was also on the horizon as AFC Bournemouth were in town. The day started off well enough and Hughton received a warm reception when he emerged from the tunnel to give the stadium a clap and the first Mull of Kintyre with a mostly full crowd was magical, but pretty much straight from kick off, Bournemouth controlled the game as Forest looked to contain a youthful Cherries side and after half an hour, the visitors broke the deadlock.

Bournemouth winger David Brooks had the ball on the halfway line and picked out Dominic Solanke, who just held the ball under no pressure on the edge of the Forest box, before playing it back into Brooks, who hadn't stopped running and proceeded to lift it over Samba and into the net. Forest responded well at least, with Taylor winning the ball on halfway and allowing Yates to run unchallenged into the Bournemouth half, where his fearsome effort rattled the inside of the post, but that was about all Forest managed to muster up in the first half.

The second half started very brightly, though. Brooks fouled Johnson out wide and from the resulting free kick, Zinckernagel's ball in was headed home by Scott McKenna. The first league goal back at The City Ground with fans and it was one of those moments where 25,000 fans felt like 250,000. The roar from A Block, Lower Bridgford making a racket, seeing the Trent End rise again...at this point, the fans started to sense something was coming. With the momentum from the goal, it felt like the three points were there for the taking. However, misfortune struck once again.

Philip Billing picked out Jaiden Anthony and while Anthony's pass into space back to him was good, the angle was well against Billing for a shot as he was wide of the six-yard box, with the near post completely covered. The best he could hope for really was a corner, or so everyone thought. Billing shot anyway and the ball inexplicably found its way through Samba and in the back of the net. Out of nothing, Bournemouth had their advantage back, but just two minutes later, Brooks found himself sent off for picking up his second yellow card.

With half an hour left against 10 men and with the home crowd behind them, the game was suddenly very much back in Forest's favour. Or...so it should've been. Bournemouth had the ball in the net again not long after, but Forest were spared by the assistant's offside flag. It was hard to tell at times who had 10 and who had 11, as Forest seemed to have no idea how to break through. The closest they came was when Lewis Grabban headed against the bar, but that was also flagged for offside. A late Zinckernagel effort was parried wide by goalkeeper Mark Travers, but that's all Forest could offer before the ref blew for full-time.

While one of the main topics of discussion was how Samba's form had fallen off a cliff, the discontent murmurings about Hughton were getting louder. For the second season in a row, Forest had lost their opening two league games, but what made it more frustrating was the manner of them. Blowing a 1-0 lead with 10 to go and failing to lay a glove against a team with 10 men for half an hour isn't good by anyone's standards, especially for a manager who hadn't been taken in by the fans. Luckily for him and for Forest, the nature of the Championship means another game is never far away and just a few days after the Bournemouth loss, they were back on Trentside to host Blackburn Rovers.

The signs it would be a frustrating evening were evident when Osei-Tutu, on his debut, had to be subbed off injured after 17 minutes. Given Forest's shortages at full back, academy boy Fin Back made his debut, with Gabriel switching to left back. Things looked like going from bad to worse when Joe Rothwell breezed past three Forest players before putting it on a plate for John Buckley, but against all odds, the attacking midfielder was thwarted by an outstanding stop from Samba. That save was just as well as Forest had offered nothing aside from one speculative Zinckernagel effort from distance that forced a save from Thomas Kaminski. Somehow, it was still 0-0 at the break, but it didn't stay 0-0 for very long.

Straight after half-time, a Harry Pickering free-kick was whipped in from wide and former Forest loanee Daniel Ayala haunted his old club as he steered his header into the bottom corner. This seemed to inject some life into Forest at least and a Johnson ball was zipped across the six-yard box to Yates, but his first touch let him down and the chance was gone. By this point, the home crowd were beginning to become restless. Thankfully for Hughton, they were eased not long after, as Zinckernagel decided enough was enough and let fly from 25 yards out, finding the bottom corner with immense precision. It felt like the only way Forest were going to score was with something special and the Watford loanee had provided it.

Bizarrely, there seemed no real urgency for Forest to push for the win. It was like Hughton was happy to settle for a point at home and given what happened in the Coventry game, it made no sense to play that way. It was therefore inevitable what would happen and with 86 minutes on the clock, it came. What was a surprise though, was the comedy or errors that took place when it happened. Harrison Chapman's free kick from the right was floated in and when Samba went to claim it, he spilled it outside the box and fell over. As he was retreating, Hayden Carter kept the move alive by crossing in and seemed to find both Darragh Lenihan and former Forest man Ben Brereton Díaz, with a combination of the two heading the ball goalbound. Gabriel valiantly defied that attempt, but the rebound fell to Lenihan, who nodded home into an empty net. To make matters worse for Forest, Gabriel was sent off for a second bookable offence a few minutes after, as his late lunge caught Chapman.

Now the pitchforks were starting to come out for Hughton. To his credit after the game, he said it was on him to make sure the team gets results, but also banged the drum for reinforcements. However, that wasn't going to wash and for the first time, it felt like he wouldn't even be in a job long enough to get reinforcements in as the fans were furious. There was also concern over Samba's form, which was worryingly poor and was costing Forest goals. Nevertheless, the Forest board and Murphy remained calm for the time-being and up next was a trip to Stoke City.

To say that Forest didn't turn up would be something of an understatement. From kick off, it was clear that the plan was to try and nick a 0-0, which was going to be an ask with Back, an academy boy thrown into the deep end, starting his first game for Forest. However, he and the back four fared very well. Stoke had a lot of the ball but couldn't really find a way to test Samba in the first half, but again Forest had offered absolutely nothing. They had Zinckernagel, Carvalho and Alex Mighten behind Taylor, but they had zero service whatsoever. It was a pathetic, lifeless and languid display, with Yates in particular looking way out of his depth, but the whole team seemed unable to complete a pass, let alone pass forward or move into space.

Stoke seemed to realise that and in the second half, stepped it up a gear. It soon led to what would be the only goal of the game, as a beautiful flowing move involving at least five Stoke players and featuring some brilliant one touch play ended with Mario Vrancic playing in Josh Tymon to fire home. Stoke had pulled the entire Forest defence apart and it was the sort of front foot football you'd happily pay to watch as a fan. For the 2,679 Forest supporters, it was the type of play they'd been starved of for too long and when Samba denied a certain goal from Steven Fletcher, they started to make their feelings known. Not even the introduction of Grabban and Johnson off the bench to try and salvage something could prevent the discontent.

By the time the ref's whistle blew for full-time, those feelings went to a new decibel as the standard cheer from the home fans after a win was drowned out by a crescendo of boos from the away end. Forest hadn't mustered a single shot on target and the fans were livid. For the second season in a row, they'd lost their first four games. For the second season in a row, any aspirations for promotion were shelved. For the second season in a row, it was worrying about how to stay up. As for Hughton, that was him done with the fans. There was no way back at that point and more alarmingly, it seemed like the players were done with him as well.

Shortly after the game, a series of WhatsApp messages from a Forest player surfaced on social media. To say they were uncomplimentary of the manager ("he's clueless"), his tactics ("I'm running round like a cunt up top pressing with no fucking help from the centre midfielders and no stepping up from the defenders") or the player's teammates – especially Yates ("never passes the ball forward") – would be something of an understatement. The Athletic would later confirm these messages were real, although they didn't state who the player in question was.

The fan anger subsided briefly when popular midfielder James Garner returned on loan from Manchester United the next day. Garner had been instrumental in Forest's survival the previous season and to have a player of that calibre back was a huge boost. What made it sweeter was that Garner had rejected other clubs to return, including Forest's fierce rivals Derby County. This was especially notable as Derby's manager was United legend Wayne Rooney, who presumably felt his contacts with his former club would've swayed Garner.

Ironically, it was Derby up next in the league for Forest, but before that was a home tie with Wolverhampton Wanderers in the Carabao Cup. Forest basically fielded a reserve side for the match, with Back, Baba Fernandes, Ateef Konate, Riley Harbottle, Jayden Richardson, Tyrese Fornah and Oli Hammond all starting, which was a source of pride for the club in a sense given they were all academy graduates. Horvath also started, but a strong Wolves side were ruthless. Goals from Roman Saïss, Daniel Podence, Francisco Trincao and Morgan Gibbs-White secured a 4-0 win for the visitors.

All real focus though was on the trip to Pride Park, the home of Forest's hated rivals. The mood going into the game was not good by any stretch. Amazingly, it had been 1,413 days since Derby had last beaten Forest – a 2-0 win in October 2017 courtesy of goals from Matej Vydra and David Nugent. The eight games played after that had seen five draws (indeed, the last three meetings were all 1-1 draws) and three Forest wins, but many fans feared that run would be coming to an end with the way Forest were playing.

However, Derby also had their fair share of trouble. It was widely known that they were in serious hot water with the English Football League (EFL) due to chairman Mel Morris' running of the club and it remained to be seen whether that would lead to points deductions or not, with the threat of administration also looming. Rooney was doing a decent job of putting that to one side though, with the Rams only losing one of their first four games and not many would've bet against them taking the bragging rights from the East Midlands Derby.

As a fan, the week leading up to that game is never pleasant at the best of times, let alone when you've lost four league games on the bounce. The thought of that becoming five after losing to Derby was just horrific and didn't bear thinking about. Separated by the A52 (or the A5-2 to some Forest fans, in homage of a truly magnificent 5-2 victory over the Rams in 2010), the two clubs are connected indefinitely by the genius that is Brian Clough, with the great man achieving unparalleled success at both clubs, but truly detest everything else about each other. It's the one game you simply do not lose, for either side.

Relations between the two sides at board level were put under the microscope as well, given Forest had bid several times – unsuccessfully – for Derby's left back Lee Buchanan. It seemed as if Morris was willing to cut off his nose to spite his face given their financial issues and it was interesting that Buchanan didn't start the game just a few days before the window closed, with Rooney instead opting for Craig Forsyth. The first chance came to Forest as a loose Nathan Byrne backpass was picked up by Taylor, but his tame shot was saved by Kelle Roos. It wasn't long before the game took a turn, as Forsyth deliberately elbowed Zinckernagel, but somehow wasn't shown a red card as none of the officials clocked it.

Forest's frustration soon turned to outright anger as six minutes later, Forsyth picked out the run of Tom Lawrence, played onside by Forest defender Gaetan Bong, who promptly fired home. Forsyth arguably shouldn't have even been on the pitch, but had played a huge role in putting the Rams 1-0 up. The ref seemed in a generous mood though and evened it up pretty swiftly. Bong's shanked clearance in the box was basically caught by defender Joe Worrall, but the referee didn't give a penalty to the home side.

After half-time, Derby continued to be the better side and Forest were given a scare when Kamil Jóźwiak hit the outside of the post with an effort outside the box. Forest grew into the game though and much like before, needed to go a goal down before deciding to play. Grabban forced Roos into a smart stop with a cheeky flick after a well worked move down the left, but Derby didn't heed their warning. With eight minutes to go, Bong's cross was allowed to bounce by Jack Stretton, falling kindly at Johnson's feet on the volley. Johnson lashed his right boot at it and Roos was unable to stop it from nestling in the back of the net. That was Johnson's first goal for the club and it had come in the backyard of the enemy – the stuff dreams are made of.

Forest now had all the momentum and you could see the panic among the faces of the Derby fans. The match suddenly had echoes of only Forest's second ever win at Pride Park; a 2-1 victory in 2015, where they came from behind to score twice in the final 15 minutes of the game, first through Britt Assombalonga on 75 and then through a dramatic Ben Osborn strike in stoppage time. There was still time for Forest to find a winner, but it appeared Hughton didn't feel the same way. Despite having the ascendancy, Forest sat off and the remaining time sort of fizzled into a non-event. While a fourth 1-1 draw in succession against the Rams allowed the person running the Days since Derby beat Forest Twitter/X account to breathe a little easier, it felt like a missed chance for Forest.

It also felt like a chance missed for Hughton to redeem some stock with the fans and probably new CEO Murphy, who must've been pulling his hair out at the brand of football served up. Hughton did have someone fighting for him at board level in the form of Forest chairman Nicholas Randall QC, who claimed that Forest were "the envy of Premier League clubs in securing his services" before the Bournemouth game, but with the club now at the international break, this was the optimum time to make a change. Hughton had mustered one point from a possible 15, but Marinakis – much like he did with Lamouchi – showed patience and backing in the transfer market instead.

First, former Derby man Max Lowe came in on loan from Sheffield United. This was important as despite Bong's assist against Derby, it was clear that he couldn't be trusted to be first choice left back, whereas Lowe definitely could. It also marked an end to Forest's pursuit of current Derby left back Buchanan, though Lowe was arguably a better option in the short-term. Then on transfer deadline day, Forest got very busy. Paraguay international midfielder Braian

Ojeda signed on a permanent basis from Olimpia, along with right back Mohamed Dräger from Olympiacos and winger Xande Silva from West Ham United.

Forest did see a reported £4m move for striker Josh Maja fall through at the 11th hour, but did manage to get the paperwork in on time to sign right back Djed Spence on loan from fellow Championship side Middlesbrough, while Rodrigo Ely, a centre back once of AC Milan, joined on a free. As for outgoings, Jordan Gabriel went back to Blackpool, this time on a permanent basis, while midfielder Harry Arter and striker Nuno da Costa went on loan to Charlton Athletic and Caen respectively.

This is where things got a bit muddled, though. The reason Syrianos and Murphy were brought in by Marinakis was seemingly because he was fed up with continuous poor recruitment, which had been overseen by former CEO Ioannis Vrentzos. Player turnover was huge and the amount of bad signings far outweighed the good. However, it appeared that in the case of Dräger, Silva and Ely especially, Vrentzos had got his mitts on transfer strategy again. Murphy and Syrianos were aligned in that they wanted young, high potential players who were extremely athletic and fast, whereas it felt like Vrentzos just wanted bodies to fill gaps.

You could argue that given Dräger's Bundesliga past, Syrianos might have recommended him. Same with Silva, who was a pacey wideman and only 24. As for Ely, Murphy and Syrianos didn't want to pay a fee for anyone over the age of 26, so the 27-year-old signing on a free could also have passed. However, Ely had just spent several months out with his second ACL injury. As such, something didn't seem to add up and it felt like wires had been crossed at board level, which no doubt made things even harder for Hughton. In fact, in the case of Ely, Dräger and Silva, Hughton would later tell talkSPORT that they were signed without his knowledge. Nevertheless, the club didn't pull the trigger during the international break and up next for Forest was a home game against Cardiff City.

New recruits Lowe and Spence started at left and right back respectively, which immediately made the defence look a lot stronger. It didn't take too long for Lowe to make an impact either, as a smart one-two with Johnson saw Lowe pull the ball back from the byline straight to the feet of Grabban, who slotted home to give Forest the lead. The pace shown by Lowe and Johnson in that one move was huge cause for optimism, but Forest were far from home and hosed as Cardiff's...agricultural, shall we say, approach was causing problems. They'd already hit the bar before the goal after Worrall failed to deal with a cross, so retreating into a low block was only going to end one way.

It appeared Hughton didn't get the message, as the second half saw the Reds try and deal with wave after wave of aerial bombardment. Eventually, the Bluebirds got a breakthrough. Will Vaulks' cross wasn't dealt with and caused pinball in the box, before falling kindly for Rubin Colwill, who lashed home for his first goal for Cardiff. It was very nearly 2-1 after Samba dropped a free kick at the feet of Mark Harris eight yards out with an open goal to aim at, but somehow Harris blazed over. Kieffer Moore then hit the post from another ball into the box, which Forest just didn't seem able to defend at all, before Colwill got his second Cardiff goal with a curling effort, past the reach of Samba.

This was entirely self-inflicted and entirely on Hughton. The football Forest played for their goal was good, so for them to then revert to playing the negative brand of football that had become synonymous with Hughton's Forest was appalling. It finished 2-1, it could've been five. Had the club revealed there and then that Hughton was sacked, he could've had no complaints. Forest were now 12 games without a Championship win (spread across two seasons) and it felt like the board had made a huge mistake not sacking him before the international break. Still though, he remained – even if there was an air of 'dead man walking' about him as he stepped out into the dugout a few days later for the midweek visit of Middlesbrough.

There was a switch in goal – Horvath had come in for Samba, whose form had become so bad that he had to be dropped. Spence was also ineligible to face his parent club, so Mbe Soh stepped in to play right back. Forest started brightly – Grabban had his blushes spared by the offside flag after somehow skying over from six yards out, but there was at least some intent to attack. Unfortunately, it was very short lived. Boro won the ball back in midfield and Marcus Tavernier slipped in Andraz Sporar, who proceeded to rattle it top corner, leaving Horvath with no chance.

Worrall then had a great chance to level the scores, but drove his volley from about eight yards out into the floor and then over the bar, leaving Hughton exasperated on the touchline. Soon after, the final nail came. A routine pass back to Horvath by Mbe Soh was woefully controlled by the American goalkeeper, with his first touch falling straight into the path of Onel Hernández, who passed into an empty net. Game over – for both the match and for Hughton. Forest fans started pouring out of The City Ground even though there was still 20 to play and those that stayed were hardly in a buoyant mood.

"Sacked in the morning" chants weren't just limited to the away end, as they were echoing all around the ground. As the ref blew for full-time, condemning the Reds to a 2-0 defeat, boos were all anyone could hear. 13 games without a win was Forest's worst run since February 2004, while the run of one draw and six losses from the club's first seven games was the worst start to a season in 108 years – leaving the Reds bottom of the table, already four points from safety. The Forest board acted immediately, to the point that the media were briefed before Hughton even came out to do his post-match press duties, although no official statement had been made yet and Hughton himself hadn't been told.

To give Hughton some credit, he remained dignified until the end. He took responsibility for the run, accepted it was on him to sort it and was big enough to admit "managers are judged on results." Deep down, as he went to speak with journalists in the glow of The City Ground, you suspected he knew what was coming next, even before it was put to him that he'd apparently been relieved of his duties. He soon found out though as the sacking was made official the next day, which was September 16. This meant that for the 20th time since being relegated in 1999, Forest were on the lookout for a new permanent manager. What on earth could come next...

CHAPTER TWO – THE HANDBRAKE COMES OFF

The initial reaction from the outside world was not good. Forest were being painted as a basket case club and the fact Hughton was sacked – as justifiable as it was – was being used as a stick to beat the club with. Hughton was well respected and well-liked by the footballing world, so there was a lot of sympathy for him. Throw in the fact that he was also proven at Championship level and to the untrained eye, it was easy to jump to the conclusion that the reason it didn't work was because of issues beyond Hughton, instead of Hughton himself.

The best example of this was from John Cross at The Mirror, who tweeted, "Another terrific and experienced manager can't make Forest work...maybe it's not the manager." The glare of the national media generally don't pay attention to the Championship unless there's a big story, so it's easy to see why they would come to that assumption. Who cares about a club having their worst start in over a century when you can run a lazy narrative instead?

That isn't to say the running of the football club was something that should've been taught to prospective football owners. It was a commonly held opinion that Forest were unconventional in their approach – however, sacking Hughton needed to be done. There were certainly no Forest fans shedding tears, even if it meant the club were back at square one and watching with intent to see who would be next to drink from the poisoned chalice. One person it would not be was Chelsea legend – and one time Forest loanee – John Terry, who publicly distanced himself, but two names did emerge as frontrunners pretty quickly.

Those names were Chris Wilder and Steve Cooper. Wilder had recently been sacked by Sheffield United after taking them from League One to ninth in the Premier League and had a pretty impressive CV, boasting four promotions and also being recipient of the LMA Manager of the Year award in 2019. Cooper meanwhile, had recently left Swansea by mutual consent after back-to-back play-off heartache. Remember the ill-fated final day implosion against Stoke? It was Cooper's Swansea who had pipped Forest to sixth, only for them to lose 3-2 on aggregate to Brentford in the semis. The year after, Swansea went one better and made the final, where they faced Brentford once more – and lost, again, this time 2-1 under the Wembley arch.

Impressively, the Swansea job was Cooper's first in club management, having previously won the U17 World Cup with England, but he left Swansea under something of a cloud after allegedly stepping down because he had concerns over the club's direction. Prior to that, the Welshman had been manager of

Liverpool's academy, overseeing the development of Raheem Sterling and Trent Alexander-Arnold among others. However, in all honesty, at the time it was hard to be enthused by either.

While it's true Wilder had Sheffield United punching, he left the Blades in an abysmal state after some haphazard recruitment and the season after they finished ninth, they went down bottom of the league – taking just two points from their first 17 games, making it the worst start in Premier League history. Wilder eventually got the chop in March 2021. As for Cooper, as soon as his name was thrown into the hat, hordes of Swansea fans rushed to the Forest Twitter/X timeline to warn us about his overtly negative style of play and how he was basically a younger Hughton.

Such was the apathy at the time, it felt like jumping out the frying pan into the fire with either choice. Could we, as fans, even afford to be picky? It was a surprise to fans to see managers of such calibre even interested given the mess Forest were in. Wilder wanted the job and made no secret of that, either. After the Nottingham Post ran an exclusive saying that he wanted it, former Manchester United and England centre back Rio Ferdinand retweeted it with the caption, "Speaking the truth...", which I'm sure had nothing to do with the fact that Wilder and Ferdinand were part of the same management agency in New Era Global Sports. Despite all the noise though, it was Cooper that Murphy and Forest wanted. And really, with an objective set of eyes, it was clear to see why.

Cooper's success was very recent, he hadn't finished any lower than sixth in the Championship and he was still young – only 41 at the time. His record with young players was phenomenal and while Premier League side Crystal Palace passed up the chance to hire Cooper, instead opting for Patrick Vieira, it was clear he was on an upwards trajectory. Swansea knew that as well, as while he had left his head coach role, he was still on their payroll – so effectively on gardening leave. As such, they were due compensation. This proved to be no hurdle though and on September 18, two days after sacking Hughton, Sky Sports reported that Forest had paid £1.2m for his services.

Before that could be moved along though, Forest had another game, with the Reds going to Huddersfield Town and still seeking their first league win of the season. As they had no manager, first team coach Steven Reid was in temporary charge and had just 48 hours to prepare the players for the match given the quick turnaround from the midweek defeat to Middlesbrough. Reid put the team in a 3-4-3 formation, a change from Hughton's rigid 4-2-3-1 and for the first time, Forest would be wearing their new third kit, which was...bright, to put it mildly. Half luminous yellow, half luminous orange and with matching yellow shorts and socks, it was certainly a sight.

It also resembled a new start as Forest played with a sense of freedom that fans simply hadn't seen for months. They were knocking the ball around nicely and their pace on the counter was causing the Terriers all sorts of issues. Eventually, that pressure told. Much like at Coventry, Forest broke on the counter and Johnson carried the ball a good 40 yards or so down the right before whipping in a cross, which Grabban stooped low for to head into the back of the net. It was an outstanding breakaway goal and it seemed to spark cathartic release in both the fans and the players when it went in.

The question now would be whether Forest would do what they'd done all season and retreat into a shell, let Huddersfield gain momentum and then throw away three points – probably late on, as well. However, those fears were unfounded. Forest limited Huddersfield to next to nothing and after winning possession high up in their half shortly after the restart, the ball made its way to Yates who shot from 25 yards out. His effort was palmed back into play by Town keeper Alex Nicholls straight into the path of Joe Lolley, who was more than happy to score past his former club, although it went down as a Nicholls own goal.

Huddersfield gave Forest – and a reinstated Samba – a few scares from corners towards the end of the game, but that was all they could offer in return and finally – at the eighth time of asking – Forest had a win to celebrate. After the game, Reid, who was brought in by Hughton, spoke very well, saying that while it was a sad week because Hughton was sacked, he reiterated to the players what it should mean to play for a club like Forest and was very pleased with the reaction. Three days later, Cooper was formally announced as Head Coach and a new chapter had begun at Nottingham Forest.

In a rather surprising move – and perhaps due to the discourse about his style of play – Cooper had given a message to the fans, which was posted on the club's website. The key takeaways? "This is a squad with lots of potential" was the first and it was refreshing after Hughton had repeatedly said it needed reinforcement. "My approach to management throughout my time coaching in the junior and senior game has been to play attacking, creative football. That will not change" was next and line by line, you could feel every Forest fan siding with their new leader.

"I recognise this is a club that demands a style and a verve in keeping with its greatest days under its greatest manager. I hardly need to tell you this club has been out of English football's top flight for too long." This was all music to the ears of supporters – a manager that was actually going to embrace the club's rich history, rather than be daunted by it. Finally, Cooper ended by saying, "We have so much to look forward to and it is a great honour to be leading Forest into what I believe is a very bright future."

It suddenly made his first game at home to Millwall all the more exciting. Like Hughton, Cooper came out a few minutes before the players did to give the crowd a clap and to introduce himself, but it was noticeable how much warmer his reception was. Words go a long way, especially words fans had been longing to hear for years. It was also interesting seeing Cooper's reaction to 'Mull of Kintyre', with the Welshman standing in awe as he was taking it all in on his first game in the home dugout. These small things do make a difference and it was clear from the get-go how genuine Cooper was.

Forest stuck with the 3-4-3 that Reid had them playing at Huddersfield to great effect and again, Forest were sprightly. Grabban forced a fantastic close range save from Millwall goalkeeper Bartosz Bialkowski after Spence had picked him out with a low cross and the Reds carried a threat whenever they had possession. In true

Forest fashion though, it was too good to be true. Sheyi Ojo slipped as he went to cross the ball, but it still managed to find the head of regular Forest nemesis Matt Smith, who outjumped Joe Worrall and headed into the bottom corner.

Previously, this would've seen Forest cave, but this was different. Half-time came, they dusted themselves down and within seven minutes, they had the score level. With Forest advancing into the Millwall half, McKenna picked out Lowe, who attempted to whip the ball into the box for Taylor. However, his aim was slightly off and his cross instead looped over the head of Bialkowski and into the top corner of the net. As first goals for a new era go, that was certainly unconventional, with Lowe being so amazed/embarrassed that he didn't even celebrate it.

Millwall were far from done though and the equaliser seemed to spur them back into life. George Saville split the Forest defence with a beautiful pass that found the feet of Ojo, but an outstretched leg by Forest defender Tobias Figueiredo managed to take the ball away from him. However, the ball fell kindly into the path of Smith, whose shot rattled the crossbar. Forest ended strongly though, with Worrall and Zinckernagel having decent efforts, but the visitors managed to hold on for a point. Despite that, the early signs of Cooperball were very, very positive.

Another midweek game beckoned and this time, Murphy would be going back to his old club as Forest made the trip up to Barnsley. The Tykes had been somewhat stripped of their assets after failing to win promotion, losing both their manager Valérian Ismaël and their captain Alex Mowatt to West Bromwich Albion, while of course the brains of the operation in Murphy was taken to Trentside. However, it was only 10 games prior for them that they were in a play-off semi-final, so Forest couldn't take it lightly. Things didn't start particularly well either, as after 20 minutes, Figueiredo clumsily held onto Cauley Woodrow and brought the striker down in the penalty box. After giving it a good think, the ref gave the pen and Woodrow sent Samba the wrong way from the resulting spot kick.

Woodrow made a point of celebrating in front of the away fans, which went down as well as you would expect and after that, Barnsley largely kept Forest at arm's length for the first half. For the second half however, it was like a different Forest side had turned up. One full of hunger, desire, aggression and ability and they turned on the style in emphatic fashion. The warning signs were there for Barnsley when Lolley drove into the box and picked out Zinckernagel, whose effort was brilliantly blocked en route to goal, but they weren't heeded.

On the hour mark, Grabban picked out Johnson and broke Barnsley's high line in the process, allowing both Johnson and Zinckernagel to bear down on the keeper. Johnson squared it for the Danish forward, who ran the ball into an empty net. Seven minutes later, Samba threw the ball through the middle of the pitch to Zinckernagel, who put a ball through to Johnson. It took a little nick on the way through, but this allowed Johnson to speed away from his man and find himself in the exact same situation as the first Forest goal, this time with Grabban alongside him. Johnson opted to shoot instead and found the bottom corner to give Forest the lead. It took just nine seconds from the ball being in Samba's hands to being in the back of the Barnsley net and Forest weren't done yet.

With 10 left to play, Mighten darted in-between two Barnsley defenders and drove forwards, before drilling it across the six yard box to find an unmarked Grabban with the goal at his mercy. He didn't miss and Forest were 3-1 up having been 1-0 down at half-time, playing some electric football along the way. Having won just one of the first seven, Forest had now taken seven points from a possible nine. Maybe the hi-vis kit, which was worn again at Oakwell, was a lucky charm after all.

The full time whistle also brought something new for Forest fans – the sight of Cooper, with a beaming smile, fist pumping the Forest support in celebration, which was made even more sweeter by the sight of Woodrow, who suddenly wasn't quite as brave as he was after his goal, skulking away down the tunnel. The result also lifted Forest out of the relegation zone and up to 20th, out of the bottom three on goal difference. That was a huge mental boost, but there was very little time to bask in the glory of victory and the leap up the table as a few days later, Forest were away again – this time at Birmingham City.

The hosts started well and Forest were perhaps lucky not to concede. After receiving a throw from Marc Roberts, Lukas Jutkiewicz was bundled to the floor inside the box by Figueriedo – who clearly hadn't learnt his lesson from Oakwell – but instead of staying down and asking the question for a penalty, the striker instead got straight back up to his feet and his rasping effort was parried wide by Samba.

Not long after, another long throw from Roberts was poorly cleared by McKenna and landed straight into the path of Tahith Chong, whose effort beat Samba and hit the post. The rebound off the post then somehow went through the legs of Jutkiewicz two yards out from goal, who was running into an area he anticipated any ricochet going and Forest survived.

Birmingham soon rued those missed opportunities – and how. Jack Colback pinched the ball off Chong near the halfway line after 11 minutes and that allowed Grabban to run through towards goal. No-one approached or put any pressure on him, so he decided to let fly an absolute rocket of a shot from 25 yards out straight into the top corner, leaving the goalkeeper with no chance. By this point, Cooper already had his own chant – "Ste-vie Cooper (clap clap), Ste-vie Cooper, he hates the Leicester, he hates the Derby, Forest are magic" and this was swirling around the away end.

Granted, it was a rehashed Aitor Karanka/Sabri Lamouchi chant and it meant calling him Stevie instead of Steve, but the sign of endearment was there. For context, the only chants Hughton got were "sacked in the morning" and "Hughton out", so that was a notable improvement. Birmingham didn't relent though and a Jérémie Bela free kick was headed goalbound by Jutkiewicz and hit the same post that had denied Chong earlier, with Samba's goal living a charmed life.

Once again though, Forest made them pay. Zinckernagel's corner found the head of Yates, who sent his header into the ground and past goalkeeper Matija Sarkic, who could only helplessly watch it hit the back of the net. It was Yates' first goal in eight months and while it was still early days, no-one was benefitting from Cooper's management more than Yates, who looked a completely different player to the one fans saw under Hughton. It was like someone had lifted a weight vest from him and he was able to perform so much more freely.

Birmingham came back again and Jutkiewicz did brilliantly to hold the ball up in the box, before firing over a low cross into the path of Scott Hogan from a few yards out, who couldn't miss. However, the official's flag went up and the goal was ruled out for offside. From a Birmingham perspective, they must've thought this just wasn't their day. Forest very feasibly could've been going in at half-time behind, yet held a two goal advantage going into the break. The half-time team talk was very clear – kill the game off with a third goal and get it early.

And that is exactly what Forest did. With just eight minutes of the second half played, Grabban carried the ball down the left into the Birmingham half before feeding it to Zinckernagel in the middle, who quickly popped a ball in behind the Birmingham defence and found Spence, who duly lashed home. Forest had scored three goals in consecutive games for the first time since the 2015/16 season, when the Reds defeated Reading and Fulham 3-1 and 3-0 respectively. Birmingham did have one more notable chance to get a consolation, as Kristian Pedersen saw his header cleared off the line by Grabban, but the football gods were very much against them on that day.

After their trip to St Andrews, Forest were up to the lofty heights of 17th, three points clear of the drop zone. Cooper was keen to keep feet firmly on the ground and bemoaned the Reds' inability to defend set pieces in Birmingham, but it was already clear that this was no new manager bounce. Forest had scored more goals in Cooper's first three games than Hughton's Forest did in seven and the style of football was so much better to watch. The Welshman hadn't just yanked the proverbial handbrake off, but he'd launched it off Trent Bridge and watched it sink to the bottom of the river.

The next task was to finally win a home league game, as the Reds were now 11 fixtures into the season and didn't have one to their name. Their next home game was against Blackpool, who arrived with Jordan Gabriel in tow, as the right back went up against his former employers mere weeks after leaving. It wasn't the happiest of returns for Gabriel as with 22 gone, Worrall hit a stunning diagonal ball over his head and into Lowe's path. Lowe took one touch to get away from Gabriel, taking him into the Blackpool box. His second touch was a pass that was rolled into Johnson's path, which the Forest forward gobbled up to make it 1-0.

Blackpool hit back well though and came close to equalising when a Ryan Wintle corner caused havoc in the box and ended up with both Gary Madine and then Tyreece John-Jules fluffing their lines, before the Reds scrambled it clear. After half-time, the Tangerines started strongly and eventually got their reward when a Josh Bowler cross saw both Samba and Spence go for the ball, with neither getting anything substantial on it. The ball then fell for Gabriel, who nodded it into the path of Jerry Yates, who thumped a volley home to equalise.

Just eight minutes later though, Zinckernagel sent Lowe down the left, whose cross found Worrall. The centre back's effort was saved, but the rebound fell straight to Grabban, who prodded home for his fifth goal in seven games. After that, Forest didn't look back and could've extended their lead even further. Some lovely wing play and quick feet from Lolley saw him fashion a crossing opportunity, where he cut it back for Grabban, but his effort had the sting taken out of it by a brilliant last ditch block from Marvin Ekpiteta. Yates also sent Lowe through on goal with a precise through ball, but despite having Grabban available to square it to, Lowe shot and saw his effort go wide of the target.

Ultimately, two was enough. Forest finally – at the sixth attempt – had their first home league win of the season. Such is life in the EFL though, the games were coming thick and fast. Up next was a midweek trip to Bristol City, with the Robins having gone 16 home games without a win. However, this was exactly the sort of game that Forest would traditionally lose. I have long referred to Forest as Charity FC and with very good reason. Haven't won in a prolonged period of time? Got a striker on a comically long goal drought? Manager under pressure and needs a win to save his job? Never fear, Charity FC are here. It always, always seems to be Forest to end these barren runs and any time you think it's a good time to play someone, Forest play them and they turn into Brazil 1970 for the day. Honestly, it's infuriating beyond words.

The trip to Ashton Gate had all the hallmarks of a Charity FC special, even despite the hi-vis kit making another appearance. The writing was on the wall in the first half, when Andreas Weimann drove forwards and picked out Nakhi Wells inside the box. Wells was tackled by Lowe, but the ball fell into Weimann's path once more. He then squared it to Alex Scott, who incredibly put the ball wide of a pretty much open goal. It was easier to score and the miss was a huge let off. Forest nearly made the Robins pay soon after, as Worrall sent the ball long and Johnson's pace caught out the Bristol City back line, allowing him inside the box. Johnson chopped onto his left and let fly, but was thwarted by the base of the post.

With 39 on the clock, Bristol City decided to go back in time and to great effect. Goalkeeper Daniel Bentley smacked the ball long, another ex-Derby player in Chris Martin flicked the ball on and the Forest defence allowed it to bounce, with no-one wanting to take responsibility for removing the danger. The ball subsequently made its way to Wells, whose shot across goal was parried out back into open play by Samba, straight at Scott's feet. This time, he didn't miss and Bristol City had scored a textbook route one goal. That Charity FC gene had kicked in once again, it seemed.

Forest started the second half strong and at times, it was like watching an attack vs defence training session. There just wasn't any cutting edge or penetration at the end of it, as time and time again Forest squandered being in good positions. They were nearly made to pay for that as Han-Noah Massengo twisted and turned down the right hand side near the halfway line and got clipped by Lowe, but while Forest stopped as they expected a foul to be given, the referee correctly waved advantage and Bristol City immediately got the ball moving. Scott worked it into Weimann, whose ball into Wells saw him breeze past Worrall and into a one-on-one, where his powerful effort was tipped onto the post by Samba.

With 10 minutes left to play, Cooper turned to his bench and brought Taylor on for Grabban. Taylor was quite the sight, as he had pink hair and pink boots, which was quite a clash with the hi-vis kit – although it was all for a fantastic cause. October is Cancer Awareness Month and for the three previous seasons, Taylor had partaken in Pink October, which is designed to raise awareness for breast cancer. This meant he dyed his hair pink and wore pink boots, as the cause is very close to his heart given he's had several family members and some family friends suffer from cancer. Taylor saw it as a conversation starter and would fundraise for Cancer Research every year, which was a very noble act.

The Bristol City fans hadn't quite got the message, because as he was coming on, Taylor was serenaded with "what the fucking hell is that?" chants. It's probably fair to claim ignorance on this occasion, as that chant has been and always will be part of terrace folklore and with some understanding, you'd like to hope the Bristol City fans wouldn't have chanted it, but it didn't half light a fire under Taylor's arse. With the game now in stoppage time and with Forest fans exasperated they hadn't scored, Yates split the defence with a brilliant ball to Spence, whose first touch carried him into the box. He barely got a chance to make a second one, as he was unceremoniously wiped out by Nathan Baker. Penalty given.

Taylor was something of a penalty specialist, but his run-up – if you can call it that – didn't half put the fear of God into fans. Taylor's technique was to walk up to the ball and then sort of skip into his last step, see where the keeper is and then choose where to place it. It had worked to great effect in similar circumstances the season before in a 2-1 win over Coventry, with Taylor scoring a 90th minute penalty that was literally the last kick that night to win the game for Forest. Here he was now to secure a point, which was the least Forest deserved. The walk seemed to take an age, but Taylor was the coolest man in the stadium. After arriving at the ball, he sent Bentley the wrong way and the ball found the back of the net – balls of steel shown and Forest were leaving Bristol with a point.

However, after scoring, Taylor sprinted into the goal for the ball and the legged it back to halfway to get going again. The message from the players was clear – we aren't content with a draw. Straight from kick off, Bristol City sent it long and Forest won the ball back immediately with a header, with the ball falling to Lolley, who immediately sprayed it out to the left to Mighten. Mighten then ran into the penalty area, but when faced with two Bristol City defenders, turned back. Lolley had covered the ground so he was an option to pass to, which Mighten duly did. Lolley then curled an effort goalbound, which Bentley parried straight into Taylor's chest. The ball then dropped for Taylor, who nudged it into an open goal, sparking serious scenes in that away end.

Bentley ran off to the officials to ambitiously claim handball, but no dice. Taylor cupped his ears to the home fans in his celebration, before knee sliding in front of the away end. Members of the coaching staff, the subs and Samba had all sprinted to him to celebrate along with the rest of the team as somehow, someway, Forest had turned a 1-0 defeat into a 2-1 win in stoppage time. The two goals were just 50 seconds apart and the Bristol City players looked completely shell shocked. A few minutes earlier, they were set to end a 16 game winless run at home – now it was going to be 17. There were still a few minutes remaining, but nothing really happened. How could it? After the game, Cooper spoke to BBC Radio Nottingham about needing to improve the final ball, but most tellingly also said, "An away point is never a bad result in the Championship, but we were never going to settle for that."

Forest finally had someone who understood the club's standards and fans were starting to dream. If that result was possible, what else was? The win had also taken Forest to 12th in the league, with the Reds now 11 clear of the relegation zone and five points off the play-offs. For context, the highest Hughton had taken Forest was 13th, where they had spent a grand total of one gameweek in the 2020/21 season. However, Forest would soon be brought crashing down to earth. As the old saying goes, pride comes before a fall. Fulham were up next for Forest on Trentside and to say it was a painful afternoon for Forest would be putting it mildly.

It was the biggest home attendance of the season so far, with 27,470 (1,546 away) inside The City Ground, but after just seven minutes, it was fairly evident how the day would go. Bobby De Cordova-Reid played in Aleksander Mitrovic, who turned Figueiredo far too easily and saw his shot deflected over from a corner. From that corner, Mitrovic flicked it goalbound and as Spence tried to block it, he inadvertently put the ball into his own net. Forest were furious that a very blatant block from Denis Odoi stopped Worrall from getting near Mitrovic, but the ref waved away their protests. That would be the spark for what proved to be a very feisty game (there would be nine yellow cards shown, five for Forest) and Forest should've equalised in the second half when Zinckernagel picked out an unmarked Grabban on the penalty spot, but the experienced striker fired miles over.

However, things went very wrong very quickly not long after that miss. In fact, all it took was nine minutes. First, Forest were caught napping from a free-kick and while McKenna did his best to stop the danger, he and Figueiredo ran into each other, leaving the ball free for Mitrovic, who passed it in. Three minutes later, Neeskens Kebano caught the Forest defence on the backfoot and ran through their half before playing a one-two with Harry Wilson, where he then beat Samba at his near post with his effort from seven yards out. Six minutes later, a Jean Michael Seri free kick was flicked towards goal and cleared off the line by Spence, but as it was falling to Odoi, Yates pulled him down for a penalty. Samba went the right way, but Mitrovic doubled his tally on the day.

For context of what Forest were up against, the Reds' starting XI came to a combined cost of around £11m - £6m of that being on one player, in Lewis Grabban. Harry Wilson cost Fulham £12m on his own. Meanwhile, Mitrovic – who had scored his 14th and 15th goals of the season, a ridiculous stat bearing in mind the season was only 14 games old, was earning £120k a week according to TalkSport. The financial mismatch between teams without Premier League money or the parachute payments relegated teams are given and those that have was (and remains) so stark.

For those unaware, parachute payments are given to teams relegated from the Premier League, basically in order to prevent them from going to the wall and being straddled with players on Premier League wages (like Mitrovic) with no way of paying them, as their income takes a huge hit following relegation. In recent years though, teams going down haven't really needed them and instead, they allow them to be stronger and even keep some of their better players. It all makes for a bit of an unfair playing field and while Forest kept battling and were unlucky not to score at least one, they lost 4-0.

While the scoreline was very harsh, it perhaps gave fans a reality check. It was only six games ago that fans were wondering how Forest would even survive in the league, so maybe a walking before running approach was wise. Still, fans went into a Friday night game at Queens Park Rangers with optimism as QPR – managed by former Forest boss Mark Warburton – were much more beatable. It was nearly a glorious start for the Reds as Johnson came close to putting them ahead after just 15 seconds, but his effort narrowly went wide. Forest then should've had a penalty as Yoann Barbet brought down Johnson in the box, but the ref wasn't interested. They could've had another when former Forest man Albert Adomah tangled with Spence in the box, but again nothing was given.

While the ire was with the ref for not giving at least one very simple decision, Forest had to be responsible for their own actions and it just wasn't falling for them. Johnson fired a ball across the six yard box and QPR keeper Seny Dieng got a hand to it, but he pushed it into Yates' path in the process. Somehow, Yates put his effort wide of the goal and behind for a goal kick. It would be a chance they rued missing as some neat play from QPR saw Adomah get the ball in the box, where he expertly turned Spence and floated a ball in for Lyndon Dykes to head home in the fifth minute of first half stoppage time. QPR hadn't deserved anything, but Forest had let them off the hook and Rangers had made the most of it mere seconds before half-time.

The second half was much more of a ding-dong, with Dykes missing a one-on-one and also being denied by an outstanding block by Spence, while Lolley and Zinckernagel both had good efforts go without reward. The ref was in the spotlight again after Mighten was pretty much punted into one of the side stands at Loftus Road after an appalling tackle from Stefan Johansen, but amazingly, this was only worthy of a yellow card. It really should've been a red and it felt like it wasn't going to be Forest's night. Entering stoppage time though, there was one more twist to be had.

With Forest piling men forward, Spence picked out Yates down the right wing. His cross was headed clear, but straight to Colback, who was lurking just outside the box. He took the ball down on his chest with his first touch, before unleashing a wicked left footed half volley with his second, which flew goalbound, taking a deflection on the way to put it past Dieng and into the bottom corner. Fine margins, as Warburton used to say, but also the very, very least Forest deserved.

The goal sparked pure chaos for those 2,885 fans in that away end, to the point I'd gone from the back row of the lower tier to being pretty much pitchside. What we couldn't see at first amongst the plumes of red smoke that had been set off from flares was Taylor slipping over and celebrating in a QPR player's face, while some of the players who went over to the away end had temporarily gone missing in the stands as scores of Forest fans sought to celebrate with them. A last minute equaliser always feels like a winner when you're on the right side of it.

While Forest undoubtedly deserved all three points on the night, Cooper's men had still left with something. The QPR players looked devastated and their fans even more so. It was hilarious walking out of the ground and overhearing a conversation from a QPR fan on the phone who bemoaned, "They celebrated like they won the fucking league," while me and my dad just walked behind smiling. Ultimately, Cooper had given fans reason to celebrate. Already, Forest had become a team that refused to accept when they were beaten and with that mindset, who knows what could be achieved.

CHAPTER THREE – A NEW OBJECTIVE

After the QPR game, Forest sat 15th in the table with 18 points – nine points clear of the drop zone, but only five points off the top six and with a lot of football to be played. However, fans were keeping their feet firmly on the floor. After the truly horrendous start to the season, the remit for Cooper was still a salvage job and until the Reds had gotten to the 52-55 point mark to secure another season of Championship football, staying afloat was still the order of the day. Secretly though, fans were starting to think what could be possible.

The late drama in the Bristol City and QPR games showed that Forest had discovered a mentality not seen in many years, while the ability to blow teams away like they did against Barnsley and Birmingham highlighted their strength in attack. There were a few question marks about Forest defensively, as ruthlessly exploited by Fulham, but if Forest could get to the January transfer window and be in touching distance of the top six, then they might have a chance. A good indicator of whether that were possible would come in Forest's next game at home, as they hosted recently relegated Sheffield United.

This is always an occasion as it's fair to say the Blades aren't exactly best friends with Forest, something that goes back to the mining strikes in 1984, but also because of a number of fiercely contested games in the early 2000s, when Neil Warnock was the Blades' boss. There's always a bit of needle and amidst the usual backdrop, the midweek fixture would be a very meaningful test of Forest's credentials. However, they would be without Lowe, who was ineligible to face his parent club. Instead of picking Bong though, Cooper opted to play Colback there instead, which was a bold call. Colback could do a shift at left back, but it did feel a bit like putting a square peg in a round hole, to paraphrase former Forest boss Billy Davies.

As such, Cooper picking him at left wing back was a surprise, but the only other alternative was Bong. Given the reason Lowe was signed was because Bong was done at Forest, it made sense as to why Cooper would opt for Colback. All that talk was put to one side once the game started however and Forest should've taken the lead after 25 minutes when Garner's corner picked out Taylor, but he could only poke wide. They came even closer just before half-time from another Garner corner, but Worrall's header across the six yard box went just past the post.

Forest remained the stronger side in the second half and should've had a penalty when Johnson was blatantly tripped by Chris Basham in the box, but while the referee blew his whistle, he gave the foul the other way and instead, booked Johnson for diving. This sparked a bit of a melee and Cooper was also booked in the aftermath for protesting the decision. It also woke the Blades up a bit and not long after, they took the lead. Morgan Gibbs-White, who had recently signed for Sheffield United on loan from Wolves, played a one-two out wide with former Forest loanee Billy Sharp and upon receiving the ball back in the box, slid the ball past Samba for his second goal against the Reds that season.

It was the only piece of Premier League quality that the Blades had shown all night and Gibbs-White, who was a part of Cooper's England U17 World Cup winning team, was beginning to become a thorn in Forest's side. However, Forest were undeterred and should've been level immediately after, as Grabban turned Garner's cross just past the post. Grabban would get a second chance soon after, though. Spence drove forwards into the box and cut the ball back, but his pass was behind Zinckernagel. Thankfully, Colback had roamed centrally to pick it up and immediately sprayed it left to Johnson, whose cross found Grabban. Grabban chested it down badly, but reacted the quickest to jab it over Blades' keeper Robin Olsen to make it 1-1.

This was the least Forest deserved and Sheffield United's lead lasted just five minutes. With just seven left to play, the game opened up as both sides chased a winner, which the visitors came closest to getting. Gibbs-White received the ball inside his own half and ran forwards, but with options either side of him, took one touch too many and this allowed Worrall to get a tackle in on the edge of his box. However, Worrall's tackle sent the ball straight to one of Gibbs-White's options in Rhian Brewster, but his effort was straight at Samba. Forest were the more disappointed at full time as they should've won, but it also showed how far they'd come in a very short space of time. As for Colback at left wing back, he was brilliant.

It was around this sort of time that the Forest fans decided it was time to give Cooper his own proper chant and not an older one that had been reworked (although that was still popular). This was quite big as Forest fans seem to find it notoriously difficult to take on catchy new chants, as the majority seemingly have a mindset of "if it ain't broke, why fix it?" – a perfect example being how Karanka, Lamouchi and Cooper all ended up with the same one. In the end, the ABBA hit 'Super Trouper' was used as inspiration and in all honesty, it worked a dream. The end result?

"And it's super, Cooper

Leads the Garibaldi

Forest having fun

Cooper, you're the one

To take us back where we belong!"

Whether you were sat in A Block, Lower Bridgford, the corner in Upper Bridgford, the Trent End or even the family areas, as soon as this started, it would spread throughout the ground very quickly. It was also deserved. There was genuine warmth from Cooper to the fans, who seemed to just get that small things went a long way. Things like clapping all four corners of the ground for home games and bringing the whole team over to the travelling fans for away games. Fans pay their money and travel all across the country to watch their team and Cooper understood that, believing that the least they deserved was acknowledgement for their support. The fist pumps came out after every victory too and with each set, it brought Cooper and the fans closer, forging a very strong bond that hadn't been seen on Trentside for a long time.

Preston North End were next for Cooper's Forest and it was far from a given that we'd see those fist pumps at full time. Preston are the archetypal, perennial example of a second tier side. They never seem to do anything but float around midtable, leading to fans constantly saying things like, "we should be beating teams like Preston." The Lilywhites wear this as a badge of honour though and you can frequently see their fans tweet #TeamsLikePreston with glee whenever they claim a result. For some reason, they seem to exist solely within the realms of 8th and 16th of the Championship – not good enough to go up, too good to go down, but good enough to beat you on their day.

This though, was not to be their day. With 30 minutes played, Yates peeled away from his marker from a Spence throw and fired a ball across the box, pretty much straight at Johnson. The ball bounced off Johnson's ankle, but as he turned around to recycle possession, he was tripped by Ben Whiteman and unlike in the QPR and Sheffield United games, the referee gave the penalty. Grabban stepped up and put the ball straight down the middle to give the Reds the lead. It was very nearly 2-0 not long after, when a Johnson cross found Yates, but his effort went just past the post.

Forest didn't have to wait too long to double their lead, however. A Zinckernagel free kick into the box was headed away by the Preston defence, but only as far as Colback, who volleyed it first time into the bottom corner. It was a beautiful, brilliantly executed finish that was made to look an awful lot easier than it actually was from the tenacious midfielder. It really should've been 2-1 before the break, as Preston carved through Forest and worked the ball out to Emil Riis Jakobsen on the right, whose low ball perfectly found Brad Potts lurking on the penalty spot. However, he incredibly fired the ball way over the goal and high into the Trent End.

That was as close as Preston got and their fate was sealed with 20 to go after Johnson ran at and beat two defenders, checked past a third and put a ball across goal to Lowe, but a Preston defender got a foot on it first. Despite this, the clearance hit another Preston player and looped up for Grabban, whose precise effort went in off to the post to make it 3-0. The game did have one other noteworthy incident, as with about 10 to go, the ref called both Taylor and Preston defender Jordan Storey over after the two were tussling a bit too heavily. Throughout the entire exchange, Taylor made mock crying faces to Storey and called him a baby, which went viral after the match.

The result took Forest just four points off the play-off spots and 10 clear of the bottom three, but speaking to BBC Radio Nottingham after the game, Cooper said that he felt that Forest played better in the 4-0 loss to Fulham and challenged his players to step up. Again, this represented why Cooper was fast becoming loved by fans – Forest had just beaten a team 3-0, keeping them at arm's length throughout and he's telling them to up the standards. It demonstrated a big club mentality that fans had craved, as it felt like someone finally understood the size of the club that they were managing.

It was then time for an international break, but afterwards, a trip to Reading beckoned and in Berkshire, all was not well. Far from it, in fact. Reading had just been hit with a six-point deduction for breaching Profit and Sustainability Rules (PSR) by £19m, dropping the Royals from 16th to 19th in the table, just four points above the bottom three. While it was only November, the deduction immediately meant they had to revisit their season ambitions, as staying up at all costs was going to have to be their new primary aim.

This wasn't ideal news for Forest, as even though it was still early in the season, the news would've immediately put Reading into survival mode and given them a siege mentality. Prior to the deduction, Forest were level on points with Reading despite giving them a seven-game head start, but this did change the complexion of the match. Not that you'd have known it from the start, as after just four minutes, Zinckernagel picked up the ball from a throw just inside the Reading half and played a cute give and go with Lolley, before he drove towards goal, rode two challenges and then rifled an effort into the bottom corner.

Reading rallied well, with Samba being forced into a couple of smart stops. First, Andy Yiadom beat Lowe far too easily and then cut it back to Danny Drinkwater. The former England international's effort was well saved by Samba, but the ball hit Worrall and that led to a heart in mouth moment as it seemed like it was going in off the defender, only for Colback to clear away. Shortly after, Lowe went off injured, which may explain why he was beaten so easily. Then, Baba Rahman drilled a ball centrally to John Swift, whose ball out to Ovi Ejaria was blocked by Yates, but fell straight into George Puscas' path, putting him in one-on-one. Samba stood firm though, but Forest were hugely fortunate to go into the break leading.

After the restart, Spence's long ball was taken down by Grabban near the corner flag and he wriggled past his man and sped towards goal, cut inside on his left and got a shot away, but it was cleared off the line by Liam Moore. While Grabban had every right to shoot, he had Zinckernagel, Colback and Johnson in better positions he could've passed to, the latter two of which would've had an open goal to shoot at. Forest rued that miss pretty quickly as a Swift corner found Scott Dann, who had gotten away from Worrall to equalise.

This seemed to jolt Forest back into life and they should've taken the lead when Garner brilliantly span his marker and played Grabban in one-on-one. Grabban rounded the goalkeeper, but his touch was a bit too heavy and he ended up hitting the side netting. The points were shared at full-time, which was probably fair as both sides would've felt they had chances to win the game. Some Forest fans quickly deduced Grabban as the main source of blame for not winning and were joined by a surprise guest in David Johnson, who is of course Brennan's dad.

Taking to his Twitter after the match, he called the Forest captain "selfish" and claimed that he'd made "the wrong choice and cost the team three points," alluding to the chance Grabban had cleared off the line when he could've passed to Johnson Jnr instead. This was less than ideal and Johnson Snr – a striker himself, who scored 50 in 165 appearances for Forest – should've known better. Yes, Grabban could've passed, but every striker 99% of the time is shooting after getting themselves into that position. Shortly afterwards, Johnson Snr deleted the tweets, but not before we'd all seen them.

The furore over that exchange somewhat overshadowed what was perhaps the best positive taken from the game and that was Garner's performance. The on-loan Manchester United midfielder had been in and out of the starting 11 for the previous few games as he struggled to find his rhythm from the season before, but he was exceptional against Reading. It was timely too, as the game against the Royals kickstarted a particularly brutal run of three games in six days for the Reds, which even by EFL standards is pushing it.

The second match in that run was a home tie against Luton Town, who under the management of Nathan Jones, were punching above their weight and found themselves five points off the play-offs, sitting a point above Forest. Jones' teams were horrible to play against. They were physical, they got in your face, they kicked off about every decision – both on the pitch and on the touchline – and they weren't afraid to smash it long to target men strikers. Of course, there's more than one way to skin a cat when it comes to winning football matches, but their robust style, as effective as it was, wasn't one for the purist.

In truth, the two were a match made in heaven. Jones' constant desire to prove himself to everyone and their dog meshed perfectly with a club of Luton's size, as it brought everyone together, got everyone fighting for each other and gave them an us against the world approach. It didn't work at bigger clubs, as Jones found out when he left Luton for Stoke in 2019 and won just six of his 38 games in charge before being sacked, but upon his return to the Hatters, he'd gotten that fire burning again. No-one enjoyed playing Luton under his management, especially when they started taking points from teams.

As such, it was always likely to be an awkward encounter. Colback was back at left back after Lowe's injury as Cooper changed to a 4-2-3-1, with Ojeda making his debut in midfield alongside Garner. The game wasn't one for the neutral, but Garner should've had an assist when his brilliant corner found the head of McKenna, but the Scotland international put it over the bar. Half-time came and went and in the second half, Taylor had a great chance to put Forest ahead after being played in by Lolley, but his effort was blocked by goalkeeper James Shea.

With half an hour to play though, things took a turn. A Luton corner was swung in and was hit pretty poorly, going above everyone and straight down Samba's throat – however, before Samba could claim it, Tom Lockyer had got the run on Colback and was subsequently hauled down. The ref had no choice but to point to the spot and things went from bad to worse for Forest, as Colback was sent off for a second bookable offence. Elijah Adebayo stepped up, but his penalty was saved by Samba's trailing leg, giving Forest a lifeline.

Weirdly, the next half an hour went by fairly smoothly for Forest as despite all of Luton's possession, they couldn't find a way through. Forest even had a penalty shout of their own when Pelly-Ruddock Mpanzu brought down Zinckernagel, but the ref adjudged it to be outside of the box. Samba did have to leap to Forest's rescue once more though, as right at the end, a Luton corner was flicked on to Lockyer and volleyed goalbound, but Samba managed to get in the way of it and the game finished goalless.

After the game, Jones bleated about how Luton had drawn with ex-European champions despite having a bottom three budget, but the real story was Samba's heroics. Cooper described them as a striker scoring the winning goal and said that he got a round of applause in the dressing room after the game. The wobbles Samba had endured at the start of the season were now long forgotten and he was looking every bit his usual self, which as one of the best goalkeepers in the league, was very good news for Forest.

It was just as well that Samba was back on form as up next was a trip to West Bromwich Albion, who had recovered well after being relegated the season before and were now sat in third. Given Lowe was injured and Colback was suspended, in came Bong at left wing back and it was fairly obvious that this would be the area that West Brom would look to exploit; especially with Grady Diangana down that right hand side, a player the Baggies had acquired for an initial £12m. It didn't take long for them to get some joy as an Alex Mowatt free kick was played down the right to Diangana, who darted at Bong and cut inside the penalty area, forcing Samba into a very good save at his near post with his effort.

In truth though, it wasn't just Bong that Forest had to worry about defensively, as they just didn't seem at it from the off. With alarming ease, West Brom picked apart the right hand side of the Forest defence and Karlan Grant managed to get by Worrall and pull the ball back to Darnell Furlong on the penalty spot, but his effort flew miles over. Throughout the first half, it felt like a matter of time until the Baggies would score, but Forest hung on until half-time. The second half went the same way and an awful first touch from Bong basically acted as a pass for West Brom, allowing Mowatt to play a precise through ball to send Callum Robinson through on goal, but Worrall recovered excellently and blocked his effort.

Eventually, Forest threw a punch back. Following a turnover in possession, Lolley carried the ball into the Baggies' half before playing in Johnson, whose effort took a deflection and nearly caught out Sam Johnstone in goal, but the England goalkeeper managed to tip it behind. With 20 to go, Forest gained a numerical advantage as just 10 minutes after scything down Garner, Jayson Molumby flew into a tackle two-footed right in front of the referee, giving him no choice. Forest couldn't make it count though, as the closest they game was when Worrall put in a brilliant cross, but Grabban couldn't quite connect with it.

It finished 0-0, but this was a valuable point on the road at a tough place to go. Forest were now unbeaten in six and had lost just one of Cooper's first 12 games in charge. In fact, they were averaging 1.75 points per game – over a course of a 46 Championship season, that's 81 points (rounded up from 80.5). Given 75 points is seen as the minimum requirement to finish in the play-offs, it was maybe time to start looking up, rather than down. Obviously no-one was suggesting Forest could maintain that and finish top six, but it certainly seemed as if they could at least challenge for a play-off spot.

Thinking aloud about the play-offs was still tetchy ground, but Forest had a chance to put some real daylight between themselves and the bottom three with their next game – a home match against Peterborough United. The Posh were 22nd going into the game, which is the final relegation place. Given Peterborough were 10 points behind, barring a collapse of biblical proportions, a win against them would silence any immediate relegation fears, which as December had just started, would've been a concept laughed at before Cooper walked through the door.

Colback came back into the side for Bong at left wing back, but despite his return, Forest made hard work of it early doors. A Zinckernagel effort from distance was well saved by David Cornell, but that was the only bright spark in an otherwise shambolic first half for the Reds. Siriki Dembele was wreaking havoc for Peterborough and should've had an assist when he played in ex-Forest man Jorge Grant one-on-one, but Grant weakly tried to chip Samba and instead looked very silly. Peterborough had the ball in dangerous areas quite often, but aside from Dembele, none of them seemed to know what to do with it and their final ball was frequently poor.

After the restart, Forest still hadn't woken up and should've gone behind when Cornell's goal kick was flicked on by Jonson Clarke-Harris to Dembele inside the box, but his effort hit the outside of the post. This did finally jolt Forest into life and with 72 on the clock, Ojeda glided into the Posh half and picked out Johnson out on the right, who fizzed a brilliant ball across the six yard box for Grabban. The Forest captain got his timing all wrong though and miskicked it, to the point it went behind him, but Garner was on hand to tuck the ball away.

12 minutes later and with just six minutes left on the clock, Garner turned provider when his corner bounced through to Yates, who killed the game off. It was somewhat ironic that one of Garner's weaker set pieces had been converted, after numerous outstanding deliveries had gone begging in recent games, but having a set piece specialist in the Forest ranks was proving very fruitful. The 2-0 victory was far from a vintage Forest performance, but it's a sign of a good team when you can play badly and win – as long as you aren't playing badly every week of course, which Forest weren't.

They would need a better performance for their next fixture, a trip to Swansea and a return for Cooper to his old stomping ground. Under Cooper, Swansea averaged 75 points a season and in his last year, the Swans conceded just 39 league goals. Cooper had made them very difficult to break down and while new manager Russell Martin was tasked with bringing back 'the Swansea way', whatever that is, it still posed a difficult challenge. Granted, Swansea had lost some key players – namely star striker Andre Ayew and defender Connor Roberts, while defender Marc Guehi and goalkeeper Freddie Woodman both went back to their parent clubs Chelsea and Newcastle United respectively – but they were still strong.

In the build-up, Cooper played down the importance of his return to The Liberty Stadium and insisted it was business as normal for him. After the backlash from Swansea fans though, which likely played a part in Cooper releasing that statement at the start of his tenure, you got the feeling he'd love to get one over them. The first half was very tentative, with Forest happy to cede possession and Swansea not really knowing what to do with it. Just before half-time, it should've been 1-0 Swansea as a Flynn Downes long ball caught the Forest defence napping and Osei-Tutu headed it straight into the path of Joël Piroe, inadvertently putting him one-on-one and with Samba out of position, but somehow Piroe blazed over with the goal at his mercy.

It was a huge let off, especially given Piroe had replaced Ayew very well – to the tune of 10 league goals already by that stage, but it was a reprieve Forest took with both hands. Just three minutes after the second half started, a Forest free kick caused a game of head tennis in the Swansea box, before the ball eventually fell to Zinckernagel about 25 yards out. He played a one-two with Grabban and upon receiving it back just inside the box, let fly an absolute missile that gave Swansea keeper Ben Hamer no chance. Two minutes later, Spence played a wonderfully weighted ball in behind the Swansea defence which Johnson ran onto, before squaring it across goal for Grabban to tap in.

Just before Forest could get comfortable though, 12 minutes later, a Ben Manning cross was half cleared by Worrall straight to Piroe on the edge of the box, who fired on the volley first time. His goalbound effort took a nick off Yates and wrong-footed Samba, making it 2-1.

It only took six minutes though for the Reds to restore their two goal lead and in comical fashion, too. Grabban picked out Osei-Tutu, who cut inside the box and fired what can only be described as a pea roller at Hamer. Unbelievably, Hamer fumbled picking it up and spilled it straight to Johnson, who did not miss when presented with an open goal.

That killed the game off, but right at the death, Taylor ran down the right wing and beat two players, before cutting it back to Cafu on the edge of the box. Cafu's well hit first time effort caught Hamer cold and nestled in the back of the net, sparking wild celebrations from the Portuguese midfielder, who had just scored his first goal for the club to make it 4-1. You'd have to possess a heart of stone to not have been happy for Cafu, who despite not being a regular, never complained, rarely let anyone down and always gave everything for the club – whether he was on the pitch or not.

Frequently seen shouting words of encouragement from the bench and joining in with celebrations from the touchline, Cafu was the true definition of an unsung hero. To see him knee slide, leap over a barrier and jump into the away end was a lovely moment – it may have put the cherry on top for Forest, but you could see how much it meant to him. It also wrapped up a really nice day for Cooper, who again stressed that everyone involved from his Swansea departure had moved on, himself included, but I bet that must've felt very good. The game was just two weeks before Christmas, so as early presents go, that one has to be up there for him.

The last game before Christmas saw Forest host Hull City and with the Reds now eighth, it was fair to say the club had a new objective – promotion. From kick-off, Forest put Hull under substantial pressure, with Grabban twice going close before Forest nearly put a goal of the season contender together. Some beautiful interplay between Zinckernagel, Spence and Johnson ended with Spence backheeling it through to Johnson, who chose to shoot instead of play it across goal, narrowly missing the target. Hull rode their luck though and shortly after the impressive Osei-Tutu was subdued with another injury, they struck first blood just before half-time.

A diagonal long ball from Sean McLoughlin caught Spence out and allowed Keane Lewis-Potter to dart inside of him and go one-on-one with Samba, which he didn't pass up. Not that there's a particularly good time to concede, but doing so right before half-time is one of the worst times you can do it. However, Forest were playing well and just needed to keep doing what they were doing and the result would come. From the restart, they posed a threat and Zinckernagel had a header well saved, before Mighten drove into the box and was fouled by George Honeyman. It was an awkward one as Mighten was stretching before being barged into, catching Honeyman in the process, but the ref gave the penalty all the same.

It came at the cost of Mighten, who needed lengthy treatment before being taken off the field and that meant Grabban had to wait four minutes before finally taking the spot kick. Once he got the all clear from the ref though, he made no mistake and Forest were level again. With 20 to go, Grabban surged down the right wing and held off several challenges before floating a ball in for Johnson, who after chesting it down, slotted past the keeper to make it 2-1. Hull had a chance late on to equalise when Forest didn't clear their lines and the ball fell to Greg Docherty just outside the six yard box, but he fired way over and Forest secured the win.

Christmas that year felt a bit more magical. Forest had gone nine games without defeat, their longest unbeaten run in the Championship since going 13 unbeaten in the 2015/16 season and were just one point off the top six. During the run, fans had been frantically rescheduling plans they provisionally had for late May, myself included (sorry Rich and Jack, but a bank holiday weekend in Wales could wait), just in case Forest made the play-off final. However, as fans know full well, there's always something around the corner. On this instance, it was a Boxing Day trip to Middlesbrough, who were now managed by Chris Wilder, who no doubt had a point to prove to the Forest ownership after being overlooked for Cooper.

From the start, Forest – minus an ineligible Spence or an injured Osei-Tutu, with Back playing right wing back – seemed sluggish. It was as if they'd been enjoying the festivities a little too much, as they just seemed second to every ball. Boro meanwhile, looked good and they didn't have to wait long until they broke the deadlock, although this came in comical fashion. Samba passed the ball to Yates, who in the face of pressure from an onrushing Boro player, put his head down, did a 180 turn and passed blind. While Yates meant to find Samba's feet, he instead found the back of his own net.

After that, Boro smelt blood. Andraz Sporar and Onel Hernández, both of whom scored at The City Ground in Hughton's last game, both wasted good chances, but the best one came shortly before the break. Some good play in front of Forest's box ended up with Neil Taylor receiving the ball out left and his cross went all the way through to Isaiah Jones, whose effort rattled the post. Unless Forest snapped out of it in the second half, the game had serious potential to get very ugly for them as they were playing in a way that was entirely out of kilter to the 16 games before.

At half-time, Cooper brought Carvalho on and he immediately made an impact, with Forest looking much better on the ball. After an hour, Johnson blazed past Paddy McNair and cut the ball across goal to Zinckernagel, but he somehow skied over from a few yards out. Shortly afterwards, Worrall surged forwards and after spraying it out wide to Johnson, continued his run into the box and met Johnson's subsequent cross, looping his header just over and onto the roof of the net.

Such is football though, Forest were made to pay for missing those chances. Some very neat interplay between Jones and Matt Crooks saw Boro forge an opening down the right and after Crooks' effort was saved by Samba, the rebound fell to Sporar, who made it 2-0. Forest still rallied and a lovely ball out wide by Carvalho allowed Colback to cut it back and find Xande Silva, but his effort hit the outside of the post. In truth, given how poor Forest were in the first half, they deserved defeat – but even then, could've had a draw had Zinckernagel and Silva been a bit luckier.

Cooper criticised the performance after the game, saying it was short of what was expected, but the good news for him was that because of the Christmas period, it was only a few days until Forest could try and make things right in their next game, which was a home match against Huddersfield. Despite Forest not starting brilliantly, with Sorba Thomas hitting the bar inside 20 seconds, the Reds were much improved and looked every bit a side that was looking to get out the league in the right way.

Twice Silva had goalbound shots charged down, while both Zinckernagel and Garner tested goalkeeper Lee Nicholls from range, before a lively Silva sped down the left and found Johnson unmarked on the six-yard box, only for his header to fly wide. The game looked like going one way and one way only, but then Huddersfield hit Forest with a sucker punch. Duane Holmes, formerly of Derby, found space and turned away from Ojeda towards goal, playing it down the left for Harry Toffolo. Toffolo then cut it back to Holmes just inside the box, whose near post effort beat Samba and found the back of the net.

Holmes took great glee in that goal, putting his fingers in his ears for his celebration towards the Trent End, but Forest weren't finished. Worrall and Garner twice shot just past the post, before some brilliant skill from Ojeda saw him hold off a Huddersfield player and lay it off to Zinckernagel, whose effort hit the crossbar so hard it probably could've been heard across Nottingham. Nicholls was again at the rescue for the Terriers with a superb stop from Silva, while after the break, he again denied Zinckernagel after the Dane wriggled his way through a sea of bodies.

Try and they might though, Forest just couldn't find a way through, with Spence, Cafu and Johnson all having half chances. Right at the end, Silva had a shot parried by Nicholls and it fell straight to Johnson with a partially open goal staring him in his face. However, Johnson could only find the side netting. At the full-time whistle, it was more a case of bewilderment than anger from the home fans. You could've played that game 10 times and nine times, Forest – who had 23 shots in the game – would've won.

It was a key win for Huddersfield as they clung onto sixth, whereas Forest had dropped down to ninth following their back to back defeats, leaving them five points behind the Terriers. Amidst the disappointment of the best team losing on the night though, the bigger picture objective was to get to January and be in touching distance of the top six, which is exactly what Forest had achieved. Against all odds having given the rest of the league a seven game head start, Cooper's Reds were in with a chance of glory.

CHAPTER FOUR – THE MAGIC OF THE CUP

With Big Ben ringing out and bringing in 2022, the January transfer window was officially open and Forest wasted no time at all in making their mark. On January 1, 23-year-old Aston Villa striker Keinan Davis signed on loan until the end of the season, while on January 4, Forest successfully pipped QPR to the signing of Bournemouth centre back Steve Cook on a free transfer. Both of these signings offered something valuable for Forest, but it was Cook that was seen as the more vital as he was the most needed. Forest had been a little shaky at the back on occasion and Cooper had pressed for his signing, given Cook's ability and leadership skills.

Interestingly, according to The Athletic, Murphy was against signing the 30-year-old defender. Given his style was to sign younger players, he perhaps felt Cook represented the type of transfer the club had repeatedly fallen into the trap of signing – ie, an older player with little resell value and would prove hard to shift in the long run. However, Cooper was convinced that Cook could play a huge part in the middle of a back three with Worrall and McKenna either side of him and eventually got his way, though it wasn't all rosy.

Following a Covid outbreak at Middlesbrough, it had emerged that Boro had a recall clause for Spence, who had now cemented himself as one of Forest's key players. His link-up with Johnson down that right hand side was integral to the club's rise up the league, so when Wilder said he'd have a chat with Cooper about the possibility of recalling Spence because he didn't have a team to field, panic struck. Thankfully, Boro's scheduled New Year's Day game with Sheffield United was eventually postponed and a few days after that, Wilder confirmed that Spence would be staying with Forest for the season as agreed.

Despite that, the experience spooked Forest. Life without Spence wasn't really worth thinking about, but if he were to be recalled for whatever reason, it was evident that the club were seriously ill-equipped to deal with his departure. As such, shortly after, Osei-Tutu had his loan spell cut short as unfortunately for the full back, he just couldn't stay fit. Instead, Forest signed pacey 27-year-old Canada international Richie Laryea from Toronto FC. Laryea was almost certainly a Murphy recommendation and Forest were now covered in that position, which was timely as up next was a break from Championship action as the Reds geared up to host English giants Arsenal in the third round of the FA Cup.

Arsenal – wearing a special all white kit as part of a campaign to combat knife crime – had all of the ball as expected, though they didn't really do a lot with it. Eddie Nketiah and Albert Sambi Lokonga both had efforts from range deflected wide and they could've had a penalty when Worrall dragged White to the floor, but otherwise, Forest were pretty comfortable. The main talking point was Davis and how he'd spent the entire half bullying Rob Holding. Davis was a defender's nightmare – physical, quick and technical and he was launching Holding around like a rag doll.

You could already see how he'd be important for Cooper moving forwards and it seemed as if Forest had found a real gem with him. The second half continued in the same fashion, though Forest had started to show a bit more belief and a lucky ricochet set Johnson on his way down the right before cutting it back to Zinckernagel, but his effort was well saved by Bernd Leno. Arsenal responded well and for the first time all game, Bukayo Saka escaped Colback's pocket and whipped in a wonderful ball for Nketiah. However, despite Nketiah evading Worrall, he got his header all wrong and it went harmlessly past the post.

The longer the game remained 0-0, the more Forest started to sense an upset was on the cards. Garner stung the palms of Leno with an excellently struck free kick about 30 yards out and Forest had a penalty appeal of their own waved away when Saka shoved Colback to the floor, but with seven minutes to go, none of that mattered. Lokonga's pass inside his own half hit Yates in the face and fell for Johnson, who carried it briefly before he played it down the right wing for Yates to sprint onto. Yates' first time cross found a flying Grabban, whose outstretched leg met the ball well enough to put it past Leno and into the back of the net.

The ground erupted and some fans from the Trent End even ran onto the pitch to celebrate with the players. A few minutes later, they had more reason to celebrate as the referee blew for full time.

Arsenal, who were sitting fourth in the Premier League at the time, hadn't even managed a single shot on target. To sum up how good Forest were defensively, Gabriel Martinelli would later go onto say that Spence was the toughest opponent he'd ever faced. This was the first time that Depeche Mode's 'Just Can't Get Enough' was used as victory music at The City Ground and while the song very much added to the winning experience, the crowd didn't really pay too much attention at first.

However, Forest couldn't afford to dwell on that outstanding result for too long as focus quickly shifted back to the daily grind of Championship football. Up next for Forest was a tricky trip to Millwall, who generally had the Reds' number whenever they rocked up at The Den. The hi-vis was worn for the occasion, although it was Millwall who started the brighter as Benik Afobe left Worrall trailing in his wake after a neat turn out wide, but after driving into the box, his effort was well saved by Samba. With Sheyi Ojo pulling strings, Millwall spent most of the first half putting Forest in awkward situations, but unable to really test Samba.

Shortly before half time though, Forest should've taken the lead. Grabban, an ex-Millwall player who was booed on touch by the home fans, jinked into the box and cut the ball back for Yates on the penalty spot, who shot straight at goalkeeper Bartosz Bialkowski. After the break, Forest didn't relent. A neat triangle with Yates, Johnson and Grabban saw the latter have a cheeky effort saved, before Yates had one cleared off the line after meeting a Colback corner. Millwall didn't clear their lines from that corner and Yates had another chance after Johnson picked him out, but his header flew wide of the goal and found Worrall, who quickly fed Colback, who then found the head of Grabban, but Bialkowski repelled him with a very good save.

Much like the Huddersfield game, Cooper's men had gotten into a rhythm and Millwall were being bombarded by wave after wave of Forest attacks. Also like the Huddersfield game though, Millwall had a chance against the run of play and really, they should've scored like the Terriers did. Mason Bennett's cross found Afobe unmarked and he fired a well hit effort on goal, but somehow Samba kept it out. With 91 minutes on the clock, Worrall won the ball back from a throw and found Johnson. Johnson then just ran forward and eventually picked out Zinckernagel in the box, whose effort was well saved by Bialkowski, but the rebound looped up and fell straight at Grabban's feet for him to prod home.

After being booed all game, it was poetic that Grabban would haunt his old club and right at the death, Forest had taken three points they very much deserved. Forest had 24 shots in total, the vast majority of which came in the second half. It was a huge win and one that highlighted Forest's resilience and mentality, but in the grand scheme of things, not much had changed as everyone around the Reds had won, so the gap to sixth was still five points. All Forest could do was keep winning their games and there was no better game to win than the one that was up next – Derby County at home.

Since the Reds last faced Derby, a lot had changed. Derby had been docked a whopping 21 points for entering administration and for breaching EFL accounting rules. Relegation seemed a certainty and the club's future seemed in grave danger, with administrators struggling to find a suitable buyer and money running out fast. In fact, the club were under a transfer embargo for failing to pay staff their December wages on time and their fans had resorted to posting a series of poems on social media to raise awareness and to 'save Derby County'.

Naturally, any club going into administration is awful, but sympathy for Derby was in very short supply. It wasn't that long ago Derby fans were openly flaunting their club making a mockery of the rules, claiming owner Mel Morris had the league "on strings," so the Forest faithful were hardly going to give spare change to their cause. Although, just before kick-off, Forest fans did choose to help out after all. Those in Upper Bridgford decided to shower the away fans beneath them with a series of fake £5 notes, some of which had Morris' face on.

Also before kick-off was an amazing Forza Garibaldi display in the Trent End, which depicted Robin Hood firing an arrow above of a banner reading 'Welcome to our Forest Kingdom' and with a backdrop of Nottingham in the middle. The work Forza do is incredible and the tifos they prepare have so much thought behind them. This one was the first for two years as a result of Covid and it all made for an electric atmosphere at The City Ground as 1,560 days after Derby had last beaten the Reds, the two East Midlands rivals entered battle once more – and this would possibly the last time for a while.

The Rams actually started relatively well and did a good job of managing a fervent crowd, to the point where they nearly silenced the home faithful 15 minutes in. A lucky deflection saw Tom Lawrence pick the ball up just outside the box and he drove in, played a delicious one-two with Colin Kazim-Richards, but fired wide of Samba's post when he received the ball back. He really should've scored and the Forest fans were quick to let him know it – amongst other things they had to say to him.

In 2019, Lawrence had escaped prison after drunkenly crashing his car after a team night out and then running away from the scene, leaving a severely injured Richard Keogh, who was his captain, behind. Instead, he received a 12-month community order and was ordered to carry out 180 hours of unpaid work, but the Forest fans clearly felt his punishment was light. Rousing renditions of "Tom Lawrence, you should be in jail" soon turned into "Tom Lawrence, you left him to die," further proving that this isn't a rivalry for the faint hearted.

After that scare, Forest grew into the game. A lovely flick from Garner was pushed into Yates by Davis, whose effort was well saved by Ryan Allsop and shortly after half-time, the Reds took the lead. A Garner free-kick was headed across goal by McKenna to Davis, who brought it down for Cook to have a shot. His effort was blocked, but the ball kindly looped up for Grabban to fire home just inside the six-yard box, sparking wild scenes from the home fans.

Derby were defiant though and should've equalised when they worked the ball into Luke Plange, who had his back to goal just outside the six yard box. He laid it off for Ravel Morrison, whose goalbound effort was heroically thwarted with a goal saving block from McKenna, which evaded the onrushing Nathan Byrne and went out for a corner. With 10 left on the clock, Forest made Derby pay for that miss. Johnson clipped the ball down the left for Zinckernagel to run onto and upon receiving it, the Dane drove into the box, looked up and caressed it into Johnson's path, allowing the Wales winger to give Forest a 2-0 lead.

Flares went off in A Block, causing red smoke to cover parts of the pitch, but there was another twist yet. Entering stoppage time, Derby broke down the left and Plange flicked the ball into the box for Lawrence, who was flattened by a late Cook challenge. It was totally needless from Cook and Lawrence rattled his penalty into the bottom corner to halve the deficit. As Lawrence went to retrieve the ball though, Samba shunted him into the net and subsequently sparked a melee, which both players were booked for.

Derby now had six minutes to rescue a point, but Forest put on a masterclass in how to manage the game and easily saw the time out. The drama wasn't over yet though, as in the 96th minute, a heavy touch from Morrison saw him try to recover the ball with a late lunge, which connected with Zinckernagel. This started another melee as Johnson – and incredibly, Samba – ran straight to defend their teammate and players from both sides had to be pulled apart. Before it could escalate further, the ref brandished the red card for Morrison, who left the field being goaded by Samba.

Shortly after Morrison did leave the pitch, the ref blew full time. It would be 1,560 days and counting since Derby last beat Forest and this time when 'Just Can't Get Enough' was played, it was like being at a Depeche Mode gig. Forest fans all over the stadium were up clapping and dancing to celebrate the win and with good reason – the Reds were now four points behind sixth placed Huddersfield, but with a game in hand. Cooper had now won 10 of his 19 games in charge and the more optimistic fans were noticing how Forest were now nine points off second with 19 games still to play.

Much like the momentous Arsenal victory though, Forest couldn't dwell on beating their enemy. It was only three days until the next match, which was a home tie against Barnsley, who were bottom of the league going into the fixture. This was some feat given Derby had been done 21 points and yet were still above the Tykes on goal difference, but after just 15 minutes, it was easy to see why. Mads Anderson, as the last man near the halfway line, was caught in possession by Davis, who proceeded to run through on goal unchallenged and score his first in Garibaldi red.

Amazingly, this was Forest's first goal in the first half of a game since that Zinckernagel rocket at Reading and while Barnsley offered some resistance, with Callum Styles having an effort cleared off the line by McKenna, it wasn't too long until they had their second. Colback split the Barnsley defence with a superb ball in behind for Johnson to run onto, who duly put it across the box on a plate for Yates to fire home. After that, Forest pretty much kept Barnsley at arm's length while still probing themselves, but with 15 to play, Spence ended the game.

After receiving the ball deep inside his own half, Spence skipped past two players as he drove towards the Barnsley box, carrying the ball some 40 yards or so in the process. As he approached the box, left back Jordan Williams tried to physically engage with Spence, but was mercilessly sent crashing to the turf as he lost a strength contest with the on-loan Boro defender. Spence then continued his run into the box and pulled it back for Johnson, whose shot nestled into the far corner. It was an assist that the pantheon of City Ground greats would've been proud of and was certainly one of the best of the season so far, while also showcasing Spence's phenomenal natural ability.

It was nearly four when Silva hit the post after being released following another Spence surge into the Barnsley half and it really should've been four when Garner picked out Silva with a delightful ball across the six yard box, but Silva fired over with an open goal at his mercy. Nevertheless, the points were in the bag and the Reds now had four straight wins under their belts. They were now up to seventh, just one point behind sixth placed Huddersfield. However, with just six days left of the transfer window, a storm was brewing behind the scenes.

Earlier that day, Brentford submitted an £18m bid for Johnson, which – if accepted – would be a club record sale for Forest, their previous being the £15m they fetched from Middlesbrough for Britt Assombalonga. What Forest had to weigh up though was whether cashing in on Johnson was worth it given promotion was fast becoming a genuine possibility. Promotion to the Premier League would generate at least £170m in revenue, which would far outstrip the £18m for arguably Forest's best player, but if the Reds were to miss out, it would be hard to say whether that money would be on the table again in the summer.

Johnson had just 18 months left on his deal and if the Reds were to hold firm, their negotiating position would be compromised in the summer as the forward would just have a year left. When this happens, clubs gain an upper hand as if it doesn't look like a new deal will be signed, lower than value offers come in as a result. Clubs are then forced to decide whether to cash in under value, or keep the player and risk losing them for nothing. This isn't always the case and special talents still command a high fee, but it's a huge risk to take. Forest would've been eligible to compensation in this event given Johnson's age, but it likely wouldn't be anywhere near £18m.

It was also heavily rumoured that Forest were very close to their PSR limit, which as we saw with Reading, can carry a points deduction if breached. Naturally, selling Johnson would make Forest more than clear and selling a key player had become commonplace for the Reds, with the likes of Matty Cash, Oliver Burke, Michail Antonio, Ben Osborn, Ben Brereton Díaz, Karl Darlow and Jamaal Lascelles all being sold to make ends meet previously, but none of those players had been sold with promotion realistically in the club's grasp with 18 games to play. As such, would Forest stick or twist?

It would appear that some inside the Forest boardroom twisted, as according to The Atheltic, the Bees believed that their bid had been accepted. So much so, that they had booked in a medical for the next day. There was a slight issue though, in that neither Cooper nor

Murphy had been told, despite kick-off being mere hours away. Predictably upon being informed, the news went down like a lead balloon. After the game, both Cooper and Murphy were adamant losing a player of Johnson's quality would be hugely detrimental to any chances of promotion and after some very honest discussions, those in the boardroom ceded and officially rejected Brentford's offer instead.

With everyone back on the same page, there was a realisation that Forest could do with a few more signings to really give promotion a right good go, but if Johnson wasn't to be sold, other departures were likely necessary. As such, before Forest's final game of January, Carvalho was sold to Olympiacos for an undisclosed fee. Carvalho was Forest's record signing for £13m as per BBC Sport, but in all truth, the club had let him down – he was initially signed to have the team built around him, which happened to great effect for six months, but managerial changes put a stop to that. In the end, the move was best for all parties.

There was a loan departure for Lyle Taylor, who joined Birmingham until the end of the season. Under Cooper, Taylor made 12 appearances, three of which were starts and with Davis signing, Taylor's gametime was only going to become even more limited. As such, that move also made sense, although Taylor's heroics against Bristol City would never be forgotten. It appeared that these two departures, on top of Carl Jenkinson being sent on loan to Melbourne City a week or so earlier, had given Forest a bit of wiggle room for some deadline day action.

Before that could transpire, the Reds went to Cardiff and did so knowing that a victory would see them enter the play-offs for the first time, as teams above them had slipped up. In fact, they could go as high as fifth with a win and on paper, they were serious favourites. Former Millwall striker Steve Morison was now manager at Cardiff having taken over from Mick McCarthy, but the Bluebirds had plummeted down the league and had won just two games all season. But for points deductions to Reading and Derby and they'd be bottom three, so this was as good a chance as any to cement Forest's play-off credentials.

After just six minutes, a McKenna pass to Zinckernagel was intercepted by Perry Ng, whose ball to Jordan Hugill allowed him to run through on goal unchallenged, eventually slotting home past Samba. Soon after, Hugill, who'd only signed for Cardiff on loan mere hours earlier, nearly had a second when he was picked out by a Tommy Doyle cross, but his effort was straight at Samba. Forest seemed shell-shocked and words were certainly needed at half time.

Whatever was said seemed to have the desired effect and Forest had a great chance to level when McKenna clipped a ball down the left and Garner set off after it, shrugging Sean Morrison off the ball and then bolted to the byline. Garner then put a lovely ball across the six-yard box, but a stretching Johnson couldn't quite get on the end of it. With 25 to go, Joe Ralls' powerful effort from outside the box pinged off the inside of the post and back into play, but Isaak Davies was the only one to run towards the ball, gifting him an open goal to make it 2-0 as the Forest defence stood and watched after being caught flat footed.

Forest kept going and should've scored when Silva turned his man, played a neat one-two with Davis that took out the entire Cardiff defence and left Silva one-on-one, but Silva fired over. In the 94th minute, Forest did eventually score as Garner's exceptional corner was nodded in by Davis, but it was too little too late and for the second time that season, the Reds had passed up a golden opportunity to break into those coveted top six places. To make matters worse, Grabban went off injured towards the end of the game and with Taylor now at Birmingham, they were short up front.

Ultimately, Forest were below par and were punished for it, but the inquest was put on hold temporarily as deadline day saw a small flurry of action take place on Trentside. Left footed centre back Jonathan Panzo, who was part of Cooper's U17 World Cup winning squad, was signed from Dijon for £1.5m according to the Nottingham Post, while Rodrigo Ely, who hadn't kicked a ball for Forest, had his contract mutually terminated. The Ely signing was bizarre, but the Panzo one made sense and also covered Forest if the imperious McKenna was unavailable for whatever reason.

In addition to Panzo, Forest signed striker Sam Surridge from Stoke to deal with the Grabban injury. Surridge had only signed for Stoke from Bournemouth a few months prior, but despite being Stoke manager Michael O'Neill's number one target, his time at the bet365 stadium hadn't gone to plan at all. Surridge had started just six times in six months and was set to go on loan to Cardiff before Forest swooped in, forking out £2.2m for his services according to the Stoke Sentinel. Much like with Panzo, Surridge was very much known to

Cooper, who'd loaned Surridge for his Swansea side in the 2019/20 season.

Finally, Mohamed Dräger also left – although only on a temporary basis, as he signed for FC Luzern on loan. Cooper now had the tools he needed to mount a sustained play-off charge and with a balanced and exciting squad at his disposal, the disappointment from the Cardiff game was soon forgotten about. Instead, all attention turned back to the FA Cup where for the fourth round, Forest would face the current holders in Leicester City at home, which would be the first time in eight years the two had done battle.

Forest's relationship with Leicester is...strange. Yes, both are from the East Midlands and yes, it is technically an East Midlands derby when the two meet...but in the same way that Chelsea v Brentford is a London derby. Relevant for one, not so much for the other. For Leicester, the Reds are their number one rivals. They absolutely hate the club and would love nothing more than to see them struggle, although this isn't necessarily reciprocated and they crave a rivalry that just isn't there. Forest fans who work with Leicester fans or live in Leicester or the surrounding areas will understandably share that rivalry, but for the majority who don't, it's nice to beat them but it's hardly season defining if Forest do.

Yes, the club are cited in chants, but hatred? Nah. When it comes to East Midlands clubs, that's reserved for Derby and Derby only – which in itself, annoys Leicester fans. To further highlight the difference, prior to the game, Forest fans were pretty relaxed about the affair. For Forest, it was a great test against the holders. For

Leicester, it was almost as big as the final they'd recently won, with Leicester defender – and boyhood fan – Luke Thomas hamming it up in the buildup to the game. "You know the fans are going to be up for it," he told the Daily Mail. "So we're going to go out there and hopefully, smash them."

Even on the day of the game, it was clear how it meant more to Leicester than Forest. The Forest social admin posted a routine matchday post ahead of kick-off, whereas about 30 miles down the road, the Leicester admin had posted a graphic of five Foxes players with the caption, "It's derby day". Meanwhile, some Leicester fans had taken it upon themselves to start trouble and smashed up the outside of a family pub in Nottingham, as their fans sought to wreak havoc on their big day out.

It was all very silly, but from the first whistle, Forest were relentless from the off and were hugely unfortunate not to take the lead when Johnson's cross was chested down by Davis and his powerfully struck effort smashed off the bar. It was just wave after wave of Forest pressure and eventually, Leicester caved. A Johnson cross again found Davis, but this time he laid it off into the path of Zinckernagel, who couldn't miss. From kick-off, Leicester played it back to Daniel Amartey, who under pressure from Johnson, played a back pass to goalkeeper Danny Ward. However, his back pass was under hit and Johnson pounced upon it before composing himself and putting it between Ward's legs and into the back of the net.

Eight minutes later, a Garner corner was met by Worrall's head and gave Ward no chance. How Worrall was even on the field was a mystery given he'd broken three ribs in the Millwall victory and was expected to be out for six weeks, but with three goals in nine minutes, Leicester's big day out was starting to resemble a dystopian nightmare. It was all too much for one Leicester fan, who in the aftermath of Worrall's goal, ran onto the pitch and punched Davis.

It was a deplorable event and thankfully he was contained very quickly, but things like that shouldn't happen at any level. Despite that moron's idiocy, Forest didn't relent, although they did hand Leicester a gift five minutes before half-time. James Maddison clipped a ball forward for Kelechi Iheanacho to run onto and Samba raced out of his goal to clear it, but missed the ball, presenting Iheanacho with an open goal to pass the ball into. It was a stark reminder that Forest never did anything the easy way and the start of the second half did little to calm nerves.

Maddison sent Patson Daka racing down the left wing, but after being left with nowhere to go, Daka gave it back to Maddison on the edge of the box, whose effort whistled past Samba's far post. However, any fears of an implosion were eased when with half an hour to play, Spence held off one Leicester player as he carried it towards goal, played a one-two with Zinckernagel and upon receiving it back, held off another Leicester player and prodded past Ward to make it 4-1. After that, barring one decent Amartey effort from outside the box that Samba saved and a courageous Worrall block with his head despite being grounded, the game sort of fizzled out and for only the second time in 17 years, Forest had progressed to the fifth round of the FA Cup.

Football was back, but we wished it wasn't. Above, Coventry (A), below, a welcome home before Bournemouth (H)

Above: Stoke (A) – possibly the worst ever. Below: Samba gears up for QPR (A)

Above: Celebrations at Reading (A) in the hi-vis. Below: Pre-match before
Arsenal (H) and another famous cup scalp

East Midlands supremacy. Above: The Forza Garibaldi banner pre Derby (H).
Below: Aftermath of Forest 4-1 Leicester (H)

It was an electric performance and one that reaffirmed the belief that Forest could get promoted. Cup games don't always show the full picture, but two very good Premier League teams had now come to The City Ground and deservedly exited the tournament. Forest couldn't afford to stand still though as next up was a trip to second placed Blackburn, who despite their league position, had started to stutter. Rovers had propelled themselves to second with a run of eight wins in 10 games, but their next two fixtures saw them take just one point, leaving them only a point above Bournemouth, having played two games more.

Blackburn started well though and really should've taken the lead when a smart Joe Rothwell free kick caught the Forest defence napping and played in John Buckley one-on-one, but Samba got a boot to his effort. The ball then fell to Ben Brereton Díaz, but McKenna was on hand to clear his effort off the line. After that, Forest struck and in special fashion. A Samba ball found Davis just inside his own half and with a Blackburn player applying pressure behind him, Davis turned inside and into the path of two other Blackburn players. Somehow, Davis' quick feet took the ball away from all three of them and set him running towards goal, where he was hauled down.

Before the ref could blow for a foul, Davis sprang straight up and popped the ball in-between two Blackburn defenders for Garner to run onto. Upon receiving the ball, Garner feigned to shoot and sent another Blackburn defender sliding in the wrong direction, before coolly slotting past Thomas Kaminski to make it 1-0. It seemed implausible that Spence's assist against Barnsley could be topped, but Davis had found a way to do so. Blackburn responded well and Brereton Díaz should've done better after meeting Ryan Giles' cross, but he headed straight into Samba's grateful arms.

Shortly after the second half, the game was turned on its head. Darragh Lenihan lunged in late and caught Colback, leaving the referee no choice but to brandish a second yellow card for the defender. Despite going down to 10 though, Blackburn went on the offensive and Forest struggled to cope, with Sam Gallagher wasting a great chance to score when he planted a header wide. Eventually, Blackburn tired and Forest then hit back. A Worrall ball down the line was turned into Johnson's path by Surridge, but despite Garner being in a better position, Johnson shot anyway and his strike was parried into Surridge's path, whose effort fizzed across goal but couldn't be reached by Garner.

In stoppage time, it didn't matter. Surridge took the ball down brilliantly in the box and span Jan Paul Van Hecke, who responded by chopping Surridge down. Johnson stepped up to take the penalty and put it straight down the middle, ensuring the points would be returning to Nottingham. Up in the away end, someone had somehow managed to smuggle a speaker in and at full time, cranked it up to full volume before putting 'Just Can't Get Enough' on. The away end went nuts and its impact as a song was very much spreading, to the point it was now synonymous with a Forest win under Cooper.

Finally though, at the third time of asking, Forest had won a game that ensured they would go into the top six spaces, with the win taking them up to sixth. It had been 567 days since Forest were last in the top six, but there was still a lot of work to do to lock in that position between mid-February and May. Next up was Stoke, who were only four points behind Forest and with a game in hand, so it was a match that the Reds couldn't really afford to lose.

The first half was pretty cagey, with the only real notable effort at goal coming in a bizarre manner as Ben Wilmot's audacious attempt from out wide hit the top of the bar before landing in Samba's arms, but the second half saw both teams step up a gear or two. Stoke hit the framework again after Lewis Baker banged a free kick against the post, but the introduction of Surridge as a sub against his former employers changed things. After picking the ball up in the centre circle, a crisp outside of the boot pass from Surridge released Lowe down the left, whose low cross from deep brilliantly found Johnson, who calmly slotted it under the onrushing goalkeeper to give Forest the lead.

With half an hour still to play, both the Leicester and Blackburn games started to take their toll on Forest and Stoke were more than happy to step up. Jaden Philogene offered a warning sign when he stung Samba's palms with an effort from range and just 12 minutes after Forest scored, Stoke were level. Nick Powell flicked a near post corner towards the back stick and Josh Maja, who Forest had tried to sign that summer, was on hand to tap in. Johnson came close to restoring Forest's lead with a vicious effort, but Stoke goalkeeper Joe Bursik was on hand to tip it over.

In the dying embers of the game though, chaos ensued. Samba collected a corner and as he ran out to try and release the ball early, Stoke defender Phil Jagielka deliberately charged into him. Samba shrugged it off but when Jagielka went past, the goalkeeper decided to punch Jagielka in the face. It was a total head loss moment and the referee had no choice but to send Samba off and award a penalty. As Forest had used all of their subs, Worrall had to go in goal and with just minutes left on the clock, Baker fired home. The drama wasn't over though and in the 92nd minute, Forest had a free kick just outside the box.

Garner stepped up and his effort smacked against the bar, but the rebound fell McKenna's way. Rather than go for goal himself, the Scotland international nodded across goal for Yates, who with an open goal at his mercy, headed home. Somehow, someway, Forest had claimed a point, despite defeat looking like a certainty. One again, it showcased Forest's newly discovered never say die attitude and you suspect Samba was a very relieved man in the changing room after the game, given his moment of madness hadn't cost Forest the match.

That being said, he would now be unavailable for three games and to make matters worse, other results went against Forest, who were now seventh and two points behind sixth placed Middlesbrough. But, with no midweek game, Forest could finally rest ahead of a trip to Bournemouth, who with seven first-team players out, were coming around at a good time. Four hours before kick-off though, with fans and players having already made the 200 mile trip, the game was postponed. Apparently, the stadium was no longer structurally sound following Storm Eunice, with some damage to the Main Stand roof enough for the Bournemouth Safety Advisory Group to call it off.

This seemed very hard to believe. Forest asked if the game could be pushed back until the day after to deal with the issues, but this suggestion was rejected. Bournemouth boss Scott Parker came out and said the club had done everything possible to get the game ahead, but Forest didn't agree. The club submitted an official complaint to the EFL as presumably in their eyes, Bournemouth had shirked the fixture because they were worried Forest would beat them given the players they had out Nevertheless, the decision stood.

Instead, Forest had to focus on a trip to midweek trip to Preston. It was a bright start and Forest should've had a penalty after 10 minutes when Colback slipped Davis into the box and he was brought down in a heap, but the referee wasn't interested. Forest were furious, but got over it fairly quickly and despite Preston largely being on top, a break down the left from Davis saw him get past his man and cut a ball back to the edge of the box to Garner, but he slipped as he shot and his effort was comfortably saved.

Preston were more lively in the second half and Cameron Archer should've done better when played through one-on-one, but Horvath, standing in for the suspended Samba, stood his ground well and beat the ball away. Minutes later, Archer was through one-on-one again and had left Cook for dust with his movement, but the forward shot past Horvath's post. It was very much a game for the defences otherwise, until right at the end when Spence charged into the box from the right, darted towards the six yard box and put the ball across goal, but no Forest player was willing to gamble and the chance went begging.

It was hardly a game for the neutral, but Horvath getting a clean sheet under his belt would've done him the world of good. That mistake at home to Boro seemed a world away now and his performance showed that the Reds had a steady back-up to Samba in their ranks. On the balance of play, Cooper said that he was happy with a point, but also stated that he knew Forest could play a lot better. They'd have a chance to showcase that a few days later as to round off February, Forest would host Bristol City and with the Reds now five points behind sixth place in 10th, a win would certainly be very timely.

After four minutes. Johnson set Davis off down the left and his cut back found Spence on the edge of the box, whose spectacular effort was matched by an even more spectacular save from Bristol City goalkeeper Daniel Bentley. It was all Forest and it seemed a matter of time until they broke the deadlock, with Cook forcing Bentley into another excellent save from a Garner corner. Eventually, it came. Spence carried the ball inside and when left with nowhere to go, sprayed it right to Johnson. Johnson carried it into the box and shot from just inside it, with his effort catching Bentley unaware and finding the back of the net.

Another Garner corner caused chaos in the Robins' box and Worrall's flick on was met by Davis, forcing Bentley into another sensational save. Somehow, it was only 1-0 at half-time, but just 10 minutes into the second half, Forest finally got the second they'd deserved. McKenna surged forwards from deep and played a one-two with Lowe, before pulling it back for Lowe when inside the box. Instead of shooting, Lowe played it into Garner's path on the edge of the box, whose precise finish into the bottom corner gave Bentley no chance.

It really should've been 3-0 when a loose sideways Tomas Kalas ball was sniffed out by Zinckernagel and put the Dane through on goal, but again Bentley came to the Robins' rescue with a great save with his feet. It finished 2-0, but despite being on the losing side, Bentley was easily player of the match. But for his heroics, Forest could've scored six. It was the perfect response for Cooper after a tricky trip to Deepdale, as a sign of a good side is one that bounces back from a poor performance/result with a good one.

To kick off March, Forest would face a tough trip to seventh placed Sheffield United, two points and two places above Forest. After a slow start to the season, the Blades had sacked manager Slaviša Jokanović and hired Paul Heckingbottom, who had put them firmly back on the right track. Given they were recently relegated and kept the majority of their team, it was a bit of a mystery they'd started as slowly as they had, but despite the fixture difficulty, this was very much a must not lose for Forest.

From the first whistle, there was only one team who looked like winning and that was a Forest side in their hi-vis kit. Within 60 seconds, Johnson had forced Wes Foderingham into a save and from the resulting corner, Davis flashed a header wide as the Reds made it clear from the off they weren't here to mess around. Davis was causing havoc and could've had a penalty when he was pulled down by his shirt, but where Davis failed to catch the ref's attention, Spence succeeded.

After weaving into the box from the right and slaloming past Rhys Norrington-Davies and John Fleck, Norrington-Davies mistimed his challenge and brought Spence down, leaving the ref with no choice but to award a spot kick. Johnson stepped up confidently, but Foderingham read him brilliantly and didn't move, batting Johnson's penalty into the floor and catching it at the second attempt. The home fans had their tails up after that and that helped the Blades make half time unscathed, but Forest were still in the ascendency after the break, with Cook's header from a corner hitting the bar.

However, those misses soon proved costly. With 20 left and against the run of play, Morgan Gibbs-White feigned a cross and took Colback out the game in the process, before checking inside and delivering a peach of a ball to the back stick for Billy Sharp to nod home. Sheffied United had deserved absolutely nothing from the game, but now had the lead and had finally woken up. A Fleck corner wasn't dealt with and Horvath had to be on hand to make a double save from Sharp and Ben Davies to keep it at 1-0. With time running out, it felt like the Reds would be shortchanged.

In the 95th minute though, Forest were awarded their 12th corner of the match and as Garner jogged over to take it, it had a very much do or die feel about it. Garner's delivery found the head of Yates, who had peeled away from his marker and steered his header across goal and into the bottom corner, sparking pandemonium in the away end. Yates' header was the eighth goal Forest had scored after the 90 minute mark, further highlighting they were built differently this time around and a draw was the very least they'd deserved.

While it only yielded a point, the signs of something special happening were there. Sheffield United fans after the game were saying they were in a unique predicament in that they were annoyed they'd drawn, but felt lucky to have even got that. They'd been incredibly fortunate to leave with anything and while Forest had let them off the hook, the Reds were still in the fight for the play-offs. That would have to go on pause though, as it was back to the cup next with Huddersfield returning to The City Ground to contest for a place in the FA Cup quarter finals.

Much like at Bramall Lane, Forest started brightly and Johnson's low cross found Surridge, who fired home for his first Forest goal. Or, so he thought, as despite being well onside, the official's flag went up and the goal was disallowed. With no VAR to overturn it, Forest were livid and two minutes later, Huddersfield took full advantage. Danel Sinani's corner found the head of Tom Lees, who powered his effort past Horvath. There was a huge sense of injustice at The City Ground, but rather than sulk, Forest rolled their sleeves up and set about putting things right.

Garner picked up the ball inside his own half and spotted a gap in the Huddersfield defence, playing an exquisite through ball for Yates, but he was thwarted by a superb last ditch challenge by Naby

Sarr. However, the ball fell kindly at Surridge's feet, who fired home to finally get his first goal in Forest colours. Huddersfield came back and hit the post through Pipa, but just eight minutes after the goal, Garner fired in a free-kick that was headed in by Yates, flipping what had been a breathless tie on its head.

After that, the game wasn't quite as open and this continued into the second half, although still fiercely contested. Horvath had to be very alert to deny Danny Ward after he was played through on goal, but Davis' introduction put Forest back on the front foot and Huddersfield couldn't cope. First, Yates played a ball in behind for Davis to run onto, which he played across goal for Spence, who blazed over in a great position. Shortly after, Davis held off two Huddersfield players before sending Johnson towards goal, with the Wales forward then picking out Garner, who also fired over in a great position.

In the end, Forest held on for a 2-1 win and had progressed to the FA Cup quarter finals for the first time since 1996. It was Huddersfield's first defeat in 18 games in all competitions and after the game, they took their frustration out on Eva's Grill, a Greek restaurant in West Bridgford. Eva's had a tradition where after every Forest win, they shot fireworks into the sky, which are of course, very visible at night and can be seen from the stadium. No-one had told Huddersfield this, whose fans seemed to think the display was just for them, hilariously sparking a tit for tat exchange with their fans online after the match.

As the fifth round was a midweek match, Forest couldn't bask in their progress for too long and up next was Reading at home. The Royals were just one place above the drop zone, but if they were coming to Forest expecting sympathy, that went out the window after 17 seconds. From kick off, Garner played it back to Cook, who passed to McKenna. McKenna then passed to Colback in midfield, who turned and gave it to Worrall. Worrall's first touch took him into Reading's half and his second released Spence down the right wing. Spence's ball into the box found Davis, who – with his back to goal – flicked the ball up with his right, before twisting and volleying past the keeper with his left.

It was the quickest goal scored in the Championship that season but after that, Forest looked a little complacent. Reading had chances, with Michael Morrison forcing Horvath into a good save and then Josh Laurent heading Tom Ince's cross just wide, but after half-time, Forest snapped out of it. Worrall gave the ball to Davis about 30 yards from goal and with two men on him, but the forward wriggled past both, drove into the box and curled one in off the post to make it 2-0. After that, Reading were done and the floodgates opened.

With 15 to go, Worrall played Spence down the right, who after coming inside, ran into trouble and laid it back to Yates. The midfielder had time to look up and take a touch before deciding to shoot, which he did to great effect as his effort arrowed into the bottom corner. Five minutes later, Worrall's long ball was flicked down the line by Davis to Silva, who put it on a plate for Surridge to get his second Forest goal. However, it wasn't all good news as Lowe and Cook both limped off at the end, which put something of a downer on the 4-0 win.

After the game, it was revealed that both would be out for a six-week spell, which was a huge blow. As solid as Colback was at left wing back, Forest were so much more fluid with Lowe there and while Cook had been a little rusty at the start, he'd quickly become an integral part of the back line. Cooper's mantra though was 'next man up' and he wasn't going to let a few injuries destabilise his hard work. Up next was fifth placed QPR at home, with the London club four points ahead of ninth placed Forest, but having played a game more. It was a great chance to maybe gatecrash the top six and a win under the lights would leave the Reds brilliantly poised.

Figueiredo came back in for Cook and Colback went to left wing back as Forest stuck to their shape, but QPR caught them cold early and it was a minor miracle they didn't score when Worrall's clearance was intercepted by Joe Willock on the edge of his own box, with Willock's tempting cut back somehow being miscued by Andre Gray and then Lee Wallace, with both missing when it seemed easier to score. Five minutes before half-time though, Gray wouldn't be so generous. With the ball seemingly glued to his foot, Ilias Chair expertly maneuvered his way out of trouble and into space before playing a delicious through ball to Gray, who left Figueiredo in a heap before planting one between Horvath's legs and into the net.

After 10 second half minutes, Zinckernagel gave it to Spence about 30 yards from goal, who proceeded to curl an absolute rocket into the top corner. To quote Andy Gray, take a bow, son. It was an amazing, ridiculous effort, fit to win any goal of the month or season award and it jolted Forest back into life. Davis and Zinckernagel both went close to giving Forest the lead and with seven left, a Garner corner was ran onto by Yates, who guided his effort home to make it four goals in four games for him. Three minutes after that, Lolley sent Surridge down the right and his ball found Davis, whose effort was saved by QPR stopper David Marshall. However, the rebound came back to Davis, so he laid it into Johnson's path to make it 3-1.

It was an excellent, gritty, hard fought win that saw Forest dig deep to come out on top. The Reds were now a point outside the top six with a game in hand, but again this result came at a cost as McKenna went off injured with 10 to go. It ruled him out of the next match, which was also the last before a timely international break, but it was the small matter of an FA Cup quarter final at The City Ground against Liverpool. It was the first time the Reds had faced Liverpool since relegation in 1999 and while there was only a few days of build-up, it was eagerly anticipated.

It would pit Cooper against his former club, adding another layer of interest to the match, where tensions are always high when the two face off anyway. This goes back to the glory days under Clough and to this day, Liverpool still sing "we hate Nottingham Forest," although many younger Liverpool fans probably see it as a case of if the shoe fits for the chant, similar to how most Forest fans feel when Leicester are cited in one. For a while though, it was real. Very real. Clough's Forest had the audacity to displace arguably Liverpool's best ever team, first as champions of England and then as champions of Europe. Along the way, Forest beat them in a League Cup final as well.

However, despite their iconic on-field battles from yesteryear, both Liverpool and Forest are forever aligned with each other in tragic circumstances. The Hillsborough disaster in 1989, which saw 97 fans go to a football match and not return home, occurred during an FA Cup semi-final between the two sides. There are no words to describe how awful the events of that day are, or the cover-up that followed. Ahead of their first meeting in two decades, Forest offered a show of support by covering 97 seats in the away end. The cover had both the Forest and the Liverpool badges on and a message reading, "97 never forgotten," in addition to the date of the tragedy, 15.04.89.

It was a lovely touch and one that was well received by the travelling support. The game itself would no doubt be very tribal as the embers of a long-standing rivalry would ignite, but some things are more important. Those embers were stoked before the game anyway as Liverpool manager Jürgen Klopp told Sky Sports, "I only know Nottingham from when I was a kid watching Robin Hood," which was incredibly patronising, especially as Forest had won more European Cups than Klopp had.

There was another Forza display too, which showed a parent with their child on their shoulders looking towards The City Ground on Trent Bridge with the caption, 'From one generation to the next', while the Trent Bridge shaped banner for the lower half of the Trent End read, 'Our desire is always to be here'. Stunning, as ever from the Forza team. With McKenna injured, Forest reverted to a 4-2-3-1, with

Figueiredo and Worrall playing as a centre back pairing. Liverpool only made a few changes and as expected, they had a lot of the ball, but they found it difficult to break through a stubborn Forest defensive set-up.

Diogo Jota was played through once but was thwarted by an excellent Worrall challenge and Konstantinos Tsimikas had a volley fly narrowly over, but Forest had dug their heels in well. It would only take one mistake though and when Colback got caught in possession near the halfway line, it appeared that was the moment. Within two passes, Roberto Firmino was one-on-one, but the Brazil international got too cocky for his own good and tried to lob Horvath, who read him like a book and batted the attempt away, allowing Worrall to clear the danger.

It was a huge let off for Forest and they managed to hold Liverpool off until half-time. The second half was in a similar vein, with Liverpool unable to find a way through and eventually, Klopp ran out of patience. With 25 to play, he made a quadruple change – off came Naby Keïta, Harvey Elliott, Fabinho and Alex Oxlade-Chamberlain, on came Jordan Henderson, Takumi Minamino, Thiago and Luis Díaz. Despite the changes though, Liverpool still couldn't find a way through and like the Arsenal game, Forest started to believe they might fashion a chance.

With 14 to play, it came. Colback flew into a tackle with Minamino and left him in a heap, but only after having won the ball first. The ball then fell to Davis, who gave it to Yates, who pinged it down the right hand side for Johnson. Johnson looked up and saw

Zinckernagel had lost Gomez and put the ball across to him, but eight yards out with the left hand side of the goal wide open, Zinckernagel put it past the right hand post. Cooper dropped to the floor with his head in hands. All Zinckernagel had to do was pass it into the left hand side of the goal and it was 1-0 Forest.

Within two minutes, that miss was ruthlessly punished. Spence tried to surge up the field but was dispossessed and the ball was played into the space he'd vacated for Tsimikas to run onto. Spence caught up with him, but Tsimikas turned inside him and put a teasing ball in, which Jota slid to get on the end of to make it 1-0 Liverpool. It did seem as if Jota was in an offside position and as such, Forest had their first time experiencing VAR, which was in effect from the quarter finals onwards. However, after getting the lines out, VAR determined Jota was just onside, so the goal stood.

Shortly after, Forest experienced VAR again. A lovely reverse pass by Garner caught the Liverpool defence out, Yates ran onto it and took it past Alisson before going down. It looked a stonewall penalty on first glance, but the VAR check showed that Yates had instigated the contact by dragging his trailing leg onto Alisson's arm. No penalty, but out of nowhere, Liverpool were on the ropes a bit. They tried to see the game out but overplayed it and lost the ball, with Surridge picking it up and sending Johnson down the right. Johnson beat Tsimikas and put a ball in for an unmarked Yates, but he got no power on his header and Alisson saved comfortably.

Before Forest could make it any more awkward for Liverpool, the ref blew for full time. Despite the defeat, the Forest fans gave the team a standing ovation – they'd performed heroically against one of the best teams in the world and on another day, could've caused an upset. Klopp took his Liverpool players over to their fans and clapped some of the Forest fans on the way, which was greeted by Forest fans telling him to fuck off and sticking two fingers up at him. Even in victory, he seemed patronising. Regardless, despite Cooper bringing the magic of the cup back to Trentside, Forest's FA Cup dream was over. It was a memorable run, but all focus now turned towards Project Promotion.

CHAPTER FIVE – COULD IT BE...?

After the Liverpool defeat, there was a two-week international break until Forest's next fixture, which would be a trip to the seaside to face Blackpool. It would also mark the start of April, which would be the busiest month of the season for Forest, with no less than eight games to cram in. The good news though was that Samba and McKenna were back for the trip to Bloomfield Road, allowing Cooper to revert back to the three at the back system which had worked so well, while another boost was that captain Grabban was back after his injury in the Cardiff defeat and was fit enough to be on the bench.

Having these three players back was a huge positive, as Samba had rediscovered his best form despite his moment of madness against Stoke, McKenna had been a consistent colossus at the back and Grabban still had so much to offer Forest despite his advancing years, chipping in with 13 goals in all competitions. Grabban's position as captain was frequently scrutinised by some Forest fans as he was never one to shout and scream at people, which is seen by some as a display of passion and a fundamental requirement in order to wear the armband. Instead, Grabban led by example as one of Forest's best players.

His influence was very notable off the field, too – even when he was injured. One beneficiary of this was Davis, who Grabban played with when he spent time on loan at Aston Villa in 2018. A video emerged of Grabban showing Davis how to position himself better for attacks, so that he was more central when the ball came into the box. Davis took this advice and when Forest scored after 18 seconds against Reading, Davis was exactly where Grabban had showed him where to be. While Forest had made many mistakes with their recruitment, the £6m they forked out on Grabban was an extremely good investment.

The match itself was a 12:30 kick-off, but being the early game ahead of the weekend's fixtures has its perks and Forest went to Lancashire knowing that a win would temporarily take them up to fifth. With that incentive on top of the two weeks the team had to stew on a harsh defeat to Liverpool, Forest came out firing and very quickly asserted their authority. After 11 minutes of Blackpool chasing shadows, Yates sent Johnson down the right and Johnson placed the ball brilliantly in-between two defenders to Zinckernagel, whose first time shot hit a Blackpool player and looped up and over the goalkeeper to make it 1-0 Forest.

Even though the game was still in its infancy, that goal had been coming. With half an hour on the clock, Spence played a one-two with Johnson before immediately giving it to Yates inside the box, who then played it back to Johnson to volley home. The pass from Yates to Johnson also took a slight nick and this allowed the ball to sit up for a volley, but it was beautifully struck by the Wales forward. Six minutes later, Blackpool goalkeeper Dan Grimshaw tried to play out from the back but his pass found Johnson on the edge of the penalty box, who proceeded to breeze past defender Jordan Thorniley and dink it over Grimshaw to make it 3-0.

After half-time, Forest were happy to keep Blackpool at arm's length and see the game out, though they did have some scares. A brilliant ball from Josh Bowler found CJ Hamilton on the edge of the six-yard box, but he could only fire over. There was also a penalty shout when McKenna sent Jerry Yates tumbling, but nothing was given. With eight to play, McKenna got involved in a more positive manner, as he intercepted a loose ball before driving into Blackpool's half and picking out Surridge with a brilliant pass. Surridge's first touch took him in on goal, his second was a crisp finish that found the back of the net.

Blackpool would at least deny the Reds a clean sheet in the 89th minute when a free-kick was poorly cleared and allowed Callum Connolly to score from inside the six-yard box to make it 4-1, but it was a thumping victory for Forest. By the time the afternoon's fixtures were complete, Forest were seventh but more importantly, were only a point behind sixth placed Blackburn and had three games in hand on them. Grabban also made his comeback off the bench and McKenna came through unscathed, so the trip home was a very happy one.

Their next challenge came a few days later in the shape of Coventry, who were five points behind Forest and knew that defeat at The City Ground would realistically end their play-off hopes, given they'd played two games more than Forest. Coventry made it a proper battle and the Sky Blues had the game's first real opportunity, as a quarterback-esque pass from Gustavo Hamer was badly dealt with by Figueiredo, who in a communication mix-up with Samba, nodded it towards Callum O'Hare with Samba in no man's land. O'Hare took the chance to chip Samba, but instead put it a good 15 metres over the bar.

Shortly after though, the Reds struck. Davis held off Ben Sheaf and played a crisp ball in behind for Colback to run onto, who drilled it across goal to Johnson. It seemed like Coventry had dealt with it through Jake Bidwell, but he seemed to fall over the ball and give it back to Johnson in the process, allowing him to smash home at the near post. It was far from the prettiest goal Johnson had scored, but it was certainly one of the more vital ones he'd scored that season. Despite the goal, it was still very fierce and very even, which remained the case up until half-time.

The second half saw Coventry come out strong, with Samba being forced into making a good save from a well hit long range effort from Sheaf, while a rapid counter saw O'Hare play in Viktor Gyökeres, who twisted past Figueiredo onto his left, but ballooned his effort way over. Where Coventry couldn't show composure though, Forest did. Worrall found Davis about 25 yards out and despite having a man on him, beat him easily and held him off before playing in Garner on goal. Garner was on his weaker foot, but his the power behind his left footed strike nearly took the net off and left Coventry goalkeeper Simon Moore with no chance.

Coventry weren't to be deterred though and had a great chance when O'Hare was played in, but a last ditch Figueiredo block took all the sting out of his effort and allowed Samba to claim it easily. At the other end and with seconds left to play, a Garner corner wasn't dealt with and Yates hit the bar, before the ref blew full time to cement Forest's fourth consecutive league win. The 2-0 win took Forest up to fifth and with the attacking options at their disposal, it felt like they were there to stay. A case in point was that Cooper could afford to take Johnson, Zinckernagel and Davis off and replace them with Surridge, Lolley and Grabban, which was outrageously good depth for the Championship.

Again though, Forest had no time to dwell on their victory as a few days later, they would host a Birmingham side who had little to play for. The Blues were the epitome of a midtable side, unable to go up or to go down and could only really improve their league position by the odd place, so in theory, it was set to be a routine Forest win. That being said, teams with nothing to play for can be the worst types of team to come up against, as players with expiring contracts will be eager to impress potential suitors, while the others can go out and play without any form of table pressure whatsoever.

Within five minutes though, those who predicted a routine Forest win looked to have been bang on the money. Zinckernagel nicked the ball off two-time former Forest loanee Gary Gardner on the halfway line and poked it through to Johnson, who sent Davis rampaging down the left wing. Davis sped past Nico Gordon and charged into the box, but he came in at an angle and with four Birmingham defenders and zero Forest players to his right, had little choice but to shoot and hope for the best. It was a wise decision, as Davis' shot flew past Neil Etheridge and nestled in the far corner.

The game was far from done though and Birmingham offered a timely reminder of that when a defensive mix up between Spence and Samba allowed Kristian Pedersen to get a shot away, but Samba dealt with it. After half-time, they had an even better chance when a deep Maxime Colin cross picked out Gordon, but his header flew miles wide. Forest regained the ascendency soon after and Davis had a good chance to double his tally after being picked out by Worrall following a surging run from the centre back, but his effort was well saved by Etheridge.

With 11 to go, Forest struck the decisive blow. A Garner corner that was frankly impossible to defend made its way to the back post and McKenna was on hand to head home. It was Garner's seventh assist from set pieces alone in all competitions and that one was the best of the lot – it was a ball David Beckham would've been proud of and it secured a vital three points for Forest. While the pre-match focus was on securing a top six spot, that win rocketed Forest up to third – six points behind second placed Bournemouth, who the Reds would have to face as part of their run-in.

The mere thought of finishing second seemed ludicrous given Forest's start to the season, but yet it still felt strangely possible thanks to Cooper's management. In order to do so though, there would be three huge tests that the Reds would need to overcome – the aforementioned rescheduled Bournemouth game, a visit to table toppers Fulham and the next match, which was a trip to Luton. The atmosphere is fierce at Kenilworth Road, as their fans are basically on top of you as the gap between the pitch and the stands is tiny. It's a horrible place to play at and this would be a big test for Forest.

On top of that, Nathan Jones' side had fought their way to fifth and had done a truly remarkable job given the tools at his disposal. Few would've predicted a Luton play-off charge at the start of the season, but here they were with only a handful of games remaining, with a top six spot entirely in their own hands. The game, which would be the first part of the Easter double header, would be nothing short of a battle and would need a very strong referee to keep control of.

Things didn't get off to a great start when the game was delayed by 10 minutes due to Sky having technical difficulties, but when the game finally started, it was clear that the referee wasn't going to control this game well. The game wasn't getting into any real rhythm as there was a foul given every few minutes and that suited Luton to the ground. The Hatters should've taken the lead when Amari'i Bell's drilled ball over the top was misjudged by Spence, allowing Fred Onyedinma to get a shot away, but Samba saved his effort well.

When Forest actually got a chance to get it on the deck and showcase what they could do, they caused problems. Davis rode a challenge superbly from Reece Burke and ran towards goal before prodding a ball behind the Luton defence for Grabban to run onto, but with just the goalkeeper to beat, Grabban didn't get any real direction and his effort was pushed away. It would soon prove costly as a long ball down the right flank for James Bree was flicked up by Bree and pushed onto Colback's arm. After a few seconds of deliberation, the referee gave a penalty for handball.

It was a harsh interpretation of the handball rule as Colback couldn't get out the way of it due to the proximity, but also because replays clearly showed Bree slapping the ball onto Colback's hand. It was atrocious officiating, but the decision stood and Kal Naismith stepped up and dispatched his penalty. After half-time, the officials would anger Forest even more. Davis gave it to Yates and with space opening up, Yates popped a brilliant ball in behind the Luton defence for Spence to run onto. Onyedinma tried to cut it out but his efforts were in vain, as his attempted block cushioned the ball nicely for Spence, who leathered it home.

However, the flag went up and the goal was disallowed. Spence was adjudged to have been marginally offside, but the decision was wrong. While Spence was in an offside position, because Onyedinma actively played for the ball and touched it, by law Spence was now onside and the goal should've stood. It's no different to a centre back passing it back to a goalkeeper and a striker in an offside position intercepts it and scores, so the decision was bewildering. It was the second dreadful officiating decision on the day and it wouldn't be long until there was a third, although this one did go in Forest's favour.

Zinckernagel sent a ball down the left for substitute Surridge, but Surridge was miles offside. However, the linesman didn't flag and upon receiving the ball, Surridge was clattered by Sonny Bradley. The ref brandished a second yellow card for Bradley, meaning Luton would face the final 13 minutes with 10 men. Forest started throwing men forwards in search of an equaliser and almost found it when Zinckernagel picked the ball up on the edge of the box, wriggled past two players and curled an effort goalbound, hitting the outside of the post. The ball fell to Johnson who checked in and shot, but his effort was well saved.

Despite huffing and puffing, Forest couldn't find a way through and Luton nearly doubled their lead on the counter when Elijah Adebayo beat Worrall and left him for dead, before checking back inside of him and getting a shot away, but Samba repelled his effort with an outstretched boot. Having blown for 32 fouls, shown 13 cards and given three abject decisions, the referee blew his whistle for full time and any dreams Forest had about automatic promotion were extinguished – at least, for now. It was a sobering reminder not to get too carried away and instead, to secure top six, which would still be a monumental achievement all things considered.

After the game, Cooper laid into the officials and understandably so. His dad Keith was a Premier League ref once upon a time and whenever there was a contentious or wrong decision, Cooper generally wouldn't make a meal of it. He, more than most, would know how tough the job is. This was an exception though, as he gave the officials both barrels over the disallowed goal, expressing his surprise that a decision that poor could happen at this level. His mood wouldn't have improved when it was made clear that Davis had suffered a hamstring injury, which would rule him out for the rest of the normal season.

This was a blow, as Davis had been so vital to Forest's style of play and was relishing the responsibility of being the focal point for the club. It also wasn't a 'Cooper injury', if you like – where Cooper would claim a player is out, only for them to mysteriously appear fine and dandy that weekend. This was serious and a huge shame. However, in true next man up fashion, it would give Surridge a chance to stake a claim and he would get that opportunity a few days later for the second part of the Easter double header – a home match against West Brom. Much like the Luton game, the match was to be shown on Sky, but whereas Forest were the early kick-off on Good Friday, they were the late kick-off on Easter Monday.

This at least allowed them to know in advance how everyone had fared, although the Reds knew they needed to win anyway to further secure that top six spot. As such, attention turned elsewhere and before Forest even kicked a ball, supporters were in a particularly buoyant mood as Derby had lost at QPR and as a result, had been relegated to League One. It made for a lively atmosphere before kick-off and Forest's energy matched that of their fans, with the Reds starting on the front foot against their opponents.

After 14 minutes, Zinckernagel was wiped out by Darnell Furlong, who was promptly booked. Three minutes later, Spence drilled a low ball into the box for Zinckernagel, who Furnell tackled – this time, cleanly, but the ball fell to Garner, whose shot was blocked by a still grounded Furnell, who had hoisted his arm up to do so. The referee pointed to the spot immediately and brandished a second yellow card for Furnell, leaving West Brom down to 10 men. The second yellow was maybe a bit harsh, but by the letter of the law, the officials were right.

Johnson stepped up and put his penalty into the bottom left corner, before doing his now trademark Robin Hood inspired bow and arrow celebration. A few minutes later, Spence bolted forwards from his own half before being tackled by Jake Livermore. The linesman gave a throw to West Brom, but the referee instead gave a throw-in to Forest. The Baggies were furious and justifiably so as the ball had come off Spence last, but while they were contesting it, Forest played on and Spence's throw picked out Johnson, who cut it back for Zinckernagel.

Zinckernagel's effort was blocked for a corner, but from that corner, another peach of a ball from Garner found the head of Yates, who powered home. 2-0 Forest and set piece assist number eight in all competitions for Garner. The saying goes that decisions even themselves out across the course of the season – if that's true, one of the errors at Luton was quickly redeemed at West Brom's expense. Shortly before half-time though, something truly remarkable happened. Deep in the West Brom half, Colback threw the ball to Johnson, who chipped it back down the left for Colback, who was now in a great crossing position.

Before the ball could bounce, Colback lashed his laces across the ball on the volley, to the point the ball violently swerved left and flew straight into the top corner, leaving the goalkeeper with no chance and with Surridge with his hands on his head in total disbelief at what he'd seen. Colback just put his hand over his mouth by way of celebration and laughed. If he'd meant that instead of attempting to cross it on the volley – which, of course, he claims he did – it's one of the best goals ever scored at The City Ground. It was a proper one in a million strike and one that pretty much wrapped up the game.

In the second half, Forest were in cruise control, while West Brom were in damage limitation mode. The nature of the game allowed Forest to effectively rest players while they were still on the pitch, as the Reds just knocked the ball around while conserving their energy. Laryea got on for his Forest debut, while Cook also returned from injury, as he came off the bench for the final 10 minutes. In stoppage time, Garner sprayed a ball out left to Colback, who passed it in-field to Zinckernagel and after taking a touch, Zinckernagel spotted a gap in the West Brom defence and played it for Surridge to pounce upon, which he did with emphatic effect as his composed effort put the icing on the proverbial cake.

The result put Forest back up to fifth and sitting on 70 points – given 75 points is seen as the benchmark for top six, Forest effectively needed five points from their final five games to do what many felt was impossible after their start. Before they could have any time to reflect, Forest were gearing up for a trip to Peterborough, who had their Championship status on the line going into the match. Peterborough's situation was precarious, with the Posh seven points behind Reading with nine left to play for, so they needed to pull some rabbits out of hats fast and hope for the best elsewhere.

Forest fans will always have a soft spot for Peterborough's stadium, London Road, as the Reds secured automatic promotion there in

1994. Fast forward nearly three decades and much like that day, it was something of a Forest invasion in Peterborough, with 3,599 Reds making up the 12,870 attendance – and that didn't include the ones undercover in the home end. Posh started well and weren't playing like a team staring the League One trapdoor in the face, with the home side not allowing Forest to make anything happen, while also probing well themselves.

In fact, they should've taken the lead. Some lovely one-touch triangle movement passing between Josh Knight, Ricky-Jade Jones and Jack Taylor ended up with Knight having time and space to shoot outside the box, but Spence got a block in. The ball fell to Harrison Burrows though and he immediately bypassed the Forest midfield with a driven pass to Jones, who span Figueiredo and unleashed a left-footed effort on goal, but Samba had read the situation brilliantly and rushed out to block the shot with his feet. It would be a decisive moment in the match, as on the cusp of half-time, Forest's quality told.

Knight tried to take Zinckernagel on just outside Forest's own box, but the Dane stuck a leg out and poked the ball through to Johnson, who saw Zinckernagel make a run forward and passed it back into his path. Zinckernagel then carried the ball into the Peterborough half unchallenged, with Johnson running alongside him on his outside, eventually releasing Johnson down the left. Johnson cushioned the ball into his stride before crossing the ball into the box, which Surridge met with his head and sent across the goalkeeper, finding the back of the net.

Surridge's finish gave Forest a huge boost going into the break, but Peterborough started quickly after it. A hopeful ball forwards to Posh striker Jonson Clarke-Harris was woefully dealt with by Worrall, whose outstretched leg sent the ball behind him and allowed Clarke-Harris a sniff at goal. Worrall was able to recover the situation, but his clearance went straight to Burrows, who gave it to Sammie Szmodics inside the box, but his effort was saved. After that, Forest decided they'd had enough of entertaining Peterborough and grabbed control of the game.

Lolley was allowed time and space to turn inside Peterborough's half and played the ball left for Colback, whose effort was well kept out by Posh goalkeeper David Cornell. Shortly after, Grabban had a goal ruled out for offside and then missed a glorious chance to double the Reds' lead after being picked out by Colback around eight yards out, but blazed over. Worryingly for Forest, not long after that miss, Grabban hobbled off clutching his hamstring. Forest still held on without their captain to win 1-0 and sent Peterborough down in the process, but the sound of the full-time whistle was laced with concern.

As a result of Grabban's injury and with just four league games remaining, the Reds had gone from having three strikers available to just one. Forest knew that Davis would potentially be available for the play-offs if they made it, but they'd have to wait and see what the medical department would say about Grabban. In any case, he'd definitely be unavailable for Forest's next fixture, which was a midweek trip to Fulham. Amidst the concern for Grabban, Forest's win at Peterborough left them seven clear of seventh placed Millwall, who had played two extra games than Forest.

It meant that the Reds just needed a single point to mathematically secure a top six spot, which in itself would be a phenomenal achievement. However, Forest had eyes on second again. Bournemouth were now five clear of Forest after drawing 1-1 against Fulham and both would be making up one of their two games in hand on almost everyone else on the same night. In order for second to still be on, Forest would need to beat a Fulham side who were one win away from securing the title and hope Bournemouth slipped up away at Swansea.

It was an unlikely set of events, but you can never say never in football. With Cooper at the helm, it certainly felt like Forest might at least hold up their end of the bargain. As such, Forest trekked down to Craven Cottage not only with Cook back in the starting XI, but with an air of optimism and also with some recognition. Two days before the Fulham game, the EFL Awards took place, which saw Johnson voted as the Championship Young Player of the Season, in addition to Yates, Worrall and Spence all making the Championship Team of the Season.

Despite his heroics with Forest, Cooper wasn't named as Manager of the Season. That accolade instead went to Nathan Jones, which was...something. This is always the issue with awards nights taking place while the season is still ongoing, but alas, it was still great for the club to be represented so heavily and of course, for the players involved. This was especially the case for Johnson, Yates and Worrall;

three academy graduates who were now starring for their home club and being recognised by their peers, which was an enormous source of pride for everyone involved with Forest.

Much like most of the season, the celebrations were short lived as there was still a job to do. The message of a job needing to be done was certainly heard by the players as straight from the off in west London, Forest were proving to be a rather sharp thorn in Fulham's side. They started with intent and had a slight opportunity when a Tosin Adarabioyo ball forward was intercepted by Garner and he immediately laid it off for Colback, but Colback's effort from range was comfortably held by Fulham goalkeeper Marek Rodák.

After 15 minutes, Forest won a throw by the managerial dugouts and with a gap forming down Fulham's right hand side, Cooper took it upon himself to get the game going again quickly by launching the ball at Colback to take the throw-in immediately. Colback obliged and set Surridge off down that vacant space and he clipped a ball into the box off the outside of his boot looking for the run of Zinckernagel. Surridge's pass was overhit, but defender Tim Ream and Rodák got in each other's way while trying to clear the ball, allowing Zinckernagel to run in and poke the ball goalbound, with the whole stadium watching in disbelief as it slowly rolled over the line.

It was one of the biggest slices of luck the Reds received all season, but they took it gladly with two hands. Unfortunately for Forest, Fulham – realising their title party in front of their own fans was in danger of falling through – decided to wake up. Pretty much immediately after Zinckernagel's chance goal, a ball over the top was misjudged by Garner and fell for Harrison Reed, who laid the ball into Fabio Carvalho's path inside the box, but his effort was straight down Samba's throat and the goalkeeper held it firmly. Forest's answer to this was to pretty much put everyone behind the ball and limit the space for Fulham, which – aside from a couple of Aleksander Mitrovic headers from crosses that flew over – worked until half-time.

In the second half though, Fulham stepped up a gear. Some neat play down the right allowed Neco Williams to deliver a wicked ball in, but Samba flew out and got his fingertips to it, just as Mitrovic was getting ready to run onto it. That faint touch pushed the ball up just enough that Mitrovic got underneath it with his head, with the ball flying over the top of the bar. As Fulham were committing men forward, they were leaving gaps behind and Forest soon started to exploit this. A long ball forward from Spence was misjudged by Joe Bryan, allowing Johnson to run down the right unchallenged. Johnson brilliantly put the ball in across the floor for Surridge, but Surridge's effort was expertly saved by Rodák.

Not long after, Johnson – who was being watched by Brentford boss Thomas Frank in the stands – had another opportunity down the right and had Bryan twisted in knots before leaving him sliding in the wrong direction after checking inside of him, but his effort was blocked. Johnson immediately called for handball, as did the Forest fans behind the goal, but the referee was unmoved and the lack of appeal from other Forest players nearby suggested it may have been a speculative shout. With Forest getting joy down the flanks on the counter, Cooper brought Laryea on for Colback to have two pace options down either side, but Fulham still carried a huge threat when in possession, which they were having a lot of.

As a fan, watching this match was excruciating. Seconds felt like minutes and it was so tense, you could pretty much hear your heartbeat through your chest. Every time Fulham got the ball, they looked menacing, but the Forest rearguard always seemed to find an answer. Still Fulham kept on coming. Rodrigo Munoz was on now and after picking up the ball outside of the box, he gave it to Carvalho in a more central position, whose fizzing effort was met by a diving Samba at full stretch. Wilson then checked inside and got a shot off, but it lacked conviction and Samba could get down to smother it easily.

And then, finally, the whistle blew. A side who had scored 99 goals that season had been shut out for only third time in all competitions all season. The noise from the away end was a sight to behold in itself, with those in attendance probably feeling as if they'd done 12 rounds with Anthony Joshua. As the police and stewards stood in front of the Forest fans, it appeared Cooper felt the same way as at the end of his fist pumps, he'd broken through the police barricade preventing pitch invaders before letting out a huge roar in front of the travelling support.

In the most improbable circumstances, in the most unlikeliest of fashions and thanks to a rather unique goal, Forest had mathematically secured a play-off spot with three games to play. The good news didn't stop there. Bournemouth drew 3-3 at Swansea and now the gap was just three points, with both teams level on goal difference. As a result, if Forest won their next three games, they'd likely be automatically promoted. In addition, Murphy had been named Championship CEO of the Year for his work that season, which was totally deserved and vindicated his decision that Cooper should be hired, in addition to his fresh approach for recruitment.

All focus turned to Saturday, where the Reds would be hosting Swansea, though in his pre-match press conference, Cooper revealed some bad news – the scans had come back and Grabban's hamstring injury was sufficient enough that he was done for the season. As Grabban was out of contract in the summer, it was possible he'd played his last game for Forest. Having scored 56 goals in 149 games in all competitions for the club, he deserved better than his potential farewell appearance seeing him limp off the field.

As before with his previous injury though, Grabban was still offering support from behind the scenes and with goal difference very much vital now, Forest potentially had to put on a show against a Swansea side now unbeaten in nine. The Swans' faint play-off chances were now mathematically over following that draw with Bournemouth, but they were still a side in good form and were hoping to finish the season strongly. Also, given the Cooper thing, their fans were very eager to put a stop to any potential automatic promotion aspirations, so this was by no means a foregone conclusion.

There was another display whipped up by Forza, this one taking place in The Brian Clough Stand. With red and white banners across it, the middle display was a picture of the Forest team in a huddle with lyrics from Oasis' 'Acquiesce' above it – 'Because we need each other, we believe in one another.' It was a poignant message and helped set the tone early. A McKenna ball over the top was contested for by Surridge and Joel Latibeaudiere, which left latter flat on his face as Surridge raced away down the left. His ball was parried into Zinckernagel's path, but with the goal gaping, the Dane hit a man on the line instead.

Shortly after, Spence beat two players down the right before zipping a ball across the box, which caused chaos at the back post between former Reds loanee Cyrus Christie and goalkeeper Andrew Fisher. Christie's first touch was terrible and allowed Colback to run in, but as Fisher tried to prevent that, the ball ended up ricocheting off all of them and ending up rolling towards goal with Christie trying to scoop it away with his hands. The ref blew and issued Christie a red card and gave Forest a penalty. But, as the ball had crossed the line before Christie got his hands to it, the ref awarded Forest the goal instead and changed Christie's card from red to yellow. It was an unconventional way to take the lead, but Forest weren't complaining.

Six minutes later though, Swansea were level. A simple long ball from Matt Grimes caught Cook out and Michael Obafemi took it down well, checked inside of Cook and then coolly slotted past Samba. Forest were still making chances though and how they didn't score before half-time is a mystery. Another pinpoint Garner corner found Surridge, whose header was expertly tipped onto the post by Arthur, but Swansea failed to clear their lines and a ball from

Johnson found Yates six yards out, though he could only plant his header straight at the keeper.

Forest's pressure didn't relent and three minutes after half-time, a Garner corner was met again by Surridge, but this time it found the back of the net. Four minutes after that, Forest broke and with Swansea short on numbers at the back, Garner surged forwards before caressing the ball into Surridge's path, allowing the former Swansea loanee to stroke the ball into the top corner with a level of precision a surgeon would be proud of. All Fisher could do was stand and watch as Surridge's majestic strike found the postage stamp area of his goal as Forest notched up another goal of the season contender, such was the finesse involved.

Despite not having much of the ball, Forest were destroying Swansea on the counter attack and making chance after chance after chance. With 20 to go, Zinckernagel released an overlapping Spence down the right and his cross looped over Fisher and hit the bar. The ball kindly rebounded to Surridge, who chested it and then volleyed into an empty net to secure his hat-trick. With six to go, it got even better as a Samba long ball up was ran onto by Mighten, who knocked it into the penalty box before firing past Fisher to wrap up an emphatic 5-1 victory.

Much like the away game, Cooper was dignified in victory against his former employers, although this time he did allow himself to get a slight dig in. Given Cooper was deemed to have not played 'the Swansea way' by the Jack Army, his comment of, "We know Swansea have a lot of the ball, but also knew they concede a hell of a lot of chances and a hell of a lot of goals" to BBC Sport was very much a chef's kiss moment. Combining both games, Forest scored nine goals past Swansea, conceding just two in response. So much for negative football from Cooper, eh?

That fifth goal had extra significance as elsewhere, Bournemouth had won 3-0 at Blackburn, so Mighten's strike meant that Forest were now one ahead of Bournemouth on goal difference. With two games to go and with Bournemouth up next, this was it. Do or die. A victory at Dean Court/The Vitality Stadium and Forest would have one foot over the automatic promotion line. Defeat and Bournemouth would officially be promoted. Forest being two wins from automatic promotion seemed impossible after their start, but it was very much a reality now.

CHAPTER SIX – FREED FROM DESIRE

As the Forest playing and coaching staff arrived at The Nigel Doughty Academy on Wilford Lane to board the coach to Bournemouth a few days after the 5-1 Swansea victory, something was different in the air. And no, not metaphorically. Plumes of red smoke from a seemingly unlimited supply of flares covered the sky as hundreds of Forest fans found a way to get there on a Monday afternoon, bringing flags and chanting in support of the team as the coach made its way through a sea of red the fans had created.

This wasn't normal, but then again games like this weren't normal. This was the biggest match for Forest in 23 years as their quest to finally return to the top flight seemed to be nearing an end. Despite this burden and expectation, the pressure was on Bournemouth more than Forest. How they had managed to turn this into a race was remarkable given their player quality and their parachute payments, but no-one was in a mood to argue. Given that the stadium hadn't blown away in the wind this time, the two sides entered battle for that final automatic promotion spot as both sets of fans prepared themselves to be put through the emotional wringer.

Forest looked sharp and after Kieffer Moore, who signed for Bournemouth from Cardiff in January, lost the ball cheaply, Spence picked it up and drove into the Bournemouth half, before splitting the defence entirely with a superb through ball for Surridge, whose effort smacked the crossbar and went behind for a goal kick. Soon after, Zinckernagel played a brilliant one-two with Colback deep in the Bournemouth half down the left, allowing Zinckernagel to cut it back across the box for Johnson to shoot, but Jordan Zemura put in an outstanding block to keep the score at 0-0.

Just before half time, the game took a dramatic turn. Zinckernagel, pretty much on the left touchline, carved open the Bournemouth defence with an inswinging pass for Surridge to run onto. Surridge took a touch to take it round goalkeeper Mark Travers, but before he could take a second, Travers tripped him and sent him sprawling. Referee Stuart Attwell pointed to the spot, but the official had flagged for offside. One issue, though. Surridge was clearly onside and the official had flagged the wrong player. Johnson was in an offside position when the flag went up, but he was nowhere near the ball and it wasn't played for him.

In a game of such magnitude, with so much at stake – financially as well as from an achievement aspect – to see a crucial decision given that badly wrong was bewildering. What made it worse is that Premier League officials were given the match, presumably to ensure it would be officiated without a hitch. That decision took the sting out of Forest's tail and after half-time, Bournemouth shut the game down tremendously well and didn't give Forest anything, to the point it felt like the occasion had maybe gotten to the players.

Whatever the reason for Forest toiling, Bournemouth stepped up as a result. After keeping the ball well around the Forest box, Ryan Christie picked the lock with a pass for Dominic Solanke, but his effort found the side netting. Then, a Lloyd Kelly long ball beat the Forest backline and Yates failed to stop Philip Billing running in on goal, but Billing was caught in two minds and Samba was able to smother his ball across the box. Bournemouth were growing in momentum and forced Samba into beating away a Jaiden Anthony effort, but despite the Bournemouth chances, it felt like the game was petering out into a draw.

Then, with eight minutes to go, McKenna wiped out Zemura on the edge of the box and was booked for his troubles. Rather than shoot though, which the Forest team expected given there was a six man wall and a Forest player either side of it, Solanke played it to an unmarked Moore inside the box to his left, who slotted past Samba. It was atrocious defending from Forest, who now needed a miracle and with time running out, Samba came up for a corner. Garner's delivery wasn't at its best though and didn't beat the first man, but it came back to him. His cross was also blocked, but fell at Samba's feet, only for the goalkeeper to hook it over the bar.

That was the last action of the match and as the whistle blew, scores of Bournemouth fans ran onto the pitch to celebrate their promotion. The pitch invasion did cause some unsavoury scenes as a few of them took it upon themselves to goad the departing Forest players, which Spence especially didn't take too kindly to, but when the dust settled, the automatic promotion dream for Forest was over. Cooper revealed after the game that Attwell had apologised to him for his official's mistake, but that didn't exactly make it much better to deal with.

Things were put into perspective soon after, however. After the game, Cook took to Twitter to congratulate his former club on promotion, but also revealed that his dad had suffered a cardiac arrest before kick-off and had to be revived by paramedics, whom he expressed his endless gratitude for. Cook was totally unaware of what had happened, hence why he took to the field as normal, but naturally, everyone was just pleased to know that his dad pulled through ok.

With Forest's fate secured and knowing all promotion hopes hinged on the play-offs, for some fans (including myself), a number of mental scars caused down the years were re-opened. Forest and the play-offs didn't go well. In fact, they went extremely badly. This would be the fifth time Forest participated in the play-off format and all four times previously had ended in defeat at the semi-final stage. It was like Forest were cursed when it came to the play-offs.

The 2002/03 season was the first time Forest experienced them, where they faced Sheffield United. They drew the first leg 1-1 and in the second leg at Bramall Lane, Forest went 2-0 up, but conceded two minutes after scoring their second, causing a dramatic implosion. The Blades scored again to level the tie 2-2 on aggregate, taking the game to extra time. In the 112th minute, Paul Peschisolido made it 3-2 on the night, before Des Walker – who cruelly scored an own goal for Forest in the 1991 FA Cup final – scored another own goal to make it 4-2. Forest got one back, but it proved too little too late and they lost 4-3 on the night and 5-4 on aggregate.

Then, in the 2006/07 season, Forest were trying to get back into the Championship at the second attempt after being relegated to League One. They faced Yeovil Town and did the hard work in the first leg, winning 2-0 away. With 10 minutes to go in the second leg, the score was 1-1 on the night, so 3-1 Forest on aggregate. Fast forward 10 minutes and David Prutton had been sent off for Forest and Yeovil had scored twice, forcing extra time. Yeovil then took the lead in extra time and while Forest immediately equalised, the Glovers found a way to score a fifth goal on the night to win 5-2 – 5-4 on aggregate.

There was to be no third time lucky for Forest, either. In the 2009/10 season, Forest had finished third in the Championship and faced off against a Blackpool side who finished nine points beneath them. Forest took the lead in Blackpool, but lost 2-1. In the second leg, Forest levelled the aggregate score after just seven minutes, but were pegged back by a DJ Campbell goal in the second half. The Reds restored their lead on the night 10 minutes later, but with 20 to go, Forest conceded three goals in 10 minutes – one from Stephen Dobbie and two from Campbell, completing his hat-trick – before scoring a consolation in the 92nd minute, losing 6-4 on aggregate.

Finally, the year after the Blackpool disappointment, Forest finished sixth and went up against Swansea. Despite Swansea going down to 10 men after three minutes, Forest couldn't find a way through and the first leg finished 0-0. In the second leg, Swansea scored two goals in five minutes, before Forest pulled one back with 10 to go. While chasing an equaliser and having sent goalkeeper Lee Camp up for a corner in the 93rd minute, Swansea cleared and managed to score a breakaway third to take them to Wembley. Forest hit the framework no less than three times on the night and had two decent penalty shouts turned down, which was perhaps the clearest indicator it wasn't to be their night. Or perhaps, that the play-offs simply weren't for them.

Despite everything Cooper had done, the blow at Bournemouth combined with the previous play-off history left some fans almost resigned to the inevitable. Before the disappointment could linger much longer, Forest still had to play their final league match of the season before the play-offs started, which was a trip away at Hull. While it was still possible Forest could finish third if they'd won due to their goal difference advantage over Huddersfield, the main aim was to just get the disappointment from the Bournemouth game out of everyone's system and to come through unscathed.

Forest made seven changes to the team at Bournemouth, with Panzo and Laryea making their first starts for the club and the game had a very much end of season feel about it, especially as Hull themselves had nothing to play for. That being said, a defensive mix-up between Samba and Figueiredo nearly allowed Allahyar Sayyadmanesh a chance to score, but as all three players involved went for the ball, it hit the Hull forward last and went out for a goal kick.

Forest made some changes in the second half and that brought some spark, with both Johnson and Surridge testing Hull stopper Nathan

Baxter, but Hull should've scored when a Tom Huddlestone through ball saw Keane Lewis-Potter leave Worrall in his wake, but when left one-on-one with Samba, Lewis-Potter blazed miles over the bar. In the 92nd minute, the game sprang to life. Surridge got to the ball ahead of Huddlestone in the box and was sent flying, resulting in a penalty. Johnson stepped up and sent Baxter the wrong way, but straight from kick-off, Hull worked the ball to the right and a deep cross from Lewie Coyle was flicked in by Lewis-Potter to immediately level.

The game finished 1-1, which was about right in terms of play, but because Huddersfield had beaten Bristol City 2-0, Forest would finish the season fourth. The turnaround under Cooper was staggering, with the Reds taking 76 points from his 38 league games in charge – two points per game, on average. It was a miraculous effort, but everyone knew there was still a job to do. And as a result of finishing fourth, Forest would reignite their rivalry with Sheffield United once more in the play-offs, with the Blades finishing fifth.

On the one hand, this was the toughest team Forest could've got on paper. Sheffield United had just come down from the Premier League, kept the majority of their team together and had players who knew what it took to get over the line. On the other hand, finishing fourth wasn't a disaster. Forest were the better team in both league games against the Blades, especially the away game. Had they finished third, they'd have come up against Luton, who seemed to be Forest's kryptonite to a certain degree. In a one-off game at Wembley, Forest would've fancied their chances, but over two legs...difficult to say.

As such, despite the trepidation around the play-offs as a concept, Forest fans were slightly optimistic going into the first leg at a Bramall Lane bathed in sunshine. For potentially the last time that season, the much loved hi-vis third kit would be worn for the occasion too, which made the Forest players look even brighter in the May sunshine. Much like the away game in the league, Forest went straight for Sheffield United's throat and even without Davis up front, were rampant. After 10 minutes, that pressure told.

Worrall clipped the ball forwards for Surridge, who could only put the ball back across the box into a dangerous area given the pressure on him. Former Forest man Ben Osborn slipped in his attempt to clear it, which enabled Zinckernagel to shoot from seven yards out, but Wes Foderingham could only parry into Colback's path, who mercilessly rifled home. It was a dream start for the Reds, although they almost conceded soon after when John Egan's header was cleared off the line by Surridge from a corner. However, Forest were not relenting.

A Garner ball in found an unmarked Yates, but he could only plant his header just wide of the post. Then, Surridge nutmegged a player on halfway before releasing Johnson with the outside of his boot, but Johnson's finish just dragged past the post. Just before half-time, Spence picked out Surridge in the box and his effort was parried by Foderingham and that allowed Johnson to swoop in and get a free header on goal, but there was no power in his effort and Sheffield United eventually scrambled clear.

By half-time, it was mystery that it was only 1-0. It could've easily been 3-0, but if Forest kept on going like they were, that second goal was a formality. The Blades pretty much went into damage limitation mode for the second half to stop Forest going on the counter, but with 20 to play, were architects of their own downfall. Egan tried to play out from the back and got caught on the turn by Lolley, who darted towards goal and with two defenders trying to stop him, calmly rolled the ball behind him for Johnson, who bent it around Foderingham.

During the celebrations, a flare came down from above, which Cook pretended was a cigar before giving it to a steward. The goal also meant that Johnson had followed in his dad's footsteps, as he also scored against Sheffield United in the play-offs for Forest – in fact, Johnson Snr scored in both legs in the 2002/03 play-off semis. The Blades remained cautious of Forest and the Reds were content with a 2-0 lead, but in stoppage time, Samba came for a Morgan Gibbs-White corner and missed it, allowing Sander Berge to bundle home, allowing Sheffield United right back into the tie.

Had you said before the game that Forest would win 2-1, they'd have gladly taken it. To win 2-1 in that fashion though was dodgy. It could and should've been about 4-0 Forest, but instead they'd handed the Blades a lifeline they frankly didn't deserve. Nevertheless, it was a lead and the second leg was at home, so the job was halfway done. And really, Cooper and his team could afford to be proud. It was a sensational performance, they'd carried out his tactical plan to a tee and but for one error at the end, would've had a perfect day.

Not everyone was happy, though. Namely, those in the Sheffield United camp. After the game, Heckingbottom beefed up the fighting talk by claiming Forest's players would've been gutted walking off the pitch and that the Reds would be "edgy" in the second leg as a result, while former Forest man Jack Robinson said that the away support was "embarrassing" for how they celebrated the second goal, for it were like "they thought they'd won the leg there and then." He then highlighted why he was never suited for Forest, by explaining how there's "massive pressure for them" to go up and how the crowd don't take too kindly if you don't perform well at The City Ground.

Aside from clearly losing their heads, this was quintessential Sheffield United. It comes from not being the biggest team in their city, as that honour belongs to Sheffield Wednesday instead. Whereas the Owls can brag about having a bigger stadium and winning eight major trophies to the Blades' five, United instead highlight reaching semi-finals they went onto lose – one of which, ironically enough, was to Wednesday. Regardless of how good their team is, whenever they suffer adversity, they always resort to type and play the little man card and here they were, like clockwork, doing it again. They were rattled, they knew they were in trouble and went straight on the offensive as a result.

It made for an enthralling second leg, as Forest would be playing a side that would be playing as if they had nothing to lose. There was another Forza display in the Trent End for the occasion. The Trent End upper display had Brian Clough and his assistant Peter Taylor in the middle, with FA Cup winning managers Harry Hallam and

Billy Walker either side of them, while Giuseppe Garibaldi, the man behind the colour inspiration of the Forest shirt, was above Clough and Taylor. The lower Trent End had a banner of the current team, with Cooper in the middle and the message was, 'We have conquered and we will conquer still', which was incredibly stirring.

Straight away though, the Blades looked sharper and they should've taken the lead when a poor Worrall ball was intercepted by Rhys Norrington-Davies and slipped through to Gibbs-White, who sent Iliman Ndiaye one-on-one with Samba with a gorgeous outside of the boot pass, but Samba shut down any angle brilliantly and saved well. With 19 played, McKenna sent a long ball down the left channel that perfectly fell for Surridge in the box, who squared it for a stretching Johnson to rifle home. By finding the net, Johnson followed in his father's footsteps of scoring in both legs of a play-off semi-final and amazingly, against the same side Johnson Snr did it against.

That did calm the nerves a bit and it seemed to knock the wind out of Sheffield United's sails, but sensing this, Heckingbottom opted to play the little man card again. As the ball went out for a Forest throw, it rolled to Heckingbottom, who proceeded to pick it up and drive it into Spence's midriff. Spence turned around and laughed, which is testament to his mentality as it would've been so easy to bite there, but Johnson was straight over to remonstrate with Heckingbottom, before being aggressively shoved by Robinson.

This sparked a melee in front of the dugouts, with both benches getting involved, before the referee eventually restored order and booked Heckingbottom for his antics. The half-time whistle blew shortly afterwards and Cooper very wisely kept his players on the pitch for a minute or so and let Sheffield United and Heckingbottom storm off, as it was clear now they'd sink to any level to try and get a rise out of Forest. For Forest now, it was just a case of managing the game well and keeping a cool head. They were 3-1 up on aggregate with 45 minutes to go.

Only two teams since Cooper took over had scored two or more at The City Ground in 90 minutes and one of those was Stoke, who only did so because Samba lamped Phil Jagielka and gave a penalty away. Of course, Sheffield United were going to go hell for leather now, but all Forest had to do was keep calm. Two minutes into the second half, a long ball forward caught the Forest backline out and allowed Ndiaye to run through. Worrall thwarted him with a last gasp challenge to force him wide, but he was able to lay it off for Berge, who squared it across goal for Gibbs-White to prod home. So much for keeping calm.

That gave Sheffield United a sense of belief and rocked Forest badly. A nervous energy swept through The City Ground, though the fans did their best to get behind the team. It was all Sheffield United and while they couldn't fashion any meaningful chances, that changed with 15 to go. Ndiaye flicked a ball down the right for George Baldock to run onto and he managed to take Colback on, before firing a ball across the six yard box for John Fleck to tap in from. Forest in the play-offs don't go. It was happening again. Forest were going to blow it in heartbreaking fashion once more, but if anything, their fans just got louder.

Two minutes after the goal, a poor Yates clearance ended up at Gibbs-White's feet, who whipped an exceptional ball into the box for Ndiaye, but the forward misjudged it and it flew off his chest harmlessly over the bar when he should've scored. The introduction of Davis and Lolley had given Forest a bit more zip and they started to fight back, but neither side could create anything meaningful before the ref blew for full-time. As the scores were level at 3-3, extra time would commence and if it were still level after that, it would go to penalties.

The first half of extra time came and went. Ndiaye, Davis and Robinson all had half chances, but nothing clear cut. The second half was a different story. Lolley robbed Oliver Norwood on halfway, sped towards goal and played it to Johnson down the right, who proceeded to cut it back to Lolley on the penalty spot, but Lolley slipped as he hit it and the ball rolled safely into Foderingham's hands. With five minutes to go, a Sheffield United corner was headed backwards by McKenna and then feebly headed up by Spence. Gibbs-White then nodded it towards Ndiaye five yards out, but Samba spread himself and got a boot to it, allowing Forest to clear.

I say this with no exaggeration, that is undeniably the best save I have ever seen in person. Samba had no right whatsoever to stop that, but somehow did. By the time the full-time whistle blew for a second time, Forest were lucky to get to penalties. It had been a total capitulation from the second half of normal time onwards, but they still weren't out of it. The penalties would be taken towards the Bridgford End and Sheffield United would go first. Norwood, being a very eager beaver, was already waiting while both goalkeepers were spoken to by the referee, which Samba noticed and subsequently took an age to get back to his goal. Even when he got there, he still took his time, keeping Norwood waiting even longer and ramping that pressure up further.

The notion that a penalty shootout is a lottery, for me, is incorrect. There is an art to it and pressure plays a big part, thus effectively making it a very high stakes game of poker. Norwood was very clearly flustered while waiting and when the ref finally blew so he could take it, he couldn't wait to do so. He sent his penalty left, but Samba flew across to bat it away to a huge roar. Norwood was kept waiting for 90 seconds and it clearly had an impact. Up next was Johnson, who'd missed a penalty against the Blades in the league game. This time though, he composed himself and made no mistake, sending Foderingham the wrong way. Advantage Forest.

Conor Hourihane was next, who Samba again did his best to keep waiting before being told off by the ref. Hourihane went down the middle, but Samba – with ice in his veins – didn't move and stuck an arm out instead, which sent the ball up onto the crossbar and away, sparking an even louder roar. Next up was Cafu, who came on towards the end of extra time for an exhausted Garner. Foderingham got half a glove on his penalty but because of the pace on the ball, the ball went behind Foderingham and in. It was a let off and Berge was next for the Blades, who Samba again kept waiting. With Samba pointing to his left as to indicate that's where he was going to dive, Berge called his bluff and sent it to his right to finally get Sheffield United off the mark.

Cook was next for Forest and while it was a bit of a surprise to see a centre back so high up the order, he was one of the most experienced players in the Forest ranks. Cook powered his penalty home before punching the air and whipping up the crowd, reminiscent of Stuart Pearce at Euro 96. Forest now needed one more goal or a Sheffield United miss and they were through. Ndiaye was next and before Samba could do too much, the ref was straight onto him telling him to get on his line. Despite missing so many good chances during the game, Ndiaye's penalty was superb.

It was Lolley's turn next and the situation was simple – score and Forest were through. However, in another twist, Lolley ballooned his penalty over the bar and the door was back open for Sheffield United. Once again, the play-offs are simply not for Forest. With Gibbs-White up next for Sheffield United, seeds of doubt started to grow among the fanbase. Some could hardly watch. However, Gibbs-White did a strange stuttered run-up and at that moment, it felt like he was going to miss. Gibbs-White paused again before going to his left, but his penalty wasn't well hit and Samba went the same way and blocked it. Incredibly, Forest had done it and for the first time since 1992, they were going to Wembley.

Forest fans poured onto the pitch in celebration, with flares going off everywhere. The Forest players and Cooper were mobbed, with Spence's mum even getting on the field and joining in with the celebrations. However, the pitch invasion did finish on a sour note. Robinson had to be escorted off the field by two police officers and with Worrall as a bodyguard, while a mindless idiot headbutted Blades striker Billy Sharp. Other fans also got in a tangle with Rhian

Brewster and Oli McBurnie, which saw McBurnie seemingly stamp on one of them.

McBurnie would end up going to court for his actions, before being cleared, but what happened to Sharp, who played for Forest on loan in the 2011/12 season, was awful. By way of apology, a Forest fan called Zoe Potts set up a fundraiser for Sharp's nominated charity – Martin House Children's Hospice – and Forest fans ended up raising £16,000 for the cause. Sharp would express his gratitude to those who donated and the gesture goes to show that a fanbase can't be stereotyped by one absolute cretin, who was rightfully jailed for 24 weeks for his actions.

The build-up to Wembley was like Christmas as a kid. Wembley looked a bit different since Forest were last there, given it had been knocked down and rebuilt with a glorious arch over it, but the afterglow following Samba's heroics was magical. In amongst the pitch invasion, a fan had found his bottle, which had taped onto it a list of the Sheffield United players and where they most commonly placed their penalties. Samba was looking at his bottle, which was covered with a red towel, before every penalty, so clearly whoever did their homework did it well.

Forest had completely sold out their end and meeting them in the final would be Huddersfield, who the Reds would be facing for the fourth time that season. Before the game, Johnson Snr told the Garibaldi Red podcast that Cooper had organised a family barbeque for the players to relax, while also inviting club legends like John Robertson and Ian Storey-Moore to attend. It was a nice way of bringing everyone together ahead of the final and when the players got to the Wembley changing rooms, they noticed their lockers were full of supportive messages from their loved ones. Cooper had requested this, giving them a reminder of the importance of family and how far they'd come to be at this point.

The day itself was beautiful. It was a lovely, sunny day and on the way up, it already felt like Forest fans were outnumbering Huddersfield by about three to one. All you could see on the trains and along Wembley Way were red shirts dotted about and the occasional blue and white one. It was one of those days where you just felt as a fan that it's gonna be your day. This feeling went up another notch as I was entering the ground. I'm a fairly superstitious person and as an A Block regular, I always go through turnstile number seven when I enter The Peter Taylor Stand. Queuing to get into Wembley, my turnstile number was K7.

There was just something different in the air. As fans started piling in and the teams did their warm-ups, the DJ, totally unaware of its new found meaning with Forest fans, played 'Just Can't Get Enough'. He must've been very puzzled as those already there on one half of the stadium were up clapping and singing along, but that felt like another sign. There was one further suggestion everything was going to be alright from a Forest perspective and that came about 10 minutes before kick-off.

As Wembley is a neutral ground, both teams had the opportunity to do their usual pre-match routines and as Huddersfield were the 'home' side, they went first. They had a video of arguably their most famous supporter in Patrick Stewart reading a poem and had some clappers to make some noise, but it didn't really feel...special. This maybe wasn't helped by the fact Huddersfield hadn't sold their allocation out, but for whatever reason, it just wasn't much to write home about. Then it was Forest's turn.

First up, was the pre-match video that starts with Robin Hood shooting his bow and arrow, complete with his theme tune. It then shows Forest players from years gone by scoring goals and winning trophies, complete with snippets from Brian Clough and Colin Fray, the latter of whom is effectively the voice of Nottingham Forest thanks to his commentary for BBC Radio Nottingham. It ends with a much loved quote from Clough, which came after Forest drew 3-3 in the first leg of the 1979 European Cup semi-final: "I hope anybody isn't stupid enough to write us off."

The roar after that video alone eclipsed anything that Huddersfield created and the fans weren't finished yet. After the video, the drumbeat for 'Mull of Kintyre' started and that was the cue for another Forza display – this one effectively making the Forest end a red wall, with a banner reading, 'Far have we travelled, much have we seen'. When it was the cue for the Forest fans to do their bit for 'Mull of Kintrye' with no music, the result was deafening. The Forest fans were up for it and you could tell they wanted it more. All was left was for the players to do their job.

Like most finals, the start was cagey. The play-off final is dubbed the most expensive game in football due to its £170m reward, so understandably, teams set out first and foremost not to lose. Forest had the first sight of goal when a Garner free kick found the head of Yates, but he could only nod wide of the post. Huddersfield meanwhile, created absolutely nothing. They forced a few corners here and there, but Forest had them exactly where they wanted them from a defensive aspect. Two minutes before half-time, everything changed.

As Forest probed for an opening, the ball went down the left wing for Davis, who with nowhere to go, passed it back to Garner, who shot from 25 yards. Garner's shot bounced before going to goal, with both Yates and Levi Colwill going for it, with Yates missing it and Colwill inadvertently clearing it straight into the top corner. Euphoria. Of all the goals Forest had scored that season, that was by far one of the ugliest, but they all count and Forest led at Wembley. The noise was off the scale when that ball hit the net and before Huddersfield had any time to process what had happened, half time blew.

Forest were now 45 minutes from being a Premier League side again. After the restart, Huddersfield had more of the ball as they were chasing the game, but still couldn't find a way through and Forest had another half opportunity when a Johnson effort from distance went across goal, but Surridge – who had come on for Davis – couldn't quite get there in time to tap in. With 73 played, the drama stepped up again. Sorba Thomas broke down the left and pulled a ball back to the edge of the area, where Colback and Harry Toffolo both went for it, resulting in Toffolo flying through the air and hitting the deck.

The ref blew his whistle, but instead of giving a penalty, booked Toffolo for diving and gave a free-kick. However, that wasn't the end of it. As the play-off final had VAR, the incident was checked and from one angle, it seems as if Colback clipped Toffolo, but from another, Toffolo clearly dives. Given there wasn't anything conclusive to say the ref had made a clear and obvious error, the decision stood. No penalty, Forest free kick. Colback could be seen on camera afterwards doing the sign of the cross, which ironically is exactly what Marinakis was caught doing at the same time.

Forest were cruising up until that moment, but that was a stark reminder it would only take one mistake for their lead to be taken away. Remember the Fulham away game when I said seconds felt like minutes? After that, seconds felt like hours. Straight after the incident, Lowe made his injury return and came on for Zinckernagel, with Colback moving into the middle to shore things up a bit, but it wasn't long until Lowe was involved for all the wrong reasons. With just eight minutes left to play, Lowe seemed to come through the back of Lewis O'Brien as both players tangled legs and went down, but neither the ref nor VAR were interested.

Whereas the Toffolo one was debatable, this one seemed pretty clear cut. It was clumsy from Lowe, but after what had happened in the Bournemouth game, maybe decisions do even themselves out. The tension levels were unbearable, but Forest did what they didn't do against Sheffield United and kept calm. They looked after the ball when they had it and made it very difficult for Huddersfield to create anything when they didn't. Right on the 90 minute mark, Samba went down and while normally you'd assume he was time-wasting, this time he actually seemed hurt and Horvath had to come on for the six minutes of stoppage time, but he had little to do. Even with nothing to lose, Huddersfield never looked like scoring. They just hadn't turned up.

With seconds left to play, Huddersfield worked it down the left for Duane Holmes – who'd revelled in scoring against Forest earlier in the season because of his Derby links – but he shanked his cross into the stand behind the goal. The clock had now ticked to six minutes played and at that point, Cooper walked over to the opposition dugout and shook hands with Huddersfield manager Carlos Corberán, sensing it was done. Amidst ear-piercing whistling from the Forest end, following that goal kick, the full-time whistle blew and sparked pure ecstasy in the Forest end, as a roar 23 years in the making rippled through Wembley. Maybe the play-offs are for Forest, after all.

When I was a kid, my Dad used to pick me up to celebrate goals at games, hoisting me into the air like I was a trophy. At Wembley, he was picking me up again – only this time off the floor as I dropped to my knees, tears streaming down my face and completely overcome with emotion as that full-time whistle went. 23 years of waiting. 23 years of hoping, dreaming and praying. 23 years of heartbreak, false dawns, implosions and questioning would it ever be our turn. Twenty three years. After embracing Dad and pulling myself together, I could just make out 'Just Can't Get Enough' fusing with Gala's 'Freed From Desire' and while I know that song's always played after a final, a song title had never been so apt.

Wherever you looked around you, it was just unfiltered happiness. Strangers hugging each other, people crying with joy, families embracing each other – it was just wonderful. Absolutely wonderful. Don Goodman said that out of all the play-off finals he'd been to with Sky, the roar at the end from the Forest fans was the loudest he'd heard by far. Apparently the gantry was shaking, such was the noise generated. As for the players on the pitch, they were cuddling each other, running around jubilantly and swirling their tops over their heads. It was also brilliant to see players like Grabban and Lolley join in with those celebrations, with Grabban eventually lifting the trophy with Worrall after walking up those fabled Wembley steps.

There was also a lovely moment when academy chief Gary Brazil, partially responsible for the development of Johnson, Yates, Worrall and Mighten, celebrated with all four on the pitch in addition to Jordan Smith, another academy graduate that played for the first team thanks to Brazil's influence. Without Brazil guiding these young men through their formative stages so well, it's unlikely Forest would've had the season they had. Promotion also brought out an all timer from Sky commentator Daniel Mann, who said at full time, "The first European Cup came 43 years ago tomorrow, the second 42 years ago yesterday...it is another glory day in May for Nottingham Forest."

The celebrations weren't going to slow down for a while. In the dressing room after, the Sky cameras got in and with champagne and beer already flowing, Cook said the plan that night was "to go full Jack Grealish" in homage of the England international who'd recently celebrated being part of Manchester City's title winning side a bit too well, while Spence posted a picture of him smoking a cigar with the trophy in front of him and called out his former Boro boss Neil Warnock, who once claimed Spence would be either Premier League or non-league. When Forest finally left Wembley, Steven Reid was seen on the coach clutching cans of beer with a cigar, as was Johnson, with the team set to party through the night.

The next day, there was a rumour that Forest would be having a parade of sorts at the Old Market Square in Nottingham city centre, which saw an estimated 20,000 Reds flock there to cheer them on. The City Ground announcer and former BBC man Mark Dennison ended up compering the event by chance, as he was initially there to check out the rumour, before being spotted and asked to do it. Speaking to Red Side of the Trent podcast though, he described how worse for wear the team were. "They stank," Dennison stated. "They stank as I don't think they'd changed! All I could smell that day was sweat and booze."

At the event, every player was paraded to the crowd and upon being called out, it emerged just how hard they'd celebrated. Davis hilariously had to be stopped from whipping all of his clothes off, while a hammered Cook not only thanked referee Jon Moss for not giving a penalty, but also started a rendition of, "It was a pen, we're in the Prem," referencing at least one of the two major flashpoints in the game. It still didn't feel real that Forest were going to be mixing it among the elite once more and that they were back at English football's top table, but it very much was.

This sense of realness was further emphasised when Marinakis took to the balcony to address the fans and said, "We will give the ammunition to Steve and his team to maintain our position in the Premier League, but also to be very competitive. The sky is the limit and in my life, whatever we have been involved with, we have always been at the top. We all know about the achievements of this club 40 years ago. We respect that history, but now is the time to write a new history that is even brighter." These were huge words from the owner that certainly underlined his ambition, although his expectations seemed a touch unrealistic given how ruthless the Premier League is.

Those discussions could wait for another day as ultimately, all of this was made possible because of Cooper, who at the third attempt, finally tasted play-off glory. Because of his managerial skills, his tactical nous, his ability to coach players and the way he made everyone believe, Forest were in this position. Amongst all the things the Sky cameras picked out in the changing rooms, it was Cooper's very brief post-match chat to the players that caught the eye. Never one to make things about him, Cooper only said two things to his Wembley heroes. "Make sure you spend time with your family today and the people that have been good to you in your life, there won't be anybody prouder than them," was first. "The second thing is…WELCOME TO THE PREMIER LEAGUE!"

CHAPTER SEVEN – A BUSY SUMMER

Once the dust had settled from Wembley and the hangovers eased, Forest had to get straight to work off the field. Through no fault of their own, in terms of prep, they were two and a half weeks behind Bournemouth and three weeks behind Fulham. As soon as those two teams knew they were up, they could plan accordingly, whereas Forest didn't know what league they would be in. Preparing for the top flight didn't just mean the playing staff either, as The City Ground had to be revamped to cater for the Premier League and all that came with it, which meant new floodlights and finding space to be made for the added media presence.

New job positions had to be created and filled, while there was also an issue with Lower Bridgford. In the Championship, Forest gave away fans 2,000 seats and had half the lower section, but Premier League rules dictate you have to offer either 10% of your stadium capacity or 3,000 seats as an allocation. This meant moving 1,000 season ticket holders to accommodate this, which led to fears the atmosphere may suffer as a result. Thankfully, the 1,000 that had to move mostly went to A Block or U1 in Upper Bridgford, which have always been good for atmosphere.

Even the training pitches were changed, with The Athletic reporting that Cooper – who constantly demands the best; not just from his players, his coaching staff and himself, but from the facilities as well – demanded new ones after concluding that the existing ones were dated. The new pitches were specifically designed to replicate the playing surface at The City Ground and came at a cost of £2.5m. Cooper's belief was that if Forest were going to be a Premier League club in name, they needed to act like one in every single aspect – a view shared by those in the boardroom.

Shortly after Wembley, Murphy told Sirius XM that he wanted to keep the five loan players at the club, but sadly, that was easier said than done. In fact, the first casualty was already known to the club – Spence. The Athletic also reported that in January, it had become clear that Spence wanted a move to Tottenham Hotspur, which would give him a chance to go back to his home city of London, to play in the Champions League and to play for an elite manager in Antonio Conte.

As much as Forest tried to convince him that he would be better off staying with the club and developing with them before making the leap to one of the 'Sky Six' (one of Arsenal, Chelsea, Liverpool Manchester City, Manchester United and Tottenham, all of whom Sky have an infatuation with), Spence had his mind made up. It was a hammer blow as Spence was so integral to Forest's success and the bad news kept on coming.

While Lowe had an awkward reunion with Sheffield United following the play-offs, according to the Sheffield Star, Forest had submitted a bid around the £1.5m mark for Lowe in January, which was swiftly rejected as the Blades wanted £5m. Now Forest had been promoted, the Blades felt his value had gone up even higher and as a result, Forest were unwilling to sign him. Lowe likely would've been a back-up player for Forest in the top flight, but he still would've been very useful to have around.

This wasn't even Sheffield United being bitter, it was more that they – and everyone else – knew Forest had money to spend and were upping their asking prices as a result. It was a similar story with Davis, as while Forest immediately explored trying to sign him, according to The Mirror, Aston Villa wanted £15m for his services. This was outrageous given a) he had a year left on his contract and b) he'd scored eight career goals (five at Forest) in 88 appearances. As such, much like Lowe, Forest felt priced out of signing him and moved onto other targets. However, like Spence, this was another hammer blow given Davis' importance following his arrival, as he thrived off being that focal point for Cooper.

Weirdly too, despite Murphy's comments, Forest weren't going to move for Zinckernagel. The Dane scored seven goals and clocked up 10 assists in all competitions for Forest, but instead he went back to Watford following his loan ending and then shortly afterwards, signed for Olympiacos for £1.7m, as per the Watford Observer. This just seemed bizarre, as like Lowe, Zinckernagel would've likely been a bench option, but he would've been a great one. You can't get a lot of value for £1.7m, so Forest passing up on him was very strange – even if he did go to another Marinakis owned club in Olympiacos.

There was some good news, at least. The Telegraph reported that Cooper was close to signing a new deal and that McKenna was awarded Player of the Season for his exploits, both of which was fully deserved. Cooper, who spent some of his time off with Celtic manager Ange Postecoglou in Greece, had achieved a miracle to some and going into a season where for the first time in his managerial career, he'd likely lose more games than he'd win, having contract security was important – especially for fans, who wanted him in the home dugout for a long time to come.

As for McKenna, even during the Hughton led start, the Scotland international was putting in consistent 7/10 performances, which not everyone else could necessarily say. Across the whole season, it was more than justified and at Wembley, it was McKenna who took home the Player of the Match award. In addition, there was still some hope Garner could be signed. The message from Manchester United was that their new manager Erik ten Hag wanted to assess him over pre-season before deciding whether to keep him or sell/loan him, but it wasn't an outright no.

Knowing that four of the five loanees realistically wouldn't be returning was a blow, however. There was still a lingering belief among fans that Spence might stay, but it didn't get the summer off to a great start as in order to survive in the Premier League, the Forest squad would need a lot of work. Including the loanees, the starting XI of Samba; Worrall, Cook, McKenna; Spence, Garner, Yates, Lowe; Zinckernagel; Davis, Johnson was strong and with the likes of Colback, Surridge and Grabban as regular first-team players, there was a solid core that with some wise additions, could be competitive enough to stay up.

The rest of the team, simply put, were not or would not be up to it. Lolley was a fan favourite, but he wasn't the player he was a few years before and many fans had accepted that was likely his last season. Cafu was much loved, but realistically, he was a backup player for the club in the Championship. When Figueiredo was on it, he was good, but there was a reason why he was replaced by Cook. Taylor didn't seem a great tactical fit for Cooper, Mbe Soh and Mighten had shown bright burning glimpses of both ability and potential, but probably needed a loan before they could be considered for PL level, while Horvath, Laryea, Ojeda and Panzo were all likely signed with the Championship in mind.

On top of those 10, you had players like Bong and Silva who were surplus to requirements, but had still played sparingly the season before. Because of the loanee situation though, Forest were effectively in the market for 17 new players and that was just to replace what was already there. The odds were against Forest as was, with The Athletic reporting that one analytic study gave them just a 32% chance of survival, but now Cooper had to effectively mould a new team from scratch if the Reds were to stand any chance of staying up.

Sensibly, a new contract had been offered to Grabban, who still had a lot to offer. Even if his role would be off the bench, he was still a valued asset and the hope was he would sign a new deal. While he was deliberating, the club got busy. Very busy. Given the scale of the rebuild, Forest were naturally linked with just about everyone in world football, though the most exciting link was Morgan Gibbs-White. He would cost though, as The Athletic stated that Wolves, his parent club, would be looking for at least £20m for his services.

While Gibbs-White had inadvertently sent the Reds to Wembley with his penalty miss, he'd easily been the best player Forest had faced all season. In five games against the Reds – one for Wolves and four for Sheffield United – he'd scored three and assisted two, racking up a goal involvement in every game he'd played against Forest. Cooper also had a brilliant relationship with Gibbs-White, whom he'd managed at England U17 level as part of his World Cup winning side and also at Swansea, when he signed the attacking midfielder on loan. Even being linked to Gibbs-White was a statement of intent, but if Forest could pull it off, it would be a colossal coup.

With Davis having been priced out, Forest looked for alternatives and it didn't take them long to find one. Despite being linked with Ukraine international Artem Dovbyk, the Reds signed Nigeria international Taiwo Awoniyi from Union Berlin for a club record fee of £17.5m. Awoniyi had just scored 15 goals in the Bundesliga for Union and fitted the Syrianos model to a tee – quick, strong, athletic and only 24. It was a very exciting signing and for the money involved, reminded everyone that Wembley wasn't a dream.

The Reds also tried to sign RC Lens midfielder Cheick Doucoure, but were beaten to the punch by Crystal Palace. Forest were also interested in PSV Eindhoven midfielder Ibrahim Sangaré, but felt the financials involved were too much. It was a similar story with Lille midfielder Amadou Onana, who Forest walked away from after his asking price turned out to be £33m as per BBC Sport, which Everton eventually paid. Ultimately, Forest had a lot to of work to do and if they were going to sign anyone for that sort of money, it would be Gibbs-White and Gibbs-White only.

Shortly after signing Awoniyi, Forest announced a pre-season camp in Spain, which would culminate in a friendly against Coventry. Upon their return, they would face Burton Albion, Barnsley, Hertha Berlin, Union Berlin, Notts County and Valencia as they geared up for their first top flight campaign in 23 years, but as The City Ground was undergoing infrastructure work, they would be using both Notts' Meadow Lane and Burton's Pirelli Stadium for their 'home' games. However, Bong and Figueiredo would not be going, as both would be released following the expiry of their contracts. Figueiredo had been a good servant and left with good wishes, while Bong just didn't work out.

In addition to Figueiredo and Bong, Carl Jenkinson was also released, but on July 1, Forest announced some very good news. In addition to unveiling their new home kit (which in itself caused issues, as many shirts had to be returned due to poor quality), the Reds had managed to tie Johnson down to a four-year deal despite Brentford sniffing around him again, which was fantastic news for the club. Amidst all the chaos, Johnson, who scored 19 goals in the season Forest got promoted, pledging his future to his boyhood club was reason to be hugely optimistic. The next day, Horvath signed for Luton on loan for the season, but Forest were soon dealt two huge blows.

The first was that coach Steven Reid had left his position as part of the coaching staff, although this was bittersweet as what Reid planned to do instead was incredibly admirable. Reid, who'd suffered from mental health issues during his playing and coaching career, was going to become a specialist coach and to help other athletes improve their mental well-being. Cooper was upset that Reid was leaving, but wished him well as really, some things are more important than football and mental health is certainly one of them.

The second was that around the end of June, rumours started to circulate that Forest were looking at a new goalkeeper, with England internationals Nick Pope and Dean Henderson some of the targets linked. The reason being? Samba had rejected a new contract and informed the club of his desire to leave, stating that he had unfinished business in France and wished to return. It was likely that Samba felt undervalued by the contract offer and subsequently decided that a return home sounded great, but it all seemed surreal – Forest had just been promoted to the best league in the world and Samba now wanted to leave?

Despite a wobbly start to his season, Samba was a crucial part in promotion and was more than good enough to play in the top flight. It also meant the minimum number of signings needed had risen to 18, but Forest had acted swiftly and on the same day as Horvath departing for Luton, signed Henderson on loan from Manchester United for the season. However, this one hurt the fans a lot. There was an acceptance that Henderson was an outrageously good signing for the club, but Samba was beloved. A few days later, Samba left for RC Lens in a £4.3m deal, according to L'Equipe.

To soften the blow, Forest brought in two defensive reinforcements a day either side of Samba leaving. First was Guilian Biancone, who signed for £5m from Troyes as per the Athletic and could play either as a centre back or a right back, while second was centre back Moussa Niakhaté, who signed for £8.5m from Mainz with a further £4.2m due in add ons, as per the BBC. 26-year-old Niakhaté, who had been captain at Mainz, was a very important signing as he could replace some of the leadership that had been lost with the departures. Both players were in the Syrianos mould too, with both being very quick, athletic and 26 or under. Niakhaté also had a long throw and was left footed, which helped with the defensive balance.

Two days later, Forest lost 3-1 in their first friendly to Coventry, with all four new signings playing the first half and Biancone even scoring. It was on that day though that The Athletic reported Grabban had rejected a new deal, instead choosing to play in the Middle East. The total number of required signings had now gone to 19 and losing Grabban, much like Samba, was a blow and also meant Forest would need a new captain. No-one could begrudge Grabban for leaving, but his departure left a void and no doubt would've hurt Cooper, who really valued what Grabban brought to the table.

Grabban's departure saw Cooper turn to Worrall as his – and Forest's – new captain, which just felt right. Worrall was an academy graduate, born in Nottingham and knew what it meant to represent the club. In addition, fellow academy graduate Yates was named as vice captain, which was a huge achievement for the academy. Worrall held the armband in Grabban's absence and led Forest out at Wembley wearing it too, so it felt right that a Nottingham born lad would lead the club into their first Premier League season in nearly a quarter of a century.

The clear-out continued as Tyrese Fornah and Will Swan both went on loan to Reading and Mansfield Town respectively, while Forest then moved on from Lowe and Spence by signing Omar Richards from Bayern Munich for £8.5m and Neco Williams from Liverpool for £17m, both fees as per The Guardian. Forest had also been eyeing up Issa Kabore from Manchester City as their Spence replacement, but instead opted for Williams, who had worked with Cooper at the Liverpool youth academy. Williams was a different profile of player to Spence, but the Cooper connection gave fans optimism.

The next day, Forest claimed their first win in pre-season as a Cook goal was enough to give them a 1-0 victory over Burton Albion. Recruitment wasn't slowing down though and the next one through the door was experienced goalkeeper Wayne Hennessey, who signed on a free from recently relegated Burnley. The Wales international represented dependable backup and had a wealth of Premier League experience, which was something distinctly lacking among the rest of the team. He also had a unique connection with Forest given his cousin is Terry Hennessey, who spent five years as a Red in the 1960s. Panzo was then sent on loan to Coventry, while youngsters Fin Back and Riley Harbottle went on loan to Carlisle United and Mansfield Town respectively.

Forest then had a busy 48 hours as they drew 0-0 with Barnsley at Oakwell and got some more minutes into the new signings, including Williams, before swooping for Costa Rica wonderkid

Brandon Aguilera from Alajuelense for about £800k, according to Futbol Central America. With Aguilera, it seemed like Forest had found a gem. The attacking midfielder was immediately loaned out to Costa Rican side Guanacasteca to aid his development, but despite only being 19, Aguilera had already played three times for Costa Rica and was likely to be on the plane for their World Cup 2022 squad.

Then, Forest compounded recently defeated Huddersfield's misery even further by agreeing a joint £10m deal for both central midfielder Lewis O'Brien and left back Harry Toffolo as per The Athletic, ironically enough the two players who had penalty shouts in the final. Also according to The Athletic, the move very nearly fell through at the 11th hour due to Toffolo's wage demands, but the left back eventually eased his stance and finally the deal could be completed. The next day, Forest announced the transfer (aptly using fireworks in Toffolo's announcement video) and celebrated by defeating Hertha Berlin 3-1, with Taylor bagging a brace and Lukas Ullrich scoring an own goal. But, there was a bigger story afoot and it surrounded Omar Richards.

A rumour had gone around on Twitter that he'd broken his leg, but this was taken with a huge pinch of salt. It seemed scarcely believable, especially with the club releasing pictures of him in training and then even naming him on the bench for the Hertha Berlin friendly. However, he was nowhere to be seen at the Hertha game and after the match, Cooper confirmed that the rumour was indeed true, but that Richards wouldn't be out for, "months and months and months". According to deep dive from The Atheltic, nothing flagged up on Richards' medical, but he started to notice some pain and swelling on his leg during his first training session.

He then went for an X-ray and it revealed he had a hairline fracture. Marinakis was furious and had some very heated conversations with Bayern Münich's hierarchy, but to no avail. Within Forest, there was a fear that if the news got out, clubs would realise Forest needed a left back again and would try to take advantage of the club financially. As such, they simply decided to pretend that nothing was wrong, especially as they were already going through a turbulent transfer with Huddersfield for O'Brien and Toffolo and felt that Huddersfield would jack the price up if they knew.

The next day though, everything changed. The Guardian had been reporting that Forest had been chasing England international Jesse Lingard on a free transfer following his release from Manchester United along with West Ham United, whom Lingard had a hugely successful stint with on loan during the 2019/20 season, but no-one really thought much of it. Lingard scored nine goals and registered six assists in 16 games in that loan spell, so it seemed inevitable he'd return to the Hammers. It just felt like agent talk to force West Ham's hand.

Until it wasn't. While West Ham were trying to force a move through with Lingard, giving him several ultimatums and leaving him feeling disrespected in the process, Forest had taken a different approach. Lingard revealed on Steven Bartlett's Diary of a CEO podcast that Marinakis had offered to fly the 29-year-old to Greece to outline his plan, while Cooper had offered to come to Lingard's house for a chat. It made him feel loved and wanted and in the end, the charm offensive worked. In a move that absolutely nobody saw coming, Lingard was announced as a Forest player, signing a one-year deal that provided flexibility for all parties.

This was a sensational coup for the club and the highest profile signing the Reds had made in at least two decades, with the media going into a frenzy over the news. While praising the signing, Worrall was keen to emphasise to the Daily Express how once upon a time, Forest had many players of Lingard's calibre at the club and that the aim was to return to that level, but while his words were true and certainly highlighted Marinakis' ambition, few could've predicted a statement signing like that.

Outside of Nottingham though, the reaction was of bewilderment and scorn. Signing Lingard changed everything. When Forest were promoted, the general vibe was, "great to have you back! It's been far too long, a proper club back in the top flight, we love to see it!" After signing Lingard, it was, "who the fuck do you think you are?! You actually want to try and compete? How dare you!" This wasn't helped by the wildly exaggerated reports on Lingard's weekly wage, which seemed to go up every day, as the media struggled to get to grips with the fact a player had turned down West Ham to sign for Forest.

This was bizarre in its own right. West Ham had finished seventh the year before and were in the UEFA Conference League, but they were hardly a footballing giant. Had Forest beaten Arsenal or Manchester United to a high profile signing, I could've maybe understood it. But

West Ham? Really? It was like Forest had committed a crime by failing to understand how the other Premier League clubs felt, in that newly promoted clubs should be seen and not heard, concede at least four points to everyone apart from the other newly promoted clubs and go straight back down. See also, Norwich City and West Brom.

On the topic of Premier League clubs, some of them weren't happy with Forest. According to The Athletic, a few felt they were distorting the market by offering players big salaries and then ultimately moving onto other targets, thus making it harder for other clubs to sign these players as the financial expectations had changed. As such, the Lingard wage claims likely went down like a lead balloon in certain boardrooms, as the reality that a newly promoted side weren't going just roll over was sinking in.

Contrary to the wild claims about Lingard's wages, including figures of £180k and £200k a week, The Telegraph revealed that Lingard's base salary was £80k a week, which could rise to £120k per week depending on performance related bonuses. What made the hysteria even funnier was that The Times claimed that West Ham had tried to make Lingard their top earner, offering bigger wages than Forest in the process. £80k a week was massive money for Forest, but Lingard effectively worked out as a £4m signing if he didn't play well, or a £6.25m signing if he did play well. All things considered, it didn't seem that bad.

Despite the media glare shining brighter than ever, Forest continued their pre-season prep and flew to Berlin to take on Union Berlin,

Awoniyi's former club, who had just finished fifth in the Bundesliga. This was a much tougher test and Forest lost 1-0, but much like the other games, the exposure to first-team football for the new signings was the most important aspect. A few days later, the Reds drew 2-2 with Notts County in a game that was treated like a cup final by the Magpies instead of a friendly, with Surridge and Cafu finding the net, before Nicholas Ioannou departed permanently for Como.

The Reds then had their final pre-season friendly, which was against Valencia and saw Lingard get some minutes in a Forest shirt for the first time. A Johnson strike earned Forest a 1-1 draw and the next day, the Reds announced the signing of Belgium international Orel Mangala from VfB Stuttgart for a fee of £12.7m, as per the Nottingham Post. Mangala, a central midfielder, was Forest's 12th signing so far and one that at least gave Cooper a starting XI and some options to work with ahead of their opening Premier League match away at Newcastle United.

There was some more squad trimming as Xande Silva and Nuno da Costa both departed on permanent fees, to Dijon and Auxerre respectively, while Ojeda (Real Salt Lake) and Laryea (Toronto FC) both went on loan. The big news though was that The Guardian reported Forest had submitted a bid worth up to £35m in add-ons for Gibbs-White, which had been rejected. That was Forest's third bid for the attacking midfielder and would've smashed their record transfer by some margin had it been accepted, so it remained to be seen whether they would return. The Athletic also credited Forest with a strong interest in Leeds United winger Crysencio Summerville, but it came to nothing.

Annoyingly though for Forest, despite pre-season ending, the situation with Garner was still no clearer. Garner had only played once in pre-season due to injury, but due to a midfield shortage at United, would be involved in and around the first team at least for the opening weekend of the season. This would likely delay any decision on his future, but all focus was now on that trip to St James' Park and Forest's first Premier League match in 23 years. Henderson, Niakhaté, Williams, O'Brien, Toffolo and Lingard all made their competitive debuts, while new signings Mangala, Awoniyi, Biancone and Hennessey were on the bench.

However, the bench itself looked remarkably weak for the level Forest were at and highlighted just how much more work needed to be done from a recruitment aspect. Mighten, Cafu, Taylor, Mbe Soh and Oli Hammond, who'd not yet played a league game for the Reds, made up the rest of the substitutes and all of those realistically would be playing their football away from The City Ground that season. It was in stark contrast to Newcastle's bench, which included the likes of Chris Wood, Ryan Fraser, Jacob Murphy, Sean Longstaff and new signing Sven Botman, who'd recently cost the club £32m.

That wasn't the only notable difference – the football itself was a world away from the Championship and to quote Colin Fray from a Red Side of the Trent episode, "It was like watching a different sport." The pace of the game was on another level. Whereas in the Championship, games are very fast paced and frenetic, this is because the player quality isn't as high and more mistakes are made. Here, Newcastle were zipping it around and finding feet every time, making no mistakes and not giving the ball away, but doing so at great speed.

After wave after wave of Newcastle attack, Joelinton decided to take matters into his own hands and darted inside O'Brien and Worrall, glided past Niakhaté and shot just wide. It was a petrifying shot across the bows that highlighted just how good these players were and that Forest could be in for a long season, let alone a long day. However, against the run of play, Lingard found space in the area and fired a dangerous effort at goal, but Fabian Schär put in a brilliant block to prevent it causing any real issues.

Soon after, Bruno Guimarães split the Forest defence in two with a sublime through ball that Almiron raced onto and put across goal, but Henderson was on hand to tip it behind courtesy of the post. Remarkably, Forest made it through to half-time unscathed, but the gulf in class was evident. Despite this, Forest were being stubborn and digging in. The second half continued in the same vein as the first, with Newcastle moving the ball about ferociously without finding a way through, but eventually Forest's luck ran out.

An Allan Saint-Maximin cross was half cleared by Niakhaté before being properly cleared by McKenna, falling to Schär about 30 yards out. Schär then proceeded to drive forwards, with none of Lingard, Colback or Toffolo in a hurry to close him down, before unleashing an absolute piledriver from outside the box straight into the top corner. This seemed to knock something into Forest and immediately after, they went straight up the other end down the right and Williams whipped in a peach of a ball for Surridge, but the striker mistimed his jump and put the ball harmlessly over.

At a moment where Forest needed to show quality, they failed to do so and with 12 to go, it cost them. A well worked move saw Saint-Maximin play Joelinton down the left and his first time low cross was met first by Callum Wilson, with the England international getting there ahead of Niakhaté and scooping it over Henderson into the corner with a first time effort from the outside of his boot. It was a majestic finish and a timely reminder that if you don't take your chances, the other team has the quality to punish you.

In truth, Forest were outclassed and did well to keep it at 2-0. It was clear they had a long way to go to be a Premier League side on the pitch, even if they were one by name. This was the case off the field too, as one thing the media picked up on after the defeat was that Forest didn't have a shirt sponsor. Their agreement with previous sponsor BOXT ended after they wouldn't pay what Marinakis wanted and so there was just nothing there. Given the club had so many plates to spin, it was inevitable some would fall, but that one seemed a strange one as any extra revenue would have helped.

To maybe help with things like this, Forest hired former Newcastle Chief Executive Lee Charnley on a consultancy basis, at Murphy's request according to The Telegraph, to help them adapt to Premier League life. Unlike in the Championship with its plethora of midweek fixtures, as there are less games in the Premier League, it's generally a week's wait until the next match. This can be a good and a bad thing, as nobody enjoys stewing on a defeat for a week, but given Forest's dire need to bolster the squad, it was a blessing.

They had some bad news as Real Betis left back Alex Moreno had a last second change of heart to join the club, while another left back target in Villarreal's Pervis Estupiñán rebuffed the Reds for Brighton & Hove Albion, but otherwise, Forest made good use of the time. The day before their first Premier League home fixture since May 1999, central defensive midfielder Cheikhou Kouyaté signed on a free following his release from Crystal Palace, while Nigeria international forward Emmanuel Dennis also checked in on Trentside, signing from Watford for around £10m as per The Athletic, while the deal could rise to £20m depending on add-ons.

Dennis' arrival was an exciting one as while Watford had gone down the previous year, he'd scored 10 goals and racked up six assists, so to have a player of that calibre was promising. Importantly though, both Dennis and Kouyaté had Premier League experience and on paper, a decent team was starting to form. There was still work to do, but the signs of progress were there. Unfortunately for Forest though, neither would be available for that first home match, which was against West Ham. After the whole furore regarding Lingard, it was perhaps fitting they'd be first up at home and it was pretty much all the media were talking about.

At a packed City Ground bathed in sunshine, Forest were ready. A Forza display went up in The Brian Clough Stand, with the message reading 'Risen' – a hark back to Forza's first ever display in 2017, which read 'Rise of the Garibaldi', but also very apt given the stage was now set for Forest's first home Premier League game in two decades. As loud as the Forest fans were, it didn't take long for the travelling West Ham contingent to make their feelings towards Lingard known, with the attacking midfielder being booed on touch as both teams looked to start with intent.

The first major chance fell to the visitors as Saïd Benrahma cut inside off the left and sent a curling effort goalbound, which Henderson inadvertently parried out straight into the path of a lurking Tomás Soucek, who was thwarted on the line by a recovering Toffolo. However, Forest had given a good account of themselves so far, with Awoniyi and Niakhaté both coming close with headers and the Reds were getting joy on the counter attack. Not long before half-time, Forest won a corner in front of the away fans and both Williams and Lingard went over to take it, with one of the two set to offer a short option.

Anticipating they'd be in close contact with Lingard at some point, some of the West Ham fans had brought wads of fake cash with them in light of the exaggerated wages reported in the media and threw them towards the corner flag, but in their infinite wisdom, threw them at Williams instead of Lingard. The error wasn't lost on Lingard, who just looked at the away end and laughed, but he wasn't laughing for very long as shortly afterwards, the Hammers had the ball in the net.

From that corner, West Ham cleared and Benrahma broke at pace, zooming past O'Brien and Lingard before laying it off for Declan Rice. Rice then popped the ball through into a gap for Benrahma, who coolly slotted home. Straight away, the Forest players were protesting and upon watching the replays, it was easy to see why. The reason why Rice could play that pass to Benrahma was because Mangala was unable to plug the gap, on the basis former Forest man Michail Antonio ran straight into him at full pelt, NFL style, sending him tumbling. After a quick VAR check, the goal was disallowed and Forest were awarded a free-kick deep in their half.

Forest generated momentum from that reprieve and right on the edge of half-time, they got their reward. Toffolo played a neat give-and-go with O'Brien and surged into the box before cutting a ball back to an unmarked Lingard on the penalty spot. Lingard, with the goal at his mercy and in front of the West Ham fans, fluffed his effort and Ben Johnson managed to get a foot in to block it. However, Johnson's block hit Awoniyi, who was running towards goal anyway and with goalkeeper Lukasz Fabianski grounded as he'd pre-empted Lingard connecting with the ball cleanly and dived early, the ball bobbled into the back of the net.

It was the first Premier League goal Forest had scored since a Chris Bart-Williams effort against Leicester on May 16, 1999 and to say the proverbial roof came off would be an understatement. It was far from an aesthetically pleasing goal, but they all count and Forest had been good value for their lead. The ref blew for half-time pretty much immediately after the goal, but straight after the restart, it seemed clear that words had been had in the West Ham changing room. Within a minute, Benrahma had gone down the left and pulled it back for Pablo Fornals, whose effort struck the underside of the bar and came back out straight to Soucek, but out of nowhere, his header was beaten away by Henderson's arm.

Forest then had the ball in the net again as a Mangala through ball found Johnson, who rifled home, but VAR showed that Johnson was offside and it was ruled out. West Ham then hit the underside of the bar again as a Benrahma free-kick cannoned off it, as the Reds' goal started to lead a bit of a charmed life. Immediately after clearing that free-kick, West Ham came straight back through Benrahma, who sped down the left and pulled it for Soucek on the penalty spot. Unlike Lingard, Soucek connected well and both McKenna and Henderson went to block it, the former doing so with his hand.

The referee missed that, but VAR didn't and after a check, a penalty was awarded. McKenna was booked for his exploits and was perhaps lucky not to be sent off for that action, but was presumably spared a red card as Henderson was right behind him and looked set to save it anyway. Rice then stepped up to take the spot kick and sent it to his bottom left, but Henderson leapt across his goalline and caught it, clutching the ball into his chest with one arm and fist pumping the crowd with the other.

With 25 still to play, Forest understandably became more cautious, but as good a job as Forest were doing killing the game, West Ham still had something left in the tank. With seven minutes to go, an inch perfect corner from Aaron Cresswell found the head of Kurt Zouma. Henderson was finally beaten at long last, but Williams had incredibly managed to scramble it clear off the line and the Reds survived. For whatever reason, the footballing gods had decided

West Ham simply weren't going to score and after nine minutes of injury time, the referee blew his whistle and Forest had their first top flight victory in 8,856 days.

The first few notes of 'Just Can't Get Enough' felt euphoric, as did Cooper's customary fist pumps after a win. Yes, Forest were fortunate, but they'd deserved at least a point from the game from their first half showing alone. In addition, both O'Brien and Mangala were tremendous, effectively doing the job of a three-man midfield between them with the amount of ground they'd covered. As an aside, it was great to see Antonio get a fantastic reception after he was subbed, with the forward racking up 19 goals and 15 assists in his 54 games as a Forest player.

Unfortunately though, the win did come at a cost. Niakhaté had to be subbed with 10 to go with a hamstring injury and was set to be out for a good few months as a result, which was a huge blow as he'd already started to impose himself and his pace was invaluable to how Forest wanted to play. This was somewhat softened by the arrival of Remo Freuler from Atalanta, with the 30-year-old Switzerland international midfielder being described as 'the conductor of the orchestra'. Freuler, who cost around £7.6m according to The Guardian, had been a Serie A gem for years and also had Champions League experience with Atalanta, so his signing felt like a real coup.

This also came at a price, though. With Forest having signed Mangala, Freuler, O'Brien and Kouyaté, with Yates still at the club, they had five players jostling for two positions. Six, if you counted Cafu. As such, they no longer needed Garner, meaning none of the promotion winning loanees would be returning. This was sad and in Forest's defence, not really their fault. It felt like United were constantly deliberating about what to do with Garner and Forest couldn't really afford to sit around and wait with the season now underway, as Cooper needed players in quickly to have with the best chance at integrating everyone.

Losing Garner was a genuine shame for Forest, not only for his all-round game and potential, but also for his set-piece delivery. Given Forest were up against it to stay in the top flight, the finest of margins can be enough to win games and having a set-piece specialist can be the difference. In addition, Lolley had been sold to Sydney FC in Australia and while it was expected he'd be moved on, there was something very cold and cut-throat about his Forest exit that a player who'd served the club like he had didn't really deserve.

Lolley revealed that the day after returning from the club's pre-season camp in Spain, he received a text from Cooper telling him that he was training with the under-23s and not allowed in the first team building from that point onwards. It was a particularly brutal way of informing someone they were surplus to requirements, especially someone who was Forest Player of the Year for the 2018/19 season. Forest had signed Lolley from Huddersfield in a rumoured £500k fee, say The Athletic and the return on that investment was outrageously good.

In total, Lolley racked up 26 goals and 27 assists in 171 games for Forest, but his two crowning seasons were the aforementioned 2018/19 campaign, where he scored 11 and assisted 11 and the 2019/20 season, where he scored nine and assisted nine. In fact, his form in 2019 was so good that his boyhood club Aston Villa were heavily linked with a £10m bid, but the alleged response from Forest was that they wanted £15m, such was his importance to the Reds. Injuries unfortunately took a toll on him physically after that second standout season and he wasn't quite the same player after, but Lolley deserved a much better exit than that.

Cooper insisted to The Athletic it wasn't personal and that it was more to do with the numbers he wanted for training sessions, but it also highlighted how ruthless he could be when he needed to be. Ultimately, professional football is merciless and despite his personable character and friendly demeanour, Cooper clearly had an edge to him that was part of the reason why he'd been successful as a manager. However, all talk about Lolley ceased pretty quickly as after weeks of negotiating, Forest had finally got their man and Cooper his main target – Morgan Gibbs-White was a Red.

Wolves had initially refused to sell Gibbs-White, but when it was made apparent to them he didn't want to sign a new deal, as per The Athletic, they eventually cashed in. According to The Telegraph, this was to the tune of £25m up front, but a fee that could rise to £42.5m – which absolutely shattered Forest's transfer record. The Telegraph also stated there was some late drama as Everton had attempted to hijack the deal at the last minute, but Gibbs-White wanted a reunion with Cooper, who he'd been close with ever since Cooper was his England U17 manager.

In fact, The Telegraph also reported that Cooper was annoyed he hadn't been hired as Forest manager earlier, as he wanted to sign Gibbs-White on loan for Forest before Sheffield United got there. But now, he finally had his man and ahead of Forest's next fixture, a trip to Everton ironically, it felt like the squad was starting to take shape. Gibbs-White, who'd started Wolves' first two games of the season, was named on the bench at Goodison Park as the Reds sought to build on the momentum generated from the West Ham victory.

Despite starting well, Henderson had to be alert after 15 minutes when Alex Iwobi found Anthony Gordon and Gordon got a shot away from outside the box, stinging the goalkeeper's palms, but Forest carried a constant threat. Shortly after Gordon's effort, Williams forced Jordan Pickford into a smart stop, before Johnson robbed James Tarkowski just outside the Everton box and fed Awoniyi, but Awoniyi was held up by Conor Coady and couldn't quite get a clean sight of goal, eventually shooting tamely at Pickford.

Unlike the West Ham game, Forest were doing a lot better defensively and while Demarai Gray had Henderson scurrying across his line to save a free-kick, the Toffees weren't offering too much from open play. In the second half though, they got a bit braver and had Forest on the ropes a little bit, with Salomón Rondón shrugging Cook away with ease and firing just wide, before Iwobi wriggled through two challenges before finding Gordon in the box, but Henderson was on hand to deny Gordon again.

After an hour, Gibbs-White was brought on for Awoniyi and immediately got himself involved, dispossessing Gordon out wide and proceeding to jink inside both Gordon and Nathan Patterson with a sublime turn. Gibbs-White's cross was cleared but only as far as Williams, whose powerful effort flashed just past the post. With nine to go, Lingard gave it to Yates outside the box and after leaving Iwobi flat footed, fired goalbound. Yates' shot was parried by Pickford, but straight into the path of Johnson, who calmly slotted it past the England goalkeeper to give Forest the lead.

Johnson's goal sparked bedlam in the away end and with just a few minutes to play and with Everton having no real ideas, it felt like Forest were set for back-to-back wins. Entering the 90th minute however, a long ball from Pickford completely caught the Forest backline out and Gray was allowed to run through on goal one-on-one, firing past Henderson to give Everton an equaliser. Despite seemingly being down and out, that goal sparked Everton into life and with seconds left, Gordon had a great chance to win the game for the hosts, but his lofted effort was well read by Henderson and the game finished 1-1.

After the game, both teams felt that they should've won, so perhaps a draw was a fair result taking everything into consideration. For Forest though, it meant that they'd taken four points from their first three games in the Premier League, which given all the new arrivals and key departures, represented a fantastic start to life as a newly promoted club. Cooper had dealt with the numerous challenges superbly and while they were far from out of the woods yet and still with work to do before the window shut, Forest were very much enjoying Premier League life again.

CHAPTER EIGHT – A RUDE AWAKENING

Before their next taste of Premier League action, Forest faced a trip to League Two Grimsby Town in the Carabao Cup second round. Cooper made 11 changes for the fixture, handing debuts to new signings Hennessey, Dennis, Biancone and Freuler, while Kouyaté and academy graduate Aaron Donnelly made their first starts for the Reds. Despite it being a competitive fixture, it had a slight pre-season fixture feel to it, with Cooper being afforded the luxury of bedding the new signings into his system without disrupting the league form.

After 18 minutes, Dennis cut the ball back to the edge of the area and Yates' half volley on his left foot found its way into the top corner. With 35 played, any hopes of a cupset were over for Grimsby when Yates robbed Kieran Green inside his own half, allowing Cafu to feed Surridge inside the box, who finished ruthlessly. In the second half, Grimsby decided to throw everything at it and hit the post through a Ryan Taylor header after Hennessey came for a cross and didn't get anywhere near it, but Surridge made sure of the win with 13 to play when Cafu again picked him out in the box, with the exact same outcome as in the first half.

Forest then signed South Korea international Hwang Ui-Jo from Bordeaux for an estimated £3.5m as per L'Equipe, but the 30-year-old was sent straight out on loan to Marinakis owned Greek giants Olympiacos. It was a very weird signing as his profile was nothing like what Forest had been seeking, let alone his immediate loan to Athens, but the striker became Forest's 17th summer signing. The volume of players coming in wasn't lost on the media, with it being frequently claimed that Forest were 'doing a Fulham' or 'doing a QPR' – both teams having bought a lot of players in previous years upon promotion and then subsequently went down.

Despite the outside noise, Cooper was keeping calm about it all. In one press conference, a helicopter flew over the building and Cooper joked that it was another one coming in now. It would be understandable though if he couldn't wait until the window was closed, so that he could solely focus on his side. There were two more league games before the summer transfer window slammed shut, neither of which were going to be easy – Tottenham Hotspur at home and Manchester City away, but Cooper had a tactical trick up his sleeve for Spurs.

Rather than start a striker, Cooper opted to have Lingard in a false nine role, with Gibbs-White and Johnson either side of him. It seemed to catch Spurs out initially, but after just five minutes, the gameplan was effectively out the window. After breaking through the Forest press with ease, Dejan Kulusevski ran with the ball into the Forest half before playing it right to Harry Kane, with the England captain using McKenna as a screen and placing the ball the other side of Henderson and into the net.

Despite the setback, Forest kept a positive outlook and were playing some really good stuff. Johnson and Williams had decent efforts, but with Spurs going into a defensive shell to try and hit Forest on the counter, it was up to the Reds to pick them apart. Shortly before half-time, they came very close when Lingard laid it back for Gibbs-White just outside the box, but his effort went over the bar. When the half-time whistle blew, despite being a goal down, it was Forest who went into the break the happier side.

Words were clearly said in the Spurs dressing room at half-time as in the second half, they started to stamp their authority. Just 10 minutes after the restart, Ivan Perišić jinked past Williams and hung a cross over Henderson right on Kane's head, but before it could land, Cook batted it away like he was playing basketball. The ref had no choice but to give a penalty and Cook could count himself fortunate he was only shown yellow. There was an ominous feel as Kane stepped over the spot-kick, but just like against West Ham, Henderson flung himself the right way and pushed away Kane's effort.

That gave Forest some belief and pretty much straight from the penalty save, Forest went up the other end and almost levelled. Lingard beautifully released Toffolo down the left after some superb skill and Toffolo's cross found Yates on the edge of the box. Yates nudged it to Williams, who drove a powerful effort into the floor, which flashed just past the post. Much like the Gibbs-White effort earlier though, Spurs punished Forest for their profligacy. After catching Forest on the counter, Ryan Sessegnon sprinted down the left, but he took too long to square it to Kane and McKenna cleared.

However, while chasing the clearance, Richarlison outmuscled Freuler to win the ball and fired in an outrageously good cross from the outside of his boot, straight onto an unmarked Kane's head for a tap in. Somehow, neither Toffolo or Kouyaté thought to mark him and that was game pretty much over. There was still some drama to come as Richarlison decided to showboat and do some keep-ups during the game, resulting in Johnson clattering him from behind and sparking a mini fracas. Spence came on for his Spurs debut to a great reception from The City Ground faithful, but it ended in defeat for the Reds.

The mood post-match was one of positivity. The players were applauded off the field despite losing as ultimately, a 'Sky Six' side that were heavy favourites going into the game were made to work for a win. Forest were maybe a little naïve at times, but losing a game in that manner was hardly something to be ashamed of. Mighten was sent out on loan to Sheffield Wednesday the next day as the squad shaping continued, but while he was getting his things ready, Forest were getting ready to announce another huge statement signing in the shape of Atlético Madrid and Brazil international left back Renan Lodi on loan.

If you'd told someone a year earlier that in 12 months, Forest would be signing a 24-year-old with 15 caps for Brazil, who'd won Player of the Match awards in the Champions League for Atleti and someone who'd knocked Man United out of the competition as recently as six months prior, you'd have laughed. But here he was, at The City Ground doing keep-ups, with sports journalist Fabrizio Romano claiming he'd signed for a £4.3m loan fee with a £25m option to make it permanent. Much like with Lingard, the Marinakis family and Cooper went on a charm offensive as per The Athletic and it worked.

Lodi had pushed for a move as he wanted to be playing first-team football ahead of the 2022 World Cup, which was taking place that winter due to it being held in Qatar, to give himself the best opportunity to be selected for the Seleção. It was an agreement that worked in everyone's favour – Forest were getting a top class player who wanted to prove a point, while Lodi could showcase his ability in the Premier League. Lodi signed in time to be given a baptism of fire of sorts though, as Forest's next game was a trip to champions Manchester City's Etihad Stadium.

No-one in football expected Forest to do anything at City other than get beat – and get beat badly. But it was these sorts of games fans craved when being promoted, as it was a chance for Forest to test themselves against the best team in the land with arguably the best manager of all time in Pep Guardiola. Cooper realised their threat and set Forest up in a 5-3-2, with Lodi coming straight in at left back, while a midfield three was made up of Freuler, Yates and O'Brien. Meanwhile, Kouyaté came in for Cook as one of the three centre backs, while Gibbs-White partnered Johnson up front, with both expected to drop in to help out.

It only took 12 minutes for that plan to go out the window. After having what felt like 99% possession, City forced a corner and opted to play it short to Phil Foden, who'd peeled away from Gibbs-White and whipped a ball in towards Erling Haaland. Yates went to intercept it and bizarrely stopped, allowing Haaland to hold Worrall off to get to the ball first, firing past Henderson with his first touch of the game. This forced Forest to open up a bit and they nearly reaped their rewards for that when a Williams cross found Lodi at the far post, but he could only head into the side netting.

A few minutes later, that miss was immediately punished. Henderson tried to find Lodi, but his kick was poor and intercepted by Bernardo Silva, who immediately fired it into Julián Álvarez on the edge of the box. Álvarez instantly laid it off for Ilkay Gündogan, who found Haaland in the box with a first time pass, allowing him to play in Foden. Foden's first touch was heavy and as Henderson rushed out to close the angle, a last ditch tackle from Williams denied Foden a shot, but instead the ball kindly fell for Haaland, who rolled it into an open net.

It was scintillating football from City, but Forest were the architects of their own downfall. Seven minutes before half-time and it was game well and truly over. A João Cancelo cross from the outside of his boot from deep was headed across goal by Foden to John Stones, who himself headed it back across the six-yard box, allowing Haaland to head home to complete his hat-trick. It was just quality from a different planet and thankfully for Forest, it was only 3-0 at half time. Cooper's message would've likely been to not let it get embarrassing, but it would appear City had other ideas.

Five minutes after half-time, Bernardo Silva found Cancelo on the edge of the box and with Yates reluctant to close him down, Cancelo fired a rocket into the top left corner. 15 minutes later, a Riyad Mahrez pass cruelly deflected off both Freuler and McKenna into Álvarez's path, who fired past Henderson first time to make it five. With three minutes to play, substitute Dennis had a free-kick that hit the wall and while the rebound came to Williams, his touch was heavy and allowed Kevin De Bruyne to stride forwards on the counter, eventually feeding Mahrez on the edge of the box. Mahrez's effort was blocked by McKenna, but the rebound fell for Álvarez, who slammed it top corner. 6-0, full time.

The last two goals had a huge element of fortune about them, but City had outclassed Forest. Every mistake, or even half-mistake in some instances, was ruthlessly punished, with no mercy spared whatsoever. The majority of the Forest fans still stayed behind to clap their team off at the end, but losing 6-0 is never fun. It was the last game before the end of the window and on transfer deadline day, Forest were busy again, as experienced centre back Willy Boly signed from Wolves for an initial £2.25m, rising to £4.65m depending on appearances and Premier League survival, as per The Telegraph.

In addition, Blackpool winger Josh Bowler – who was long admired by Cooper and someone Forest eyed up as a direct Johnson replacement in the event he was sold to Brentford in January, as per The Athletic – signed for around £2m, but was immediately loaned to Olympiacos, which, much like the Hwang Ui-Jo signing, seemed very weird. Given how Cooper clearly rated him, why were Forest signing him now, presumably as backup to Johnson, only to loan him straight out?

It was very bizarre, as was the proposed move for Chelsea striker Michy Batshuayi, which The Athletic reported fell through at the last minute. Going for Batshuayi suggested things were disjointed behind the scenes, as there was no way he was a Syrianos recommendation. Finally, another centre back in Loïc Badé signed on loan from Rennes. This made more sense as Badé was only 22 and was very fast, so there seemed to be methodical thinking behind that move.

While the transfer window had now closed, the free agent market was still open and as Forest had until the start of the upcoming international break to finalise their squad, it was likely that despite making 21 signings and spending around £150m, they weren't done yet. Before that though was a home game against fellow promoted side Bournemouth, who had just sacked Scott Parker following a 9-0 defeat at Liverpool. After tough opponents in Spurs and City, many saw Bournemouth at home as a great opportunity to get the ball rolling again and to get three points on the board.

Forest started on the front foot and didn't look like a team who had just lost 6-0, probing well and getting into decent areas, although without really hurting Bournemouth too much. After half an hour though, a Gibbs-White corner was met by the head of Kouyaté, who powered his header home to give Forest a well-deserved lead. The Reds kept the pressure on and just before half-time, a Williams effort in the box was charged down by Lloyd Kelly, who blocked the ball with his hand. The ref pointed for a penalty immediately, but VAR weren't so sure. After a five minute wait, the ref was prompted to look at his screen, but he stuck with his decision and Johnson stepped up to fire home to give Forest a 2-0 lead going into the break.

That half was the perfect tonic and Forest seemed set for victory. However, you should never take anything for granted in football. Interim Bournemouth manager Gary O'Neil made a few tweaks at half-time and after just six minutes, they'd already paid dividends. Lingard was rushed by Lewis Cook inside his half after taking down a McKenna clearance, allowing Cook to give the ball to Philip Billing 30 yards out. After taking a touch, Billing unleased a rocket of a strike that found the back of the net, leaving Henderson with no chance and giving Bournemouth a lifeline.

It was now all Bournemouth and 12 minutes later, Forest's worst fears were being realised. Kelly got away from Forest's Cook from a corner and nodded across goal for Dominic Solanke, whose acrobatic effort took a deflection off Worrall and went over Henderson to make it 2-2. Forest brought Awoniyi pretty much immediately after and he almost restored the Reds' lead when he was picked out by Johnson near the six yard box, but his effort went wide. With both teams pushing, there was a feel that a winner was coming and with three minutes left, it came.

Bournemouth launched a long ball forward down the channel and McKenna took it down by the touchline under pressure from Solanke. Rather than put it out, McKenna attempted to pass back to Henderson on his weaker foot, but scuffed his effort and sent

Solanke racing through on goal. Solanke put a simple ball across goal for Jaiden Anthony, who stroked the ball past Henderson to cap off a remarkable comeback for Bournemouth and a horrendous capitulation for Forest.

There was still time for one last twist, though. A long ball forward from Worrall was flapped at by Bournemouth goalkeeper Neto and McKenna nodded it into Awonyi's path, but despite having his back to goal and with Dennis to pass to in a pretty much goal guaranteed position, Awoniyi swivelled and fired wide. The ref blew for full-time shortly after and somehow, despite being 2-0 up at half-time at home, Forest had lost. The tone in mood compared to the City and Spurs defeats was completely different and understandably so.

It was at this point that alarm bells started ringing quite loudly. It was one thing losing to elite sides, it was another blowing a 2-0 lead to a team who came up alongside you. Boos were heard at full time as while everyone was aware of the insanely difficult job Cooper had to mesh all these players into a cohesive outfit, that wasn't an excuse for imploding like that. To his credit, Cooper held his hands up at the end and stated that Forest had thrown away a win, but the next game couldn't come soon enough to try and get that out of the system.

That would be against Leeds United at Elland Road and accompanying the Forest team would be experienced right back Serge Aurier, who was signed as a free agent to make it 22 signings for Forest, which was a British record for one window. Aurier made the 25-man squad, but the Reds were unable to shift Cafu, Lyle Taylor or Arter, so all three wouldn't be registered to play. However, the day after Aurier signed, Queen Elizabeth II sadly passed away and as part of the nationwide mourning, the Football Association (FA) postponed all games set for that weekend, from Premier League to grassroots, as a mark of respect.

As such, Forest's next fixture would be back at The City Ground and also against a newly-promoted side, as Fulham came to Nottingham. After 10 minutes, a clipped ball from Yates allowed Johnson to fly down the wing and cut it back for Awoniyi, but his effort on goal was blocked for a corner. Gibbs-White's corner found Yates, but he'd jumped a bit too early and got his header on goal all wrong. However, Yates' effort unintentionally fell kindly into Awoniyi's path at the back post, who headed home to give Forest the lead.

Aside from that, the first half wasn't much to write home about. Forest were mostly in control, Yates was picked out by Lodi but fired wide and Fulham had a few efforts that Henderson dealt with pretty comfortably, but once again, it seemed like the Reds were in a good place. However, this rapidly changed nine minutes after half-time, when Tosin Adarabioyo peeled away from Yates to meet a Willian corner and planted his header just inside the post to level proceedings. Three minutes later, Kenny Tete found João Palhinha on the edge of the box unmarked and Yates was too slow out to him to stop his first time effort, which whistled past Henderson and into the top corner.

Three minutes after that, Bobby Decordova-Reid was released down the left and he crossed a ball into the box, which an unmarked

Harrison Reed ran onto and put past Henderson. Within six minutes, Forest had gone from looking good value for three points to being pretty much out the game. The defending for the Reed goal was awful, with Lodi and McKenna on different wavelengths, allowing Reed to be unmarked. Soon after, Forest nearly made it 3-2 in an identical scenario to Awoniyi's goal, with Worrall flicking a Gibbs-White corner to the back post for the Nigeria international, but he nodded wide.

Forest did make things interesting with 13 to go as a lovely first time ball over the top from Lingard set Johnson off down the right, but his ball across goal to sub Surridge was cut out. However, the ball fell nicely for another sub in O'Brien, who fired home to get his first Forest goal and to give the Reds a chance. Despite efforts from Williams and Yates though, Forest couldn't find a way through and for the second game running, had lost 3-2 on the banks of the Trent. Despite their promising start, Forest were now 19th, two points from safety and with a goal difference of -11.

The table made for grim reading, although nothing was settled in September. There was a general consensus that Forest hadn't really deserved to lose the Fulham game, but fans were bewildered at the six minute collapse and some of the defending involved. Again, it felt like every mistake – no matter how minor – led to a goal. Take Fulham's second; yes, Yates couldn't get there in time and was actually desperately unlucky not to block it, but few players in the Championship are stroking that into the top corner, first time, with enough power to beat any goalkeeper in the league. Despite all the upheaval, Cooper had done a brilliant job gelling a team together, but Forest were being caught out by mistakes and player brilliance.

Not that the wider media saw it this way, though. In fact, quite the opposite. Maybe it was because Forest fans weren't used to the intense media glare that comes with the Premier League, or maybe it was because parts of the media genuinely wanted Forest to fail, but it felt like a clear narrative had been struck that Forest were destined for the drop after signing an unprecedented amount of players. It felt like every defeat wasn't looked at from a fair perspective and it wouldn't have mattered how Forest lost a game, it would always be because Forest had signed so many players.

An example of this was from The Athletic journalist Adam Crafton, who famously went viral when he was working at the Daily Mail after making a combined Arsenal and Tottenham team full of 11 Tottenham players the day before a North London Derby. Arsenal subsequently won that game 2-0. Immediately after Fulham's six minute salvo, he tweeted, "Forest have gone full QPR 2012 haven't they." Again, no analysis into why Forest had to sign so many players, only comparisons to previous sides who signed lots of players and went down.

Saying that, Forest didn't exactly help themselves with a few of these signings – namely Hwang and Bowler and a few days later, goalkeeper and free agent Adnan Kanurić became another one for the list. The Bosnian became signing number 23 and went straight into the development squad, effectively becoming fourth choice goalkeeper, even though it appeared he would have little to no chance of ever playing a single minute for the first team. It all seemed a little odd, but at long last, the Reds' summer business was done.

Next for Forest was the shortish trip to Leicester City, who were the only team in the league below the Reds in the table. The Foxes had taken just one point from their first seven games and amassed a goal difference of -12 in the process, which was surprisingly poor given they were expected to challenge for the European slots. Much like the cup game, their fans went into overdrive at the prospect of facing Cooper's side, especially at The King Power Stadium and their fans had prepared a 'display', which is a term I use very lightly, for the occasion.

The display was former Forest man Wes Morgan lifting the Premier League trophy for Leicester, but it had notable gaps and tears in the material, which took all the focus away. There was also a jab thrown to Forza Garibaldi on a banner, with the insinuation that the Leicester displays were done properly, weren't copy and pasted and weren't printed out – although this was ironic, as the Leicester fans hadn't exactly put up a great advert for their alternative. Much like their obsession with Forest, it was just a bit tinpot.

Cooper, perhaps in an attempt to be a bit more solid, had gone for a 4-2-3-1 formation, but the early signs weren't great. Leicester were finding space far too easily and things looked ominous. Despite this though, Forest were competing well and with 20 minutes played, Lingard found Gibbs-White on the half turn, who proceeded to deliver an inch-perfect through ball for Awoniyi to run onto. The striker held off Wout Faes with ease and found himself one-on-one in a central position just inside the box, but while his effort beat goalkeeper Danny Ward, it hit the post and Leicester could recover.

It took just three minutes for that miss to be incredibly costly. A Harvey Barnes shot was blocked to the edge of the Forest box and while Lingard went to clear it, he sliced it straight into James Maddison's path. Maddison took it down and fired goalbound, with his effort taking a deflection off McKenna and leaving Henderson stranded as it found the back of the net. Two minutes after that, Leicester broke on the counter and Jamie Vardy cut it back for Barnes on the edge of the box. Under no pressure from Williams, Barnes picked his spot and whipped it past Henderson, making it 2-0.

Eight minutes after that, Kouyaté wiped out Kiernan Dewsbury-Hall on the edge of the box, receiving a yellow card for his troubles. From the resulting free-kick, Maddison bent it around the wall and his effort went in off the post. Much like Forest had done in the FA Cup game, Leicester had scored three goals in 10 minutes and the game was effectively over. At half-time, Cooper rang the changes. Off came Williams, O'Brien and Kouyaté, on came Aurier for his debut, Freuler and Yates – though the shape would be the same.

Whether it was because of the changes in personnel or because Leicester were in game management mode due to their lead, the second half was much more even as a contest. In fact, Forest really should've pulled a goal back when a thumping ball over the top by McKenna caught out Leicester's back line and allowed Awoniyi through on goal, but he rushed his effort and Ward was able to parry away. The ball fell at Johnson's feet with an open goal to aim at, but

Johnson opted to take a touch rather than shoot and his touch was a shocker, taking him miles clear of goal and allowing Ward to reposition.

Leicester would have their icing on the cake moment, though. A powerful low Maddison ball across goal fell to Patson Daka, who let it run across him before audaciously flicking it towards goal to make it 4-0. Despite the result, which sent the Reds bottom of the league, the Forest fans – those that were left – continued singing Cooper chants and doing their best to support the team. They realised the task Cooper had been given was ludicrously difficult and this was something Forest fans online were very aware of, too. Cooper came over at the end to clap them off and to apologise, but the fans had his back and could see the bigger picture of what he had to deal with.

It wasn't something the owners seemed to be aware of, however, as reports after the game started to emerge that Cooper's job was heavily at risk, with The Athletic stating that the likes of Rafael Benítez, Bruno Lage, Sean Dyche and Nuno Espírito Santo were in the frame. John Percy claimed that Murphy wanted to bring Leeds manager Jesse Marsch in, while The Times went one further and said that Benítez, who had won La Liga twice and the Champions League once as a manager, had actually been approached. There was just one problem – the Forest fans were absolutely seething at developments and made their feelings very known, especially on Twitter.

Within minutes, thousands of Forest fans shared their support for Cooper and their immense displeasure at the notion he could be sacked. Lage had just been sacked by Wolves and the season prior to his dismissal, they scored a dismal 38 goals in 38 games. Nuno, while magnificent at Wolves, had a very rough run at Tottenham and had recently gone to Al-Ittihad in Saudi Arabia, which seemed like accepting semi-retirement. Benítez had won some of the biggest honours in the game, but his football was outdated to put it mildly and his last stint at Everton was a total disaster, setting them back several years in the process.

That just left Dyche, who was on Forest's books as a kid, although he never played for the Reds. Dyche had not long been sacked by Burnley after 10 very successful years all things considered and was seen as the best option out the four, but even then, none of those managers felt like an upgrade on Cooper at that moment in time. They all would've had the exact same situation to try and fix with the influx of players, but none of them – not even Dyche, who likely would've brought Forest icons Ian Woan and Steve Stone with him as coaches – would've had the connection that Cooper had with the fans.

Cooper, whether the owners wanted to accept it or not, was the glue. He was holding everything together, in nearly impossible circumstances. He was the man that had taken Forest out of the doldrums after 23 years. He was the man the Forest fans would go into battle for, if he'd asked them. Taking away sensationalisms, he'd also not done anything to warrant being sacked, as the season was only eight gameweeks old and he had 23 new players to make a team out of.

To the surprise of everyone – including the backroom staff, who thought it was all over – the Forest board relented. The fans were heard and instead, Cooper finally signed a new deal, tying his future to the club until summer 2025. This had been in the pipeline since the summer, but hadn't been signed. It was reported by The Athletic that one reason for this was because Cooper wasn't happy with the news about his contract extension being leaked, but at long last, his future was secure on paper. However, the same security wasn't offered to others at Forest and it felt like if Marinakis couldn't sack Cooper, he'd sack others instead.

Filippo Giraldi – former Watford Technical Director, who oversaw the hugely successful signings of Richarlison and Abdoulaye Doucouré – was announced as the new Sporting Director and according to The Telegraph, after conducting a review on Forest's summer transfer business with Marinakis, Syrianos and Head of Scouting Andy Scott were both sacked. This all seemed ridiculous, especially given Marinakis' son, who had clearly taken more responsibility for transfers, came out of the inquest seemingly unscathed, but even from an objective viewpoint, it seemed absurd.

No-one in football has a 100% success rate when it comes to transfers and when you sign as many as Forest did, of course they aren't all going to play at their very best the second they walk onto the pitch. Some of the new signings hadn't even been given their debuts yet, so how a thorough inquest into the summer dealings could be done after eight games of Premier League football was baffling. This is before you mention that Syrianos approved signings played a huge part in getting Forest to the Premier League to begin with. However,

Forest were now in full reshuffle mode and it didn't look good for Murphy either.

The Athletic had revealed that Murphy was already taking legal action against Forest after the club had gone back on a contractual agreement to reward him upon promotion, but with a huge ally of his in Syrianos gone, the writing was on the wall for someone who only a few months earlier had been named Championship CEO of the Year. The Telegraph had suggested that Charnley could step into his shoes, but for now, Murphy would remain – although from the outside eye, his position looked untenable. Murphy and Syrianos saw things the same way and if Mariankis found fault with Syrianos, how could Murphy remain?

Before any more questions could be asked, Forest had a home game against Aston Villa to prepare for – who themselves weren't having much fun, hovering just above the drop zone. Prior to the match, Villa manager – and arguably Liverpool's best ever central midfielder – Steven Gerrard expressed his sympathy for Cooper, stating that he wouldn't want to be in Cooper's, "extremely tough and extremely challenging" position and that it takes time to bed in a few players, let alone 23. One wonders how those comments went down in the Forest boardroom, especially from someone of Gerrard's stature within the game.

The Forest fans made sure their support for Cooper was well known before kick-off, giving him a rapturous reception as he emerged from the tunnel, while Forza put up a banner across the Trent End reading, 'We've come so far and we've only just begun'. If that was too subtle for the boardroom, Lower Bridgford had a tifo of Cooper with a banner underneath reading, 'Leader of the Garibaldi'. The message was very clear, but as soon as the whistle went to start the match, it was full focus on getting behind the team and trying to arrest a five-game losing streak.

Cooper had his own method of trying to fix that and switched to a 4-3-1-2 formation, with Johnson and Dennis acting as wide forwards and Yates, Kouyaté and Freuler making up a midfield three. It was clear Forest were being overran in midfield with just two there, so a third body in there seemed smart. There were also changes at full back, as Aurier was given his first start, while Toffolo came in for Lodi. Perhaps predictably given the form of both teams, the game was very cagey, but after 10 minutes, Tyrone Mings fouled Dennis by the touchline. Gibbs-White put a ball into the box and Dennis had to do very little to escape Mings for a second time, nodding Forest into the lead in the process.

Just seven minutes later though, a John McGinn cross from deep was headed across the penalty box by Ollie Watkins and while Yates bravely headed it away, taking a hefty whack for his troubles, the ball fell to Ashley Young outside the box. Young's first touch took him more central and neither Dennis nor Freuler could get out quick enough to stop him shooting with his second, with Young's effort flying into the bottom corner. It was the seventh game in a row that Forest had conceded from outside the box and the eighth game out of nine that it had happened.

Not much else happened for the rest of the first half, or in the second for that matter. The returning Matty Cash received a genuinely warm reception by the Forest fans, but otherwise it felt like two teams who didn't want to lose and were happy with a draw. For Villa, it was a point on the road and that's never normally a bad thing, while for Forest, it offered them a platform to build on, stopped the rot and as a result of Leicester's defeat to Bournemouth that gameweek, took them off the foot of the table.

Forest's next fixture was away at Wolves, who were just a point and a place above them, but the main sub-plot going into the match was Gibbs-White's return to Molineux. The Wolves fans were not pleased, to put it mildly, at Gibbs-White's decision to leave the club and had made it very much known on social media that they would be giving him a hostile reception. On the morning of the game though, all focus shifted towards the actions of the Forest's social media team. Bizarrely, the official account posted a photoshopped picture of Dennis playing with three wolf cubs in the centre circle at Molineux, with the caption, 'Playtime'.

This type of fighting talk was incredibly unprofessional, least of all given Forest hadn't won a league game in two months and while The Athletic reported a senior Forest official demanded it be deleted, by that point it was too late. The wider footballing world had seen it, including the Wolves team, with captain Rúben Neves sending it into the players' group chat before the game. It got the Wolves fans' backs up even more, welcoming the players to a ferocious atmosphere and fuelled by a desire to put the Reds in their place.

Gibbs-White was booed on touch, but he very nearly had an assist when his brilliant corner found the head of McKenna, but McKenna powered his effort over. Wolves retaliated when an Adama Traore cross found the head of Rayan Aït-Nouri, but like McKenna, he also headed over. Wolves were starting to stamp their authority and were getting a lot of joy down both flanks, with Toffolo and Williams both struggling. A Daniel Podence flick sent Adama down the wing again, clipping a ball onto the head of Max Kilman, who planted his header onto the inside of the post, back out into play and into Henderson's arms.

Half-time was very much needed for Forest, but just 11 minutes after the break, Wolves' pressure told. Adama cut inside off the right and his effort hit Toffolo's hand inside the box as he was trying to put it by his side. Somewhat harshly, this was ruled by VAR to be handball and Neves blasted the penalty home. After that, Wolves were happy to sit on a 1-0 lead and Forest struggled to make an impact, leading to Cooper bringing on Lingard and Mangala to try and change things. With 11 to go, a Gibbs-White corner caused chaos in the Wolves box, with Yates dropping to the floor after Matheus Nunes was all over him, while Adama jumped into Gibbs-White's ball in with his arm.

Wolves cleared, but when the ball went out of play next, VAR intervened. Even before it could make a decision, Lingard and Johnson had snatched the ball and made their way into the Wolves penalty area as the feeling amongst the Forest players was that at least one of the two incidents would be given. As it turned out, they were right and the handball was flagged, allowing Johnson a chance to level from the spot. However, Johnson didn't hit it well and goalkeeper José Sá went the right way, beating it away. There was one last chance for Forest as another Gibbs-White set piece caused havoc, with Cook heading across for Yates, but Yates headed over.

Ultimately, in a game of two penalties, Forest lost 1-0. Wolves didn't take long to retaliate, posting a picture of an axe in a tree stump with the caption, 'Playtime's over', while a banner behind the stump read, 'Safe trip back Notts Forest', knowing full well many Forest fans would insist it's Nottingham Forest, not Notts. Despite the result and the performance of both full backs, there was some improvement at least, which was a positive for Cooper. He would need to make something from that though, as after 10 games of Premier League football, Forest were bottom of the league and four points from safety. Welcome back, indeed.

CHAPTER NINE – LEARNING TO ADAPT

Forest didn't have long to process the Wolves defeat as they were soon trekking down to the South Coast for a rare designated Premier League midweek fixture, seeing them face off against Brighton and Hove Albion. The Seagulls had been flying and were seventh going into the match, but had been recently rocked by manager Graham Potter's departure to Chelsea. New manager Roberto De Zerbi was still chasing his first win after losing his first two games in charge and with Forest in town, few would've bet against it being third time lucky for the passionate Italian.

Cooper made a few changes, with Aurier, Lingard and Mangala coming into the starting XI for Toffolo, Dennis and Kouyaté, while Williams was positioned at left back. Immediately, the Reds pretty much had to ride out wave after wave of Brighton attacks, with Henderson being called upon on numerous occasions and Brighton spurning several good chances. The closest they came in the first half was when a scintillating passage of two-touch passing completely cut

Forest open and the ball fell to Leandro Trossard on the edge of the box, but his rasping effort hit the top of the crossbar.

The second half went exactly the same way, with Brighton again inexplicably getting things wrong in front of goal, despite carving through Forest repeatedly. Danny Welbeck put a free header wide of the post and a Tariq Lamptey ball was flicked centrally by Welbeck for Pascal Groß, whose volley into the ground was brilliantly kept out by Henderson, but Brighton – despite having 19 efforts on goal, seven of which were on target – couldn't find a way through. Forest offered nothing in return, not mustering a single effort on target, but by the time the full-time whistle blew, they'd secured an away point and chalked up just their second clean sheet of the season.

Was it deserved? Probably not and Forest undoubtedly rode their luck, but few in that away end cared. The only negative was Toffolo coming on as a substitute and having to go off again with a hamstring injury, but despite the fortuitous nature of the point, it was still a point – and a clean sheet – to cherish. It would be very difficult for Forest to ride their luck like that against their next opponents however, as just seven months after last facing them on home soil, Liverpool were on Trentside again, this time for a Jürgen Klopp special – the Saturday 12:30 kick-off.

Klopp notoriously hated the Saturday lunchtime kick-off, repeatedly moaning about it and there was an underlying feeling among the fanbase that Forest could exploit that. This only intensified when Klopp opted to go with a midfield three of Fabinho, Curtis Jones and Harvey Elliott, which felt more like a cup midfield than a Premier

League one. Cooper also made some interesting changes, with Kouyaté coming back in for Mangala, while Awoniyi came in for Johnson and was subsequently given the chance to lead the line against his former club, whom he never played a single game for before being sold to Union Berlin in 2021.

Straight from the off, Forest looked much better than they did against Brighton. They looked significantly more compact, while Kouyaté and Yates especially were relentlessly bullying Jones and Elliott. Liverpool still carried a threat and had the first chance of the game when Roberto Firmino lost Cook from a corner and nodded wide, but from open play, Forest were keeping Liverpool at bay and also causing problems of their own. A brilliant ball from Gibbs-White released Awoniyi, who passed into an onrushing Lingard's path and while Lingard's first time effort from just outside the box was well held by goalkeeper Alisson, Forest were finding cracks in Liverpool's armour.

Another set-piece from Liverpool caused concern as a great cross from James Milner found the head of Virgil van Dijk, but the centre back headed across goal and harmlessly out of play, despite it appearing easier to score. When the half-time whistle went, Forest were decent value for at least a point and had massively frustrated their opponents. The second half went the same way as the first, with Forest coping with everything Liverpool – Champions League finalists only a few months prior – had to offer in open play, while looking menacing when in possession.

10 minutes after half-time, Joe Gomez was booked for taking Awoniyi out just inside the Liverpool half. Gibbs-White took the free-kick and expertly picked out Cook running down the right hand side, who volleyed the ball across the box for Awoniyi, who hit the post. However, the ball bounced back out straight at Awoniyi's feet, who calmly passed into an open net to give Forest the lead, which was met by a roar for the ages. It was the least Forest had deserved. They'd limited one of the best teams in Europe to next to nothing and made them pay for it, but there was still a long way to go.

That goal sprung Liverpool into action though and immediately after the goal, Milner slipped in Elliott inside the box, but his effort was beaten away well by Henderson. The game had now opened up massively with Liverpool aggressively searching for an equaliser, but leaving themselves open defensively in the process. Lingard robbed Elliott and sent Awoniyi running down the right wing, with two options free to his left. Awoniyi picked out Gibbs-White, but just as he pulled the trigger, a superb last ditch block from Milner prevented it from being 2-0.

Soon after, Klopp brought on Trent Alexander-Arnold and Jordan Henderson as Liverpool looked to turn the tide in their favour, but Forest continued to pick Liverpool off on the counter. Gibbs-White sent an onrushing Kouyaté down the left and his ball across the box found substitute Johnson, but Alisson pushed his effort away. Liverpool started to look after it a bit better and had a great chance to level when Andy Robertson picked out Alexander-Arnold, but his powerful header was beaten away by Forest's Henderson.

With time running out, Fabinho was robbed on halfway by a mixture of Mangala and Yates, which allowed Gibbs-White to run down the inside left. Despite being held off by Gomez and Liverpool's Henderson, Gibbs-White chipped a glorious ball in-between them for Yates to run onto and upon receiving it, Yates unleashed with his left foot towards goal. Somehow, defying all logic, Alisson's reflexes were sharp enough for his arm to get a faint touch on it and make an unbelievable save, taking it over for a corner.

The fourth official indicated six minutes of stoppage time and once again, Liverpool stepped up a gear, desperately hunting that equaliser. Freuler fouled Elliott and from the resulting free-kick, Alexander-Arnold picked out van Dijk perfectly, but his left footed effort inside the six yard box went past the other side of the post. Shortly after, Liverpool won a corner and such was their desire to get a goal, sent Alisson up for it. Robertson's ball was a peach and was forcefully met by the head of van Dijk, but Forest's Henderson displayed lightning quick reflexes to get down low and push it back out, allowing Forest to scramble clear.

It was a remarkable save from Henderson and a few minutes later, it was a save that proved to be the difference between one point and three. There were no patronising claps towards the Forest fans this time from Klopp. Forest had ended a run of nine games without a win by beating Liverpool for the first time since March 1996 and goodness me, did they deserve it. Williams had completely pocketed Mohammed Salah, Kouyaté played like Yaya Touré in his prime, Lingard was sensational, as was Gibbs-White, Yates, Freuler, Aurier,

Cook and McKenna. Henderson was an unbeatable force in goal and really, every single starting player was a 9/10 or higher.

The win capped off a pretty impressive turnaround, too. Forest had gone from conceding 18 goals in five matches to two goals in four. They had lost one of those four games and that was because of a missed penalty, while also securing back-to-back clean sheets. Despite the jubilation at full-time, which saw Lingard bouncing down the touchline and Henderson run into Lower Bridgford to celebrate with the fans, Cooper was very calm. His usual fist pumps to all four stands after a win were replaced by a much more modest set towards The Peter Taylor Stand.

The message was clear – yes, this is a great win, but beating Liverpool or not, we're still in a position we don't want to be in. With a trip to table toppers Arsenal next, it wasn't likely to get any easier either, although the gap to safety was now just two points. Above all else though, the performance against Liverpool showed that Forest did belong in the Premier League and that despite the upheaval, Cooper was doing a very good job in getting a team of strangers to perform as a unit. There were going to be many inconsistent performances from Forest while the team was still gelling, but the Reds set off to north London in a buoyant mood after their landmark victory.

It took just five minutes for that mood to be shattered at the Emirates. A poor ball from Yates was intercepted and switched at pace to Bukayo Saka, whose cross was headed in by Gabriel Martinelli. One mistake is all it takes against the elite sides. Martinelli nearly had another one soon after when he was found unmarked in the box, but Lodi was on hand to clear off the line. Forest recovered well and had two great chances to level before half-time, firstly when Cook put a Gibbs-White corner wide and secondly when William Saliba blindly passed across his own box to Lingard, but Ben White closed his shot down superbly.

All things considered, 1-0 at half-time wasn't that bad. Forest ended the half strongly and could've been level going into the break, so it at least seemed a repeat of the Man City mauling wasn't going to happen. Just four minutes after the restart though, Thomas Partey picked out Martinelli in acres of space approaching the box, who found Gabriel Jesus and he passed it to Reiss Nelson as the spare man on the right, with the Forest defence all at sea. Nelson checked inside and got a shot off, which was saved by Henderson. However, the rebound fell back to Nelson and he didn't miss at the second time of asking.

Three minutes later, Nelson was on the scoresheet again when he met a simple ball across the six-yard box from Jesus. Five minutes after that, Nelson turned provider as he found Partey outside the box, who under no pressure from Freuler, unleashed a rocket into the top corner. Three goals in eight minutes and another collapse from Forest. With 12 to go, a bad day got worse for Forest when Jesus fed Martin Ødegaard who, despite having three players in Kouyaté, McKenna and Cook surround him, found space to get a shot away inside the box, beating Henderson and making it 5-0.

As implosions go, this one was pretty bad. It felt like the club had taken four steps forward since the Leicester game and now been sent five steps back. Ultimately, Forest's season wouldn't be defined by a trip to the Emirates in October, but to lose 5-0 after battling so well in the first half didn't seem possible. Yes, Arsenal were an exceptional side, but absolutely no-one was betting on 5-0 at half-time. Cooper said after the game that Forest only had themselves to blame and he was right, as the same frailties that had plagued them earlier on in the season – conceding several goals in a short space of time and conceding from outside the box – reared their head again against the Gunners.

Given the manner of the defeat, Cooper would be forgiven for wanting to ring the changes for Forest's next fixture, which was a home match against Brentford. Despite the heavy defeat to Arsenal though, Cooper didn't make many changes, although we knew before kick-off that Biancone wouldn't be one of them. The defender had unfortunately suffered a very serious knee injury during training in what was described as an innocuous incident, ruling him out for the rest of the season. Given Biancone only played a handful of times for Forest, he hadn't really left any notable mark on the club, but it was clear he'd imposed himself as a very likeable figure in the changing room and his injury was a blow.

There were some changes as Williams, Johnson and Dennis came back in for Lodi, Awoniyi and Lingard respectively, but that was all. Immediately, Gibbs-White sought to put his mark on the game and after receiving a deft header from Johnson out wide, the attacking midfielder surged through the Brentford half, shrugging off challenges as he went, before expertly finding Johnson inside the Brentford box. Johnson then stung the palms of goalkeeper David

Raya with a strong effort as Forest started well, playing much more on the front foot than they had been recently. They also had a penalty shout waved away when Yates was shoved over by Josh Dasilva in the box, but VAR wasn't interested.

With 20 played, Dennis chested down a long ball into Gibbs-White's path and the Forest number 10 proceeded to wriggle through two challenges as he approached the edge of the Brentford box, before letting fly into the bottom corner. Replays showed Gibbs-White's effort took a deflection, steering it past Raya, but the breathtaking skill to sidestep two Brentford players was extraordinary and Forest had a lead. Approaching half-time, Forest seemed comfortable and Brentford were struggling to create too much, but you can never rest on your laurels in the Premier League.

A loose crossfield ball by Freuler was intercepted by Bryan Mbuemo and he instantly sent Yoann Wissa running through on goal, but as Wissa tried to take it round Henderson, he tumbled and fell over as the ball rolled harmlessly out of play. Everyone thought that was that, but VAR took a deeper look and after sending the referee over, he deemed that the faintest of touches from Henderson was deemed enough to send Wissa tumbling and awarded a penalty. It was ludicrously soft and Henderson was booked for his troubles, while Mbuemo sent the goalkeeper the wrong way to level the scores going into the break.

Forest felt incredibly aggrieved by the situation, with Henderson lucky to avoid a second yellow after booting the ball away after the penalty, but knew they had to dig in and do it all over again after half-time. They came close to restoring their lead when Cook headed a Gibbs-White set-piece just wide, but with 15 to go, a hopeful long ball over the top by Mathias Jensen caught the Forest defence napping and Wissa ran through on goal, dinking it over Henderson to give the Bees an underserved lead with little time remaining.

Chasing the game, Cooper threw on Awoniyi, Lingard and Surridge in an attempt to find an equaliser, but the Reds just couldn't seem to find their composure in front of goal, with Gibbs-White, O'Brien, Awoniyi and Yates all missing half chances or better. With just two minutes remaining, an O'Brien ball to the back post was nodded back across by Surridge, which Raya leapt out to punch away. Raya's punched effort though hit a Brentford player and fell into Gibbs-White's path, but his goalbound shot was blocked on the line by Ben Mee. However, Mee's block ricocheted off Zanka and went back towards goal, with Mee acrobatically clearing it away on the line and then into a grateful Raya's arms. As Raya was holding it though, the ref's watch indicated that the ball had crossed the line and Mee was unsuccessful in keeping the ball out, giving Forest an equaliser at the death.

It was the absolute least that Forest deserved and after a lengthy VAR check, the goal was given and it was another point on the board for the Reds. The main topic of conversation after the game was the VAR controversy for the first Brentford goal and Forest were subsequently given an official apology by the Professional Game Match Officials Limited (PGMOL), who are the refereeing group that officiate all Premier League matches. It was deemed an incorrect decision and while on the one hand it's good they claimed responsibility for that, on the other, an apology doesn't really change anything.

Entering the final week before the 2022 World Cup break, Forest would shift focus away from the Premier League, as they hosted Tottenham in the Carabao Cup third round. However, before the game, Lodi received some bad news in that he would not be selected as part of Brazil's 26-man squad for the World Cup. It was hard not to feel sorry for Lodi, who had maybe been guilty of trying too hard while playing for Forest and as such, performed inconsistently, but he'd have been especially gutted given he was in Brazil's penultimate squad before the tournament.

Despite that setback, Lodi was one of nine changes that would start against a strong Tottenham side, with Lingard, Surridge, Mangala, O'Brien, Worrall, Boly, Hennessey and Awoniyi also coming in, with only Aurier and Yates retaining their places from the Brentford draw. Even with all the changes, Forest started brightly and nearly took the lead in bizarre fashion when a heavy Awoniyi touch was cleared by Davinson Sánchez on the edge of the Spurs box, but his clearance cannoned off Awoniyi and hit the post. The rebound looped up nicely for Lingard, but his headed effort was saved well by Fraser Forster.

Even though Spurs had a strong team out, they were labouring a lot and should've conceded a penalty when a Lodi cross was handled by Ryan Sessegnon, but they survived until half-time. Just five minutes into the second half though, a loose ball was pushed into Lodi's path by a Lingard slide tackle and the Brazil left back proceeded to cut inside of Sánchez and then release a beautiful curling effort with his weaker foot, which went round an outstretched Forster and into the net.

Seven minutes later, Aurier burst down the right wing and lofted in a cross to the back post, which was nodded across goal by Surridge into Lingard's path. This time, Lingard's header found the back of the net and the England international finally had his first goal in Forest colours. Finally, it was Forest's turn to score a few goals in quick succession. Spurs boss Antonio Conte acted pretty much immediately, bringing on Richarlison, Dejan Kulusevski, Bryan Gil and none other than Djed Spence, as he sought to shift the tie back in their favour.

Spence did inject some life back into Spurs, but with 15 to go, Mangala – already on a yellow card – scythed down Richarlison from behind and gave the referee little choice but to show him a second yellow and send him off. The man advantage massively swung things in Spurs' favour, but apart from a Spence header that forced Hennessey into a reflex save to tip over, Tottenham offered very little and a superb Forest progressed to their next round. You wouldn't have known who was bottom and who was fourth unless someone told you and Cooper had another cup scalp to his name.

In the build-up to the final Premier League match before the break, which would be at home to Crystal Palace, more World Cup squad announcements came through and Freuler (Switzerland), Kouyaté (Senegal), Johnson, Williams and Hennessey (all Wales) would all be representing their nations, while Forest loanees Aguilera (Costa

Rica), Horvath (America), Dräger (Tunisia) and Hwang (South Korea) would also be in attendance. This meant that Mangala (Belgium), Lingard and Henderson (both England) missed out. This was especially harsh in Henderson's case, who had a brilliant claim to be picked for England's goalkeeping pool, but it was more understandable for Lingard and Mangala.

Regardless of Lingard finding some momentum heading into the World Cup break, he hadn't delivered the sparkling form West Ham got out of him in that 2020/21 loan spell, while Mangala had been in and out of the Forest side. It was strange with Mangala, because while you could see he was a very good footballer and started brightly, it felt like Cooper was still finding ways to get the very best out of him. Nevertheless, even if expected, it was still a blow for both – especially for Lingard, given that he'd stated that his hopes were to get back into the England fold when he signed for Forest initially.

Before the tournament for the biggest prize in football could commence though, Forest faced off against Crystal Palace with the aim of getting off the foot of the table and to avoid being the dreaded side who finds themselves bottom of the Premier League at Christmas. Of the previous 30 installments of the Premier League, only three teams who were bottom at Christmas found a way to survive. Admittedly, this would be a bit flawed for the 2022/23 season due to the World Cup break, which saw teams play around two games less before Christmas than they would normally, but it was still a moniker that nobody wanted.

Prior to the game, Cooper spoke candidly about the task he was given for the first time. "Normally with a promotion team, there is that momentum," he said to The Athletic. "We have not been able to experience that, because we've had to change the team. This has been my toughest coaching challenge. But it will have been one of the players' toughest challenges as well, as they not only try to compete in the best league in the world, but do so in a team that is starting from scratch."

He wasn't wrong and it probably didn't help that Cooper was still trying new things out. Palace's visit was no different as Cooper pretty much completely changed the backline, with Lodi and Aurier either side of a centre back pairing of Boly and Worrall. Lingard was also restored to the starting XI, as Forest again lined up with a false nine formation. This nearly worked within the first 15 minutes as Gibbs-White split the Palace defence wide open with a pinpoint through ball to Johnson, but Johnson's driven cross/shot flashed just past the far post while an onrushing Lingard couldn't quite get there in time to tap in.

There wasn't much excitement other than that, but with five minutes to go of the first half, Jordan Ayew put a ball across the box for Wilfried Zaha, who span Worrall in the box before being clumsily hauled down by the centre back, resulting in a Palace penalty. Zaha dusted himself down and stepped up to take it, but thankfully for Forest – and Worrall – Zaha rolled his penalty against the outside of the post and behind for a goal kick. It was a huge let off for Forest and they went in at half-time level.

Forest came out for the second half brightly and when an Aurier cross was charged down, Freuler was on hand to mop up and played it back to the right back, who this time played it to Johnson just inside the box. Johnson fired a low effort towards goal and it was powerful enough for Palace goalkeeper Vicente Guaita to parry back into open play, straight at the feet of Gibbs-White who prodded into an empty net. Before the celebrations could start though, the official's flag had gone up for offside, but VAR weren't so sure. After a lengthy check, it was decreed that defender Marc Guéhi was playing Gibbs-White onside by the barest of margins, so the goal stood.

Despite going a goal down, not much changed from a Palace perspective, who lacked penetration and guile. The Forest midfield three of Freuler, Kouyaté and Yates were working brilliantly together, while the back four were doing their duties to a tee. There was a heart in mouth moment when Yates lunged in recklessly on Jeffrey Schlupp and was awarded a yellow for his actions, but not without VAR checking to see if it was a possible red card offence. In the end, they were happy with the yellow and Forest came close to doubling their lead late on when a low Gibbs-White ball across the box was tapped into Lingard's path by Johnson, but Lingard's effort went just past the post.

When the full-time whistle went, it marked a huge three points for Forest that was indeed enough to take them off the foot of the table. It wasn't enough to take them out the bottom three, but it left them 18th and just a point from safety. Much like after the Liverpool win, Cooper initially tried to be low key with his celebrations, but reverted back to delivering his trademark fist pumps to the crowd, to huge fanfare. Forest were still in trouble, but this win was a big stride forward and it capped off a very successful week for the Reds.

Because of the World Cup, the players were given a short break, though some chose to knuckle down and keep working in a hotter climate than England. Lingard, fresh off the back of his very powerful documentary focusing on mental health and his personal story airing on Channel 4, linked up with his former United teammate Danny Welbeck for some warm weather training, while Lodi went back to Athletico Paranaense, the Brazilian club he came through the ranks at, to train with them in order to stay in shape. Lodi also claimed the Goal of the Round award for his effort against Spurs in the Carabao Cup, which was richly deserved.

The break also gave Cooper some time to reflect on his start to Premier League life and how he could best get a tune out of his side. It seemed from the outside that he didn't fully trust either Awoniyi or Dennis, with both regularly coming in and out of the team, while it also seemed like he was struggling to get the most out of Lingard and Gibbs-White in the same side. With both players preferring to play in that central attacking midfield position, it perhaps wasn't a surprise that both players' best games so far – Lingard v Spurs in the Carabao Cup and Gibbs-White v Brentford – came when only one of the two was playing.

Forest's solution to that was...to sign another attacking midfielder. Charismatic Brazil international Gustavo Scarpa, who had won the best player in Brazil award for his exploits with Palmeiras, had been training with the Reds with Cooper under the impression that he was running the rule over whether Scarpa would be a good fit for Olympiacos or not. Instead, according to The Times, he was signed for Forest anyway, despite the coaching staff stating that they felt Scarpa wasn't athletic enough for the Premier League. Regardless of their protestations, signing number 24 of the year was in and Cooper had to work out how to bed another player in.

In addition, he had a lot to think about defensively. Cooper still seemed no clearer to knowing his best central pairing – with Badé not even being used and making just one matchday squad – and really, the only mainstay in the backline was Aurier. Signing the Ivory Coast international was perhaps questioned by some at first, but it was proving to be a genius move and he'd been brilliant since he came into the side. However, it also meant a £17m signing in Williams was left on the bench, albeit deservedly so due to a mixture of questionable performances and Aurier's form.

On the plus side, Lodi had generated some momentum and the midfield trio of Kouyaté, Yates and Freuler was working well – but even then, that couldn't last and Cooper had another issue to navigate as Kouyaté picked up a severe hamstring injury at the World Cup, leaving him out of action until March. The Telegraph had reported that Forest were angry with Senegal for how they handled the injury, believing that Senegal had diagnosed it poorly and showed a lack of care for Kouyaté in the process.

The injury did give Cooper a chance to continue his 'next man up' policy though, with Mangala and O'Brien in support, but even that had a catch as O'Brien suffered an illness in October and came back looking a lot weaker physically. Cooper also had Forest's away form to find a solution for, as the Reds were still yet to win away from home in the league. For some reason, as soon as Forest left the banks of the Trent, they just didn't seem the same side.

Ultimately, this inconsistency was always likely to happen given the sheer volume of players coming in and being thrown together at once. Some were going to shine, others were going to struggle and finding consistency was going to be difficult for any coach – the fact Forest weren't already dead and buried was testament to Cooper's managerial ability. The break did allow Cooper a mini pre-season of sorts though, as several friendlies were set up to get minutes back into legs while everyone waited for domestic football to return, which would allow Cooper to gel his team further.

First up were Stoke City, who defeated the Reds 2-1 (Gibbs-White scoring for Forest) at Loughborough University, while defeats also came against Greek sides Atromitos (3-2, Yates and an own goal for Forest) and Olympiacos (1-0 with former Forest man Pajtim Kasami scoring the winner). Forest ended their run of friendlies in impressive fashion though, as they were invited to play Valencia as part of the Spanish giant's 100th year celebrations for their iconic stadium, the Mestalla.

Back in 1961, Forest were the first European side that Valencia hosted and in 1980, Valencia defeated Forest to win the European Super Cup, so it was fitting that the two would face off for the occasion. Forest legends Ian Storey-Moore, John McGovern and Garry Birtles were invited by the Spanish club for a special ceremony and Forest opted to play in an all red kit for the affair, in recognition of the kit Forest wore for that meeting back in 1961. Both teams treated it very seriously and Forest ran out 2-1 victors thanks to goals from Awoniyi and Dennis, the latter being set up by Scarpa on his unofficial Forest debut.

Before a return to Premier League football though, Forest had a fourth round Carabao Cup tie at Blackburn Rovers to contest. Blackburn had been flying in the Championship and sat in third, but opted to make 11 changes for the match, which perhaps showed where their priorities were. It didn't take Forest long to turn the screw, with Awoniyi forcing goalkeeper Aynsley Pears into a brilliant save after being picked out by Johnson. Johnson then rode an Adam Wharton tackle en route to the box, but was sent sprawling inside the area by Wharton's brother, Scott. Johnson took the penalty and sent Pears the wrong way to make it 1-0.

Forest didn't take their foot off the pedal and managed no less than 16 efforts on goal in the first half, but it all counted for nothing as on the cusp of half-time, Scott Wharton made amends for giving a penalty away when he met his brother's free-kick and smashed a header into the top corner. Despite the setback, Forest started the second half in the same manner they approached the first and it took just seven minutes for them to restore their lead, as Lingard's deflected free-kick wrong-footed Pears and ended up in the back of the net.

From here, Forest didn't look back and made it 3-1 when a sublime Lingard pass allowed Awoniyi to run onto it and after shrugging

Scott Wharton off, Awoniyi composed himself and slotted home. Progression was secured when Surridge sent Johnson down the right and despite having O'Brien lurking on the edge of the box, Johnson went for goal and found the bottom corner, giving Forest a 4-1 win away from home and a place in the League Cup quarter-finals for the first time since 1993/94. It was a very nice early Christmas present for fans and a nice return back to competitive football for Forest, too.

With a space in the last eight of the Carabao Cup confirmed and with Christmas dinners eaten, a return to Premier League football beckoned, with Forest's Boxing Day fixture (pushed back to December 27 for TV) a game that every Forest fan had a look for when the fixtures came out – Manchester United away. Forest had avoided the Red Devils entirely since their relegation in 1999, so to stand toe to toe with one of the biggest clubs in the world was a challenge that many supporters were eager to see. As per his loan agreement, Henderson was unable to face his parent club, so Hennessey came in for his league debut for Forest, while Awoniyi and Mangala came in for Gibbs-White and Kouyaté respectively.

It didn't take long for Hennessey to be called into action, when a Tyrell Malacia volley was stopped by a mixture of the goalkeeper and the post, as United started strongly. With 19 gone, a Christian Eriksen corner along the floor fooled everyone and Marcus Rashford ran onto it unchallenged, firing past Hennessey to give United the lead. From a defensive standpoint, it was a terrible goal to concede and four minutes later, United had the ball in the net again. A long ball set Rashford off down the left and his cut back to the edge of the box found Anthony Martial, whose effort managed to squirm past Hennessey, despite the goalkeeper getting a firm glove to it.

Forest managed to quell the tide for the rest of the half and just before the interval, an excellent Lodi free-kick from deep was met by Yates' head and via a deflection from Boly, found its way into the back of the net. However, it was put under the magnifying glass by VAR and after spending three minutes debating whether Yates had handballed it or not, they realised that actually, Boly was offside anyway. As such, the goal was disallowed, but it's fair to say the experience left a bitter taste in the mouth for Forest fans as it just felt that VAR were actively looking for a way to disallow it.

That knocked the stuffing out of Forest a bit and in the second half, United just held Forest – who lost Lingard to injury shortly after the restart – at arm's length. Hennessey went some way to make amends for the second goal when he brilliantly denied Antony, Martial and Rashford, all of whom had been found in acres of space in front of goal, but with three minutes to go, a loose pass from Dennis inside his own half was intercepted by Casemiro, who charged forwards and picked out an unmarked Fred, who slotted past Hennessey to give United a 3-0 win.

It was alarming how United managed to get into dangerous positions so easily and it spoke volumes that Hennessey was still Forest's best player on the night. Ultimately though, much like the trip to Arsenal, whatever happened in the red half of Manchester was never going to define Forest's season. Losing in that manner would've been disappointing for Forest, but not many would've had the Reds on their betting coupons. Despite Forest only losing one out of their last five before the trip to Old Trafford, the media woke up in the aftermath of the game and again beat the drum about all the signings.

The most notable criticism came from Luke Edwards at The Telegraph, who spoke as if Forest had been relegated that night. "If I'm being brutally honest, it's never looked good for Nottingham Forest from the start of the season where they signed two completely new teams worth of players," he stated to BBC Sport. "I don't think that's ever worked in the history of football. I've never seen it work in the Premier League." Now, had Forest lost 3-0 to a team in the relegation picture, I'd have got it. But that level of criticism after losing away at Manchester United? In December? With 21 games of the season still to play? Come on. It was like they couldn't wait to stick the knife in the second Forest faltered.

With Chelsea next for Forest on New Year's Day, the media probably wouldn't have to wait long to run that narrative again. Much like the match at Old Trafford, few made Forest the favourites going into the match. However, Forest had been largely resolute on home soil and Chelsea, despite their expensively assembled squad, had been out of sorts by their standards following Clearlake Capital's takeover of the club, so it wasn't quite a foregone conclusion that the Blues would win.

Imagine saying anything like that 12 months earlier after Forest lost back-to-back games to Middlesbrough and Huddersfield. Big Ben gearing up to bring in a new year always brings reflection and 2022 had been a truly incredible year for Forest. From the FA Cup quarter-finals to winning promotion at Wembley, to landing punches in the top flight to getting to the quarter-finals of the League Cup – the highs were as high as a generation of fans had ever felt. If 2022 was anything to go by, 2023 was going to be another wild ride.

CHAPTER TEN – NEW YEAR, NEW HOPE

To kick off the new year, Forest would, at long last, have a shirt sponsor and the Reds opted to go with UK for UNHCR – the United Nations Refugee Agency. This was an incredibly bold but brave move, with Forest standing in "solidarity for families who have been forced to flee their homes and communities," as per the club's official statement. The club wouldn't be receiving a fee for the sponsor, instead making a charitable donation of their own accord to UNHCR, but it did send an incredibly powerful message and allowed them to use their platform as a Premier League club to convey that.

Top flight football can be seen as cold at times, but this was a genuinely good act from the club and they deserved credit for taking a stand like that. Taking to the field against Chelsea armed with their kit now looking complete by modern standards, Forest started well. After a Blues attack broke down and was cleared to Awoniyi, he fed Gibbs-White who proceeded to dink a beautifully weighted ball over the top of the Chelsea defence for Johnson to run onto, but

Johnson's effort wasn't the best. Chelsea stopper Kepa Arrizabalaga did parry it back to Johnson, but the follow-up wasn't much better and Chelsea managed to see out the danger.

After 16 minutes, Mason Mount split the Forest defence open as he sent Christian Pulisic down the wing and his cross was bizarrely dealt with by Boly, with the Ivory Coast defender backheeling it behind him and onto the Forest crossbar. The ball kindly fell to Raheem Sterling, who gobbled up the chance to put Chelsea ahead in somewhat unconventional fashion. Not much else happened for the rest of the half, but Forest immediately sought to grab the game by the horns as the second half got underway.

As another Chelsea attack broke down, Gibbs-White sent an exquisite ball down the right wing for Johnson to run onto and suddenly, Forest were two on two. That soon became two on one as Johnson left César Azpilicueta chasing his shadow, with Thiago Silva unsure whether to approach Johnson or to block any pass to Awoniyi. As Silva made his decision to approach Johnson, Johnson took another touch which subsequently took the pass to Awoniyi off the cards due to Silva's positioning and he proceeded to fire straight at Kepa, allowing Chelsea off the hook.

Remember after the Reading away game when Johnson Snr called Grabban out for not squaring it? Well, this was about 100 times worse given Johnson was never likely to score from that side angle. Awoniyi, understandably, was furious at Johnson, but Forest continued to apply pressure. Johnson fed Yates on the edge of the box, who played it back to Gibbs-White. The attacking midfielder crashed a half volley off the underside of the bar, but agonisingly for Forest, the ball didn't go over the line.

With just over an hour played, a Gibbs-White corner was looped up into the sky by Kai Havertz and nodded towards Aurier by Boly, with the right back taking the ball down on his chest before squeezing the ball through Kepa's legs to level the score. It was the least Forest deserved and bar one half scare late on, when a deep pinpoint Hakim Ziyech cross almost found the head of Pierre-Emerick Aubameyang in the six-yard box, they held on for a valuable point that meant Forest were now level with 17th placed West Ham, only in the relegation zone because of goal difference.

It only took a few hours for the conversation surrounding Forest to switch back to players though, as The Telegraph released an article saying that the Reds were ready to cut ties with Dennis and that the third goal conceded against United, where Dennis ceded possession cheaply inside his own half, was the last straw for the coaching staff. There was an issue, however. FIFA laws dictate that a player can only play for two clubs in a matching league season (August-May) and given Dennis had already played for Watford, he couldn't be transferred to anyone in Europe, unless he went back to Watford.

He could go to Saudi Arabia or the United States of America due to the nature of their league seasons and The Athletic reported interest in him from both countries, but neither were providing any serious proposals. The fans were quite split on the news, as Dennis had polarised the fanbase a bit. Some wanted to see him get a fairer crack of the whip as there was a belief there was a player in there, while others didn't think he could be trusted defensively and thought he was too much of a maverick.

In any case, it wasn't a good situation for anyone and the news didn't stop there, either. The Telegraph article also stated that Lingard would be out for a month with injury, which was a massive shame as he'd just started to show his true ability, while the Reds would be targeting a few more signings, namely a centre back, a defensive midfielder and a striker. The thought of signing yet more players was insane, but given the injuries to Biancone and Kouyaté respectively, there was half an argument to recruit in those positions.

There was also a conclusion to the Badé saga, as he returned to Rennes without playing a competitive match for Forest, only appearing in one matchday squad. It turned out that, according to Le Telegramme, Rennes saw the situation unfurl and asked Forest not to play Badé in a competitive game, thus avoiding a situation similar to Dennis. Forest obliged and Badé was soon sent to Sevilla, who despite being 18th in La Liga, were still in the Europa League. The whole saga left fans wondering what might have been as there clearly must have been a good player in there to catch Sevilla's eye.

Nevertheless, the show had to go on and the next stop for it was a midweek one to Southampton, as Forest faced up against the team bottom of the league and with a huge chance to get out of the bottom three, while further condemning a relegation rival. However, Southampton had already done a pretty good job of condemning themselves. The reason for that was Nathan Jones had not long left his post at Luton to take over at Southampton and to say the Saints weren't keen on him would be something of an understatement.

There was no honeymoon period for Jones and the fans had already decided they wanted him out, despite him only being there two months at that point. The football was terrible and the club were sleepwalking towards relegation, with Jones' press conferences and team selections infuriating Southampton fans. Everything that happened to Jones in his ill-fated tenure at Stoke was happening again at Southampton, just under a much bigger magnifying glass. Despite the animosity within the fanbase at St Mary's, Jones had a tendency to get a result against Forest, so it was never going to be an easy game.

Southampton nearly had a perfect start when Kyle Walker-Peters' clipped ball caught the Forest defence flat-footed after just seven minutes, allowing Che Adams – a long time Forest target – to run in behind and latch onto it, but Adams' shot was wayward. Forest then should've taken the lead when Yates found Johnson just outside the six-yard box, but his powerful effort hit off the crossbar and cannoned out of play. Both chances should've led to goals, which was perhaps the perfect way to describe a team in 18th playing a team in 20th.

Saints had another chance to go ahead when a clumsy Yates foul on the edge of the box allowed renowned dead ball specialist James Ward-Prowse a perfect chance to flex his free-kick taking skills, but the England international's effort went over the bar. With 27 on the clock, Lyanco played a loose ball just inside his own half and Johnson pounced upon it and darted towards the Southampton goal, with Awoniyi running alongside for the square ball. This time, Johnson did play it across goal, allowing Awoniyi to stroke home and score only Forest's second away goal of the season.

The noise explosion from the Forest end told you all you needed to know about how important that goal was – as did the stunned silence from the home fans. The "how shit must you be, we're winning away" chants did little to improve the mood among the Southampton contingent and they made their feelings very much known at half-time, booing their team off and launching numerous verbal volleys at Jones. Things were so bleak for Jones that the Forest chants of "Nathan Jones, what a wanker, what a wanker" were being applauded by some parts of the home end, while other parts joined in.

The second half was something of a non-event. Southampton had a lot of the ball, but couldn't really do a lot with it, while Forest were happy just to keep them at bay. Southampton's defenders were caught again in possession inside their own half, this time by Awoniyi, but the striker had no real options and opted to go for goal himself, lofting an effort over the bar. It seemed the World Cup break had done Awoniyi the world of good, as he looked a completely different player to the one who started the season for Forest – he looked stronger, more confident and with a better understanding of the league.

Shortly after that attempt, Awoniyi gestured to the bench and seemingly asked to be subbed. No sub was forthcoming and a few minutes later, the game had to be stopped as Awoniyi had to be taken off injured. Quite why he didn't come off instantly is baffling and it was typical of Forest's luck that just as he started to get going, he was likely to be out for a sustained period of time. Surridge came on for him, while Scarpa also came on for his debut and didn't take long to endear himself, as he sprayed a delightful first time ball out to the wing, bringing a bit of joga bonito to proceedings in the process.

Southampton upped the ante and had sustained spells of pressure, but Forest kept repelling everything Saints had to offer. As the referee blew for full-time, you could almost feel the relief from the Forest fans as they'd finally secured their first away win of the season. The Reds hadn't been anywhere near their best, but they didn't have to be to leave with three points and a clean sheet – three points that took them out of the relegation zone and up to 15th. Southampton didn't even register a single shot on target as the pressure on Jones grew, with the Reds finally getting the better of one of their many nemeses.

After the match, Cooper refused to get carried away, stating that while the Reds were out of the drop zone, there was still a long way to go. Deep down though, he must have been ecstatic. Cooper told BBC Sport that he'd challenged both the players and the coaching staff to get that first away win over the line, so to do so and to be out of the relegation zone must've felt huge. The next day, Bowler returned from an unsuccessful loan spell at Olympiacos and was sent straight on loan to Blackpool, his former club, as they were the only other side he could play for given the FIFA ruling.

On the topic of Blackpool, they were next up for the Reds by way of The FA Cup, although Bowler would be ineligible for the Tangerines. Given how the FA Cup run was used as a springboard for league success, the prospect of playing a struggling Championship side seemed a great opportunity to get another away win on the board and build some momentum. In the build-up to the game, Cooper sought to quash the rumours regarding Dennis and took aim at The Telegraph for reporting the story, hinting that Dennis would get some minutes at Bloomfield Road.

As it turned out, Dennis was one of 11 changes, as Cooper changed the entire team. Hennessey; Williams, Cook, McKenna, Toffolo; academy prospect Billy Fewster, Colback, O'Brien, Scarpa; Dennis and Surridge was the starting XI, which was more than enough on paper to put Blackpool to the sword and secure progression to the fourth round. Instead, quite the opposite happened. After 15 minutes, Blackpool took the lead after a CJ Hamilton from the left caused pinball in the Forest box following an awful attempt to clear it by O'Brien and Marvin Ekpiteta was on hand to finish.

Soon after, Dennis was unlucky not to score when his curling effort hit the bar, but Blackpool survived until half-time. After the break, Forest came out with serious intent and should've scored when Dennis twisted his way into the box and pulled it back for Surridge, but Surridge fired over. Dennis then missed a one-on-one after being played through by Scarpa and it felt like a goal was coming. And it did – but not for Forest. An atrocious ball back to his own goal by Williams from the halfway line went straight to Jerry Yates inside the penalty box, who put it across goal for Ian Poveda, who left O'Brien in a heap as he passed into the net.

With 20 to go, Kenny Dougal chipped a wonderfully weighted ball straight into the box for Hamilton to latch onto, leaving Williams for dead before proceeding to volley into the far corner to make it 3-0. Forest had imploded and with a few minutes to go, a Poveda cross found Jerry Yates, who slammed home to make it 4-0. In stoppage time, Toffolo's crossed to Forest's Yates and he headed home for a consolation goal, but the Reds' FA Cup run was over before it even started and ended in embarrassing fashion.

Of the starters, only Scarpa and maybe Dennis could leave with any credit and Cooper was understandably livid, telling BBC Sport that the players fell short in every area of the pitch, that there was, "too much entitlement in our game" and that what transpired could never be repeated again. It also raised severe questions about Forest's depth and its suitability, but before the inquest could commence much further, the club announced that Murphy had left his role as CEO by "mutual consent...in order to pursue other opportunities".

Murphy's work had revolutionised the club and set the wheels in motion for Forest to be a Premier League side once more, so it felt like a mistake to usher him out the door. Murphy's statement was from the heart and he stated that, "Nottingham is a community of people who put the work in before the talk" and that, "the unbridled passion for this football club, passed down through generations, reverberates throughout the sport." It was a classy exit for a classy man and a man who fans – and the owners – owed a great debt to.

Prior to Murphy's arrival, Marinakis' unrelenting and much admired ambition was being wasted on poor recruitment and poor ideology. From the outside, many felt the boardroom had underestimated just how hard it is to get out of the Championship, especially without parachute payments, but within 12 months of Murphy's processes being followed and his managerial choice being hired, Forest had done so. Few begrudged him the Marsch thing and instead, people were more concerned they'd lost a very good CEO.

Attention soon turned to the Carabao Cup though as Forest took on Wolves in the quarter-final and it was no surprise to see Cooper make 10 changes from the Blackpool debacle, with only Scarpa keeping his place in the starting XI. With Awoniyi out, Gibbs-White and Johnson operated as a front two, with Scarpa in attacking midfield behind them, while Henderson, Lodi, Boly, Worrall, Aurier, Mangala, Yates and Freuler all came back in. Forza had a display for the game too, with the top half of the Trent End transforming into a card cutout of the trophy, while the banner underneath it read, 'New team, same dreams,' with a picture from each of Forest's League Cup victories in 1978, 1979, 1989 and 1990 on display.

Forest got off to a flyer as after 18 minutes, a Gibbs-White corner was flicked onto the bar by Aurier and the rebound fell for Boly, who tapped home on the line against his former club, refusing to celebrate by way of respect to his old side. Wolves responded well and cut Forest open on the counter when Mangala lost the ball deep in the Wolves half, resulting in Raúl Jiménez playing a crisp one-two with Hwang Hee-Chan on the edge of the Forest box and going one-on-

one with Henderson, but the goalkeeper stood firm and made a great save to deny the Mexico forward.

Soon after, Mangala again gave the ball away cheaply and sparked a Wolves counter, this time allowing Jiménez to turn provider as his cross found Hwang at the back post, but Henderson again came to the rescue with an excellent one-handed stop. Forest clung on until half-time, but the second half saw them try to defend their one goal lead and it felt like a matter of time until Wolves equalised. With 25 to play, Matheus Nunes carried it forward and found Matheus Cunha on the wing, whose first time ball across goal was tapped in by Jiménez at the far post. It was superb football and frankly, it had been coming.

Forest half responded when subs Dennis and Colback tried to do a one-two, but Colback's return pass hit Semedo and instead bobbled towards goal, hitting the post. It was the last meaningful action of the game and as per Carabao Cup rules, a draw at full time means straight to penalties. Forest were up first and Surridge strolled up confidently, but his woes in front of goal continued as José Sá flew across his goal to save his effort. It was the second penalty Sá had saved against Forest in the space of a few months and Wolves immediately had the advantage.

Rúben Neves was first for Wolves, but unlike in the league match against Forest, his penalty wasn't hit well enough and Henderson guessed the right way to prevent it going in. Freuler was next for Forest and at a time where a cool head and experience was required, the Swiss international calmly placed his penalty into the bottom corner to give Forest the advantage. Daniel Podence then stepped up for Wolves and hammered his penalty into the roof of the net, just above Henderson's arm, as still nothing could separate the two sides.

Worrall was next and blasted his penalty straight down the middle, but Nunes responded well by sending Henderson the wrong way and finding the top corner. It was then Gibbs-White's turn, at the same end he missed for Sheffield United to send Forest to Wembley and against his former club, who hated him for leaving. Gibbs-White stuttered his run-up and sent it left, but Sá went the right way, to cheers from the Wolves fans. Thankfully for Gibbs-White though, despite Sá getting two hands on it, there was enough power on the ball to still go in.

That cheer suddenly looked very premature and in response to this, Gibbs-White stood in front of the away end with his index fingers in his ears for a good few seconds, causing the Wolves fans to descend into fits of rage at their academy graduate's actions, while the Forest supporters lapped it up and cheered. Cunha was up next for Wolves and powered his penalty into the bottom corner, before mimicking Gibbs-White's celebration in front of the Forest fans. Whoever said football wasn't theatrical?

With the shootout now at sudden death, Colback stepped up and much like Worrall, smacked it straight down the middle, before also doing the Gibbs-White celebration in front of the Wolves fans. Joe Hodge then had to answer for Wolves to keep them in the tie and went to his left, but his effort was met by an outstretched Henderson who batted the ball away, before sprinting towards the fans to celebrate. Forest were in the semi-finals of the League Cup for the first time since 1992.

Amidst the players embracing Henderson, Gibbs-White went straight over to the Wolves fans and slid on his back in front of them, fingers in his ears, before being mobbed by Henderson and the rest of the players. You could tell that one meant the world to him and it cemented another iconic night at The City Ground. A cup run had been a catalyst for Forest's promotion the season before, so could another be a catalyst for Premier League survival? Time would tell, but the omens were looking good and the Reds were three games from silverware.

After the game, Cooper said above all else, he was delighted for the fans – the older fans got a chance to reminisce about being in a semi-final again, while the younger ones got to experience one for a first time. Given all the upheaval, it was a notable achievement and the Reds would only have to wait two weeks until the first leg of their semi-final. Before that though would be two league games, the first being at home against Leicester. 12 months earlier, Forest had blown the Foxes away in a 4-1 win and Cooper was hoping for a similar outcome, albeit with different players.

One player from that day came back in though, as McKenna returned to the XI instead of Boly, while Scarpa got another start in the 10 role as Cooper opted to go with a front two of Gibbs-White and Johnson. Forest started brightly and had a good chance to take the lead when Freuler picked out Yates unmarked in the box, but Yates got his header all wrong and the ball went behind for a goal kick. Leicester rallied and soon had an even better chance to open the scoring when Marc Albrighton swung in a delivery that found an unmarked Harvey Barnes' feet on the penalty spot, but Barnes somehow missed the target completely.

The rest of the first half was a bit cagey, with both teams relatively cautious in their approach bar a few efforts from distance, but the start of the second half was explosive. A loose ball from McKenna gifted possession to Youri Tielemans on the edge of the Forest box and he picked out Barnes immediately, but despite the angle suiting him perfectly, he fluffed his lines again and put his effort just past the far post. Six minutes later and moments after coming on for Scarpa, Surridge picked out Gibbs-White, who cut the Leicester defence in two with an outstanding through ball for Johnson to run onto, taking it round goalkeeper Danny Ward with his first touch and passing into an empty net with his second.

The flag went up immediately for offside, but VAR determined that Johnson was just on and the goal stood. From there on out, Forest were in full control. Surridge was inches away from getting on the end of an excellent Aurier cross to give the Reds a second, but with just six minutes left to play, Gibbs-White twisted and turned to give himself some space, before firing an inch perfect ball off the outside of his boot to Johnson. Johnson had Surridge to pass to, but as his touch took him away from his marker, he was well placed to shoot and did so with aplomb, firing past Ward and doubling Forest's lead.

Once the ref blew for full-time, for the first time all season, Forest had made it back-to-back Premier League wins. If Barnes had his shooting boots on, it could've been a different story, but Cooper deserved credit for his tactical tweaks in the second half. By having a focal point in Surridge, Gibbs-White could drop deeper and grab the game by the scruff of the neck, which is exactly what he did to great effect. The result put Forest up to the dizzying heights of 13th, five points clear of the relegation zone and it felt like things were really falling into place.

Behind the scenes, Forest had finalised some more transfers. First, Brazilian 21-year-old midfielder Danilo signed from Palmeiras for about £16m according to BBC Sport, thus becoming the 25th signing of the season. With Danilo though, there was a real case of excitement. A few months prior, Arsenal had two bids rejected for Danilo according to Metro as they sought to bolster their midfield options, so it felt like Forest had landed a real coup by acting quickly to tie him down to a six-year deal at The City Ground.

In addition to Danilo, Forest also signed another striker, as 31-year-old forward Chris Wood signed on loan from Newcastle to become signing number 26 of the campaign. The Athletic reported that the loan deal for the experienced New Zealand international contained an obligation to buy for £15m if Wood made just three appearances in the matchday side, which seemed quite steep for a 31-year-old, but Wood had been hugely successful in relegation threatened teams at Premier League level before. As such, the hope was that he could do similar with Forest.

However, the win against Leicester did come at a cost. Approaching stoppage time, Henderson kicked the ball up the pitch and immediately felt discomfort. After receiving medical assistance, Henderson saw out the rest of the game, but hobbled through the final minutes and after the game, Henderson needed scans on his thigh to see what had happened. The results were that he'd suffered a tear and would be out for between four to five weeks, which was a huge blow for Forest as Henderson had been such a vital part of the team.

The England international's injury massively took the shine off the fact that at the halfway point of the season, Forest were actually doing alright. It was way too early to call off the relegation threat there and then, especially with Henderson injured for the short term, but there was also cause for careful optimism that Forest might be ok. It felt like Cooper had a team that was fighting for both him and the badge, that he was starting to see results and that he now had some of the extra reinforcements needed.

As such, Forest went to Bournemouth with the hope of making the old 'like London buses' adage come true – only this time, for away wins. Bournemouth had lost their last six games in all competitions, so fans were in confident mood. Wood was thrown straight into the starting XI for the match, taking Scarpa's place in the team and allowing Gibbs-White to drop back into the attacking midfield role, while Danilo was on the bench. Forest could've taken the lead early when Aurier was released down the right by Johnson and pulled a ball back to the penalty spot for Gibbs-White, but the midfielder's effort was well saved by Neto in the Bournemouth goal.

Soon after though, that pressure paid off. A Gibbs-White set-piece was headed across goal by Boly into Yates' path, who nodded home. However, once the celebrations had ceased, VAR intervened and ruled that Boly was offside in the buildup, so the goal was disallowed. The reprieve gave Bournemouth life and with half an hour played, Dango Ouattara sped past Lodi and put a low ball into the penalty area, which Jaiden Anthony got to ahead of Worrall and slotted home. You could see the relief amongst the Bournemouth team once that goal went in and they had their tails up as a result.

Not long after, Joe Rothwell completely split the Forest defence in two with a through ball to Kieffer Moore inside the box, with Moore then attempting to round Hennessey for an open goal. Hennessey slid and poked the ball away, but only as far as Jordan Zemura, whose goalbound effort was cleared off the line by Worrall as Forest desperately begged for the half-time whistle. When it came, the score still 1-0 and that allowed Forest to regroup, with Danilo coming on for an injured Yates at the interval to make his Forest debut.

Danilo didn't take long to stamp his authority and the Reds were much the better side in the second half with him pulling the strings in midfield, although Anthony was still causing havoc. After sending Worrall one way and then the other, he pulled a ball back for Ryan Christie, whose effort was going straight to the top corner but for a vital block by Boly. Chasing a goal, Cooper sent Surridge on against his former club in place of Wood and before even touching the ball, Surridge was roundly booed by the home fans.

The day the play-off curse ended. Above: A slightly blurry Forza display before kick-off. Below: The scenes at FT

Above: The Red Side of the Trent boys! From left to right, Reiss, me, Lee & Adam. Below: Calm before the storm

The results of winning at Wembley. Above: Joyous scenes. Below: Premier
League football returns to Trentside

Above: The Reds' new talisman, Morgan Gibbs-White. Below: Forest over land and sea! Me and Dad at Valencia (A)

The battle would take a brief break though, as Forest went to fight on another front – the Carabao Cup. Manchester United awaited them in the semi-finals, but with the first leg being at home, there was a real belief that Forest could go to Old Trafford with something to defend. Barring a few hiccups, Forest had been imperious on home soil and it was the main reason why the Reds had a chance of survival, so confidence was high. Ahead of the game, Johnson was awarded Player of the Round for his exploits against Blackburn, with fans hoping he could replicate that performance against the Red Devils.

It took just six minutes for any plans of getting to the final to be in serious danger. Forest started bravely but after a turnover deep in the United half, Marcus Rashford sped down the left wing and carried it inside the Forest half, darted inside both Freuler and Worrall and then slotted past Hennessey to make it 10 goals in 10 games for him since the World Cup. It was breathtaking quality from the England international, but poor defending from a Forest perspective, with both Freuler and Worrall culpable. One, if not both, should've stopped Rashford, but neither did and Forest found themselves a goal down.

The response was brilliant, however. Forest stepped up several gears and after Danilo intercepted a Rashford ball and released Gibbs-White, the Reds found themselves in a three-on-three situation just outside the United penalty box. A deft ball from Gibbs-White allowed Surridge a shot at goal and his expertly hit curling effort gave goalkeeper David De Gea no chance, nestling into the bottom corner and taking the roof off in the process. However, for the second time in two games, as soon as the celebrations died down, VAR decreed that the goal was offside. Surridge had gone a fraction early and the equaliser that the Reds deserved was ruled out.

Forest's didn't let up though and when a Gibbs-White corner was cleared to the edge of the box, Scarpa hit a first time side footed volley that had De Gea scrambling across his goalline to keep out. Forest were playing some lovely stuff and looked a huge threat on the counter, which was proved again when Scarpa released Johnson, who seemed to have beaten Aaron Wan-Bissaka, but sort of stopped and allowed the defender to catch up with him, before tamely firing at De Gea despite having Danilo running unmarked to his left.

Towards the end of the half however, United stepped up. A warning sign came when Antony was played in one-on-one by Bruno Fernandes, but Hennessey stood tall and managed to block his effort. On the cusp of half-time though, Antony flicked the ball up on the edge of the box and volleyed it towards goal and while Hennessey saved it, he parried it straight into the path of Wout Weghorst, who fired into a pretty much empty net. Forest didn't deserve to be going in behind at half-time, let alone being 2-0 down, but that's what happens when you don't take your chances against the elite sides.

After half-time, you could see the wind had been taken out of Forest's sails and United sought to keep Forest at arm's length. Christian Eriksen hit the bar with a vicious effort from outside the area and while Forest kept trying to probe, they just didn't cause any real problems. With three minutes to play, Facundo Pellistri was sent through on goal and while Williams did brilliantly well to thwart him with a recovery tackle, his attempted clearance didn't leave the penalty area and allowed Anthony Elanga to chip the ball to Fernandes on the edge of the box, who drove an effort into the bottom corner.

It was by no means a 3-0 game, but again Forest paid the price for not taking their chances. Gibbs-White and Danilo especially were sublime, neither of whom deserved to be on the losing side as a world class defensive midfielder in Casemiro was given the runaround all night from the pair of them. On the topic of Gibbs-White though, there was a concern as he had come off injured with 15 to play. He would need to be assessed ahead of Forest's next match, which was the second leg of the semi-final, but given that the tie was basically done, it was unlikely he'd be risked for the occasion.

Before the second leg could take place, there was some news that did lighten the mood significantly – Cooper had been nominated for Manager of the Month. With two wins and two draws in the league, Cooper would go up against Arsenal's Mikel Arteta, Aston Villa's Unai Emery, Brentford's Thomas Frank and Brighton's Roberto De Zerbi for the award, all of whom also had unbeaten records in January. Arteta would ultimately win it, but even being nominated was outstanding recognition for the job Cooper was doing and once again, demonstrated that keeping him was the right decision.

There was also transfer deadline day, which was on the horizon. Prior to the United match, Dale Taylor and Mbe Soh agreed loan moves to Burton Albion and Guingamp respectively, while after it, Aguilera – who had returned from his original loan at Guanacasteca

– was sent out on a temporary basis again, this time to Portuguese outfit Estoril. The real news though was on incomings and on deadline day itself, Forest were very, very active.

First, Atletico Madrid defender and Brazil international Felipe arrived in another statement signing. According to the Daily Mail, the 33-year-old signed for a £2m fee, but despite the centre back's advancing years, Forest had signed a player of real quality. Felipe had only played eight games that season, which was a concern, but he was elegant on the ball, could read the game magnificently and was hard as nails – prior to the current season, he'd been a mainstay in Atletico's backline and like Lodi, a big part in their title winning success in 2020/21.

As well as Felipe, Forest had also added some experience to their midfield, with the signing of 30-year-old Jonjo Shelvey from Newcastle United. The Athletic reported that the six-time England international had signed on a free transfer and like Wood, the belief was that Shelvey's experience in surviving relegation battles would pay dividends. It turned out that Cooper was eager to get both in for that very reason, but given the extent of Yates' injury was yet to be confirmed, it meant that Cooper wasn't left short in midfield while Yates recovered.

Despite Cooper's belief though, this deal didn't seem wise. While it was true Newcastle reluctantly let him go, with manager Eddie Howe paying tribute to him after the move was confirmed, Shelvey had been out of the frame completely – his only start all campaign was a Carabao Cup game. This was partially down to injury, but partially because Newcastle had simply moved on from him and had better players. It felt like the exact signing Murphy went out of his way to avoid – a player on the way down with no resale value and on big money. Indeed, The Telegraph reported that Forest had offered Shelvey upwards of £70k a week.

Still, if anyone had earned the trust of the fans, it was Cooper. If he felt Shelvey was the answer, then so be it. In any case, all talk of Shelvey stopped pretty quickly as remarkably, Forest had one more in them and it was a signing that shocked the footballing world. Goalkeeper Keylor Navas, formerly of Real Madrid and a three-time Champions League winner, had signed on loan until the end of the season from Paris Saint-Germain. Considering the 36-year-old was still seen as one of the best goalkeepers on the planet, jaws collectively dropped across the footballing landscape.

How had Forest pulled that one out the hat? So many pieces had to fall into place and it just so happened that this time, all of them did. PSG had signed Gianluigi Donnarumma from AC Milan in the summer, who was much younger than Navas and at a similar, if not better, level. As such, Navas had seen his gametime greatly reduced in Paris and wanted to play, but PSG didn't want him to leave as they felt his presence alone ensured Donnarumma couldn't afford to drop his standards.

As soon as Henderson got injured in the Leicester game, Forest went on the lookout for another goalkeeper and according to The Telegraph, it was Marinakis who actually suggested Navas, with the belief being that if you don't ask, you don't get. To the very pleasant surprise of those at Forest, Navas was very keen on the move and even eyed up the Carabao Cup semi-final with United as a game to play in. The deal was very complicated to do – so much so, that on deadline day, it seemed completely dead in the water – but Navas kept pushing and eventually, PSG gave the green light.

PSG were also covering a large portion of Navas' wages, which was a huge bonus for Forest. Signing Navas prompted big questions on Henderson's future though, as both jostling for the number one shirt was likely to go Navas' way. After all, as exceptionally good as Henderson was, Navas was a genuinely world class goalkeeper and he wouldn't have left PSG to sit on the bench at Forest. However, the same report stated that Henderson had another scan on his thigh and was expected to be out for another four weeks, so that wouldn't be a debate for a while yet.

It also transpired that there was a genuine risk that Henderson would be recalled by United, such was his impressive form, but the England stopper had told the Red Devils that he wanted to stay at Forest. The Telegraph also stated that if Forest were to survive, Henderson – who'd also won Player of the Round in the Carabao Cup for his exploits against Wolves – would be one of their key targets for the summer and they were very enthused by his decision, feeling that it really showed his commitment to the club. You could see it in the way he operated that he'd really taken to his new surroundings, but for it to be confirmed behind the scenes like that was notable.

Even with Navas hogging the headlines, there was further drama at Forest from a transfer perspective. Jordan Smith's loan departure to

Huddersfield was straightforward enough, but with the new arrivals, Forest had some big decisions to make for their 25-man squad and as such, O'Brien and Cook would be taken out. Blackburn took advantage of this and moved for O'Brien on loan, with the player passing a medical, posing with a kit and doing all of his media duties before the deadline, with Lancashire Live stating that there was an obligation to buy O'Brien on a permanent basis if Blackburn were promoted. It all seemed to be going swimmingly, until it didn't.

It turned out that Blackburn hadn't got the relevant paperwork sent over in time, citing "mitigating reasons" and as such, the move fell through. This left O'Brien in footballing limbo, as he was now unable to play a league match for the rest of the season given he wasn't registered for Forest's Premier League squad. Blackburn's Director of Football, Gregg Broughton, issued an apology to O'Brien and stated that the club would appeal the decision, but Cooper and Forest were not impressed, with Cooper stating that Rovers had let the player down.

Neither O'Brien nor any of the new signings were part of the matchday squad for the second leg against Manchester United, despite Cooper going with a rotated side and with several academy graduates on the bench. It was clear the tie was up barring a very improbable miracle, but it was a game the Reds had to play all the same. Forest were dealt a blow before kick-off as Lingard pulled up in the warm-up on his return from injury, allowing Dennis an opportunity, but otherwise defended well and restricted United to very little from open play. The Red Devils' best effort in the first half came when Casemiro met Luke Shaw's free-kick brilliantly, but Hennessey's outstretched leg denied him.

In fact, it was Forest who forged the best chance from open play in the first half when Johnson got past Casemiro down the right and crossed into the box for Dennis, who caught the ball beautifully on the half volley and fired it goalbound, with United goalkeeper Tom Heaton caught flatfooted. However, Surridge inadvertently got in the way of the shot, denying Forest a goal and allowing United to clear in the process. The second half saw Wout Weghost hit the post from a Casemiro cross, but with half an hour to go, United really turned the screw.

First, Alejandro Garnacho twisted and turned in the box and stung Hennessey's palms with a wicked effort, then with 73 on the clock, a through ball wasn't cut out by Boly and United were suddenly three-on-two, with Anthony Martial leading the charge. Martial laid it off for Marcus Rashford, whose effort was blocked by McKenna, but the ball kindly fell back at Martial's feet and he fired home. Three minutes later, a Bruno Fernandes ball found Rashford at the back post, who flicked it across the six yard box for Fred to tap in. Just like that, Forest were 2-0 down.

With passage to Wembley secured, United eased off the pedal a bit and Cooper gave Oli Hammond some valuable first team football experience, in addition to giving Detlef Esapa-Osong his professional debut. With time running out, Forest had a great chance to grab a consolation as Dennis sent Danilo through, whose effort was well saved by Heaton, but the rebound came to Surridge with an empty net at his mercy. Despite this, Surridge couldn't get the rebound on target and instead fired over, with the full-time whistle coming shortly after.

Forest's best League Cup run since 1992 had come to an end with a 5-0 aggregate defeat at the hands of Man United, but it had been a brilliant adventure for all involved with the club. Cooper was very gracious after the game, wishing luck to both the Red Devils and Newcastle for reaching the final, as full attention reverted back to the Premier League with half a league season still to play. There would be one more addition for the ranks too in the shape of Andre Ayew, Cooper's trusted striker at Swansea, who signed for the Reds on a free transfer.

By signing on the dotted line, Ayew became signing number 30 for the season. *Thirty.* Almost three entire XIs, all in one season. That's a lot of initiation songs (apparently O'Brien's rendition of Stevie Wonder's 'Superstition' is a knockout). There was no denying Forest needed a heavy influx of players, but if Forest survived, recruitment would simply have to be more joined up the following season – especially as it already seemed as if some new signings were already surplus to requirements. After a disappointing temporary spell at Olympiacos, Hwang's loan was cut short so he could be loaned to FC Seoul, while Kanurić had also departed on loan to Oxford City.

It felt like a case of too many cooks at times and while this approach was understandable to a point, given the short timeframe and significant turnover, a calmer approach would be needed moving forwards. That would be a conversation for a later time though and

Forest had a chance to make conversations of that nature more likely when they hosted Leeds United at home, with the Whites having a torrid time in the league – winning just two of their last 16 matches.

Navas was brought in for his debut and was called into action very early when Luis Sinisterra nodded a loose ball past Boly and darted into the box, but Navas saved well and showed brilliant agility to smother the ball before Sinisterra could get to the rebound. With 14 played, a Gibbs-White free-kick from out wide was half cleared by Leeds to the edge of the box, where Johnson was lurking and powered a venomous volley into the bottom corner. It was a superb goal and one that gave Forest a very valuable lead, but the Reds were far from home and hosed.

Leeds should've immediately levelled when Luke Ayling pinged a ball over Williams to Wilfried Gnonto, whose cutback was met by Sinisterra, but the Colombia international fired over. Soon after, Patrick Bamford noticed Williams was out of position and sent Gnonto rampaging down the wing, who cut it back for Bamford, but his shot was scuffed. Despite the miskick, it fell kindly for Ayling, who forced Navas into another good save to preserve Forest's lead. Leeds weren't letting up and Jack Harrison again noticed Williams out of position, firing a ball over. Williams adjusted his positioning and recovered, but headed it straight to Gnonto inside the box, with Navas coming to the rescue with an excellent stop.

It was a surprise to just about everyone that Forest made it to half-time with their lead intact and Cooper wasted no time making subs as Aurier and Colback came on for Mangala and Danilo, with

Williams moving to the right of the midfield three. Immediately, Forest gained control of the game and with Aurier at right back, Gnonto was nullified completely and Leeds seemed to have no other ideas as to how to get through Forest. The second half came and went and in the end, Forest secured three valuable points, keeping them in 13th but taking them six points clear of the bottom three.

Navas was voted Player of the Match on his debut and looked every bit the world class goalkeeper we'd been used to seeing on Champions League nights, while Ayew also got the opportunity to make his Forest debut late on. The gloss did come off the win a little in the aftermath, mind. Before kick-off, Bamford – a Forest academy graduate – emerged from the tunnel holding a bouquet of flowers, in homage of former Forest chairman Nigel Doughty, as it was the anniversary of his death the day before.

When asked why he brought the flowers out, Bamford – who was incredibly close to Doughty and is best friends with his son, Michael – explained the situation, but also expressed his disappointment that Forest hadn't done anything to commemorate it. Bamford had a point. The academy is named after Doughty for his service and dedication to the club during his tenure as owner and given it was so close to his anniversary, Forest should've done something. Like Bamford said to the Yorkshire Evening Post, everyone at Forest owed a lot to Doughty, so it was a shame that was missed.

Forest would face a trip to Fulham next and it felt like Cooper would be making some changes for the match, especially by how the first half against Leeds went. This turned out to be the case as Cooper not only changed personnel, but changed formation too – switching to a 4-2-3-1 and bringing in Aurier and Scarpa for Williams and Danilo, although Scarpa would be playing on the left wing, which seemed strange. After just seven minutes, Forest's plans were in tatters as both McKenna and Boly had to come off injured. Worrall and Felipe came on, the latter for his debut, but that was perhaps a sign Forest had used most of their luck up in the Leeds game.

10 minutes later, a Fulham free-kick was poorly cleared by Lodi straight to Willian, who feigned to go right, sat Lodi down, chopped onto his left and curled an unbelievable strike into the top corner. Soon after, Willian found Mitrovic inside the box, who breezed past Worrall, feigned a shot and tricked Felipe into sliding to block it, before rattling an effort on goal, which Navas did tremendously well to keep out. Forest were penned in and it was nearly two when Worrall cheaply gave possession to Andreas Pereira, who allowed Bobby Decordova-Reid to fire a rocket towards goal, hitting the bar in the process.

The second half went the same as the first, with Fulham swarming Forest and fashioning multiple chances. Willian was allowed time and space to cut inside and his right footed effort hit the post, before Pereira forced Navas to tip a free-kick over the bar. Cooper made some changes, taking off Scarpa and Mangala for Dennis and Shelvey and this seemed to work, with Shelvey – on his debut – swinging in a peach of a ball for Aurier, who was only denied by a point blank save by goalkeeper Bernd Leno.

They would soon rue that save as Fulham burst down the right and when the ball was cut back to Pereira on the edge of the box, Aurier and Worrall both darted towards the ball, leaving two players unmarked. Pereira simply looked up and found one of them in Manor Solomon, who had time to pick his spot and take the game beyond Forest. It was the sort of defending you'd expect to see in a kid's game, not in the Premier League. The result meant Forest dropped a place to 14th, but remained six points clear of the drop.

Naturally, Cooper was frustrated after the defeat and certainly by the manner of it, but his mood no doubt would've been even worse when the scans came back and ruled McKenna out for six weeks and Boly out for three months. Due to the nature of the injuries, especially to Boly, Forest submitted a request to the Premier League to see if they could deregister Boly and re-register Cook, as they now had two fit centre backs on the books. This was an unprecedented move, but it was perhaps worth a try. Sympathy was few and far between elsewhere mind, with people questioning how Forest could have an injury crisis having signed 30 players.

The injuries made the prospect of Forest's next match even more daunting, as Manchester City rocked up on Trentside. With memories of the 6-0 still fresh in fans' memories, the overriding hope was that it wouldn't be a repeat. Cooper sought to contain City, going for a 4-5-1 with Johnson acting as a lone forward, while Colback, Shelvey and Freuler made up the midfield, with Gibbs-White and Danilo just ahead of them. From the get-go, Forest were happy to let Pep Guardiola's side have the ball and just defend, which was a bold strategy – albeit a very understandable one.

It was largely working, too. City were struggling to create much as there was no space, although Rodri came close with a header when Kevin De Bruyne picked him out with a pinpoint cross. Just before half-time though, a City corner was cleared to Jack Grealish, who picked out Bernardo Silva on the edge of the box and with a first time strike, found the back of the net. It was exceptional quality and Forest went in at half-time a goal down – not that you'd know it by the fan reaction, who loudly applauded the team as they left the field. Ultimately, as much as fans hate admitting it, there are some occasions in football where your team simply faces a much better side. This was one of those occasions.

The second half carried on where the first left off, with City dominating possession and Forest seeking to contain – however, City were much more dangerous in the second half. They'd upped a few gears and whenever Forest decided to venture up the pitch a bit, City hit back – hard. An example of this was when Ilkay Gündogan found space in behind and sent Phil Foden through on goal, with Erling Haaland beside him. However, Foden slipped as he was about to square it and Felipe nipped in to take the ball away.

The pressure kept mounting. De Bruyne found the head of Aymeric Laporte on the six-yard box, but he could only plant his header straight at Navas. Then, Foden cut inside and shot towards goal, with Navas spilling his effort straight at the feet of Haaland. Haaland's first effort came back off the bar, but the rebound fell back to him inside the six-yard box, only for Haaland to inexplicably fire over. It was a miss that had to be seen to be believed from anyone, let alone the most prolific striker in the Premier League that season.

Shortly after, Gündogan forced Navas into a fingertip save from a free-kick, as for some reason, the ball just wouldn't go in.

Around the 75 minute mark, you could see that City were starting to tire a bit. They'd expended a lot of energy pushing for that second goal and had nothing to show for it. And subsequently, Forest started to believe. They started to be braver. They sensed the tide was turning and so did the crowd, roaring them on passionately. Football is and can be an incredibly stupid sport. You can find yourself under intense pressure for 89 minutes of a match, but if a decisive blow hasn't been struck, you are very likely to have one moment to swing the game in your favour. And Forest felt like theirs was coming.

With about seven minutes left to play, Forest were patiently moving the ball around in their own half as they looked for a way through, with Navas, Felipe, Mangala, Toffolo, Ayew, Freuler, Williams and Worrall all knocking it around between them. Eventually, the ball was worked down the right, where Williams found Gibbs-White, who turned and quickly fed Johnson. Johnson sped into the penalty area and slipped it back to Gibbs-White on the outside when he was faced up by Rodri. Gibbs-White then sent a ball across the six-yard box and Wood was there to tap in. Pandemonium.

Forest had put together a 19 pass move, involving all 11 players, which culminated in a scintillating, beautiful team goal that the finest teams to ever grace the sport would've been proud of. Forest had out Pep'd Pep. The noise around The City Ground was so loud, that Guardiola could barely hear himself think. "Forest are magic, on and off the pitch" reverberated round at a decibel level that could've probably been heard in space, but rather than go for the kill, Forest – perhaps wisely – went back to their gameplan. City were spent and despite the array of attacking players on the pitch, couldn't fashion another meaningful opening. At full-time, the outpour of noise was colossal and despite drawing, 'Just Can't Get Enough' was given a spin – which I can't imagine Marinakis was particularly pleased about, given Forest didn't actually win.

That being said, it was a draw that felt like more. City were just that good and Guardiola's side dropping points felt about as rare as a solar eclipse. After the game, Cooper was delighted that Forest got that one moment against a team he believed were the best on the planet. The draw took Forest back up to 13th, although their lead to the bottom three was now five points, but fans were in too much disbelief to care. Their team had just bloodied the nose of an elite side. Yes, Forest had been lucky, but Cooper's gameplan worked and if Forest could take points against the champions, who would get in their way as they sought to secure Premier League survival?

CHAPTER ELEVEN – "IT AIN'T ABOUT HOW HARD YOU HIT…"

For Forest fans, the glow after the City draw was stupendous. Not even the Premier League rejecting Forest's appeal to include Cook in their 25-man squad could dampen it. A year earlier, Forest had drawn 2-2 with Stoke and would draw 0-0 at Preston in their next match. Going toe to toe with a side chasing the treble (Premier League, FA Cup, Champions League) and getting a point was just a slight upgrade on that and the feel good factor around the club was very prominent. Remember Adam Crafton's smug tweet when Forest lost to Fulham, comparing them to QPR 2012? With 15 games left to play, Forest had already matched QPR's 2012/13 points total of 25.

The good mood wasn't letting up either as with a trip to 18th placed West Ham next, Forest had a huge opportunity to put serious daylight between themselves and the bottom three. Securing an eight point gap with 14 games to go wouldn't make anyone safe there and then, but it would certainly have you looking up the table rather than down. Above all else, it was imperative that Forest left the London Stadium without defeat – a draw would be a very good point on the road and was perhaps more likely given their struggles away from home, but it would also ensure the five point gap remained.

Cooper opted for a midfield three of Shelvey, Freuler and Colback, while Williams came in for Aurier at right back. The first half was by no means one for the history books and the closest anyone came to a goal was when Lucas Paquetá fired into a congested six-yard box and the ball deflected off Felipe and hit the post. Forest had a pretty solid penalty claim when Johnson tangled with West Ham's Ben Johnson just before the break, but neither the referee nor VAR were convinced.

The second half started in pretty much the same manner, with the Match of the Day team probably already penciling in the match to be shown last on that night's broadcast. West Ham were mostly restricted to shots outside the box and they did come close when Jarrod Bowen hit the post with one, but by and large, Forest were comfortable. With around 25 minutes left, Cooper opted to roll the dice and withdrew Shelvey for Ayew, switching to a 4-2-3-1 as he went in search of a win.

Shelvey looked bemused when he came off and immediately, West Ham made that extra man in midfield count. Just four minutes after the change, Bowen danced into the Forest box and put a ball over for an unmarked Danny Ings, who'd completely escaped Worrall's attention, to give the Hammers the lead. Two minutes later, Williams was caught running towards his own goal by Paquetá, who fed Säid Benrahma inside the box and Benhrama's ball across goal was tapped in by Ings.

Five minutes after that, Benrahma teased Williams with the ball and under no pressure, passed it back to the edge of the box for Declan Rice, who curled home a wonderful effort. Seven minutes after Rice's goal, Williams stood off Aaron Cresswell, who played it down the line for Pablo Fornals. Johnson was covering and managed to halt Fornals briefly, but the ball fell kindly for Fornals to cross in. Again, Williams stood off and again, Forest were punished as Fornals' cross was powered home by Michail Antonio, who easily outmuscled Toffolo to get to the ball first.

Four goals conceded in just 14 minutes of football. As tactical tweaks go, it's fair to say this one was a complete disaster from Cooper. Bewilderingly, Forest had lost a 'must not lose' game that looked nailed on to be a 0-0 draw by four goals to nil. Due to results elsewhere, the gap to 18th was four points – West Ham leapt out of the bottom three as a result of their emphatic victory, but Forest still had breathing space. Cooper said to BBC Sport after the game that it was "not acceptable", "our own fault" and that "it was a mentality thing and we were punished".

However, the blame had to lie with him just as much as the players. While it was for positive reasons as he rolled the dice seeking a win, it was his decision to take a man out of midfield, which subsequently left it exposed and overrun. Cooper had more than enough in the bank for fans to take it on the chin, but equally it didn't seem right that he was putting sole responsibility on the players when they were carrying out his instructions.

The next game couldn't come round soon enough for Forest and it was another huge one, as the Reds faced the team in 18th once again – this time in the shape of Everton. Like Forest, Everton had just been smacked 4-0 by a London opponent (Arsenal for them) and victory on home soil for the Reds would take them seven points clear of the drop zone. It was perhaps because of this dangling carrot that the alarm bells weren't ringing just yet after the West Ham debacle, especially given that Forest were on an eight-game unbeaten run at home in the league.

There was another subplot to the game as Sean Dyche, shortlisted to replace Cooper back in October, was now in the Everton dugout and after just 10 minutes, the Toffees boss couldn't believe his luck. Some pinball in the Forest box led to neither Colback or Freuler committing to clearing a loose ball and instead, it bobbled towards the edge of the box. As Shelvey went to remove the danger, he proceeded to kick Dwight McNeil instead of the ball, resulting in an Everton penalty.

It was a woefully timed challenge and Demarai Gray made no mistake from the spot, sending Navas the wrong way. Instantly, Forest started moving through the gears, resulting in Gibbs-White playing a delicious one-two with Wood before firing goalbound, forcing Jordan Pickford into a brilliant one-handed save. Unfortunately for the England number one, the rebound was immediately mopped up by Johnson, who finished with aplomb. Everton's lead lasted just nine minutes and Forest were still upping the ante, with Wood and Johnson both having efforts blocked.

277

Approaching the half hour mark, Colback tripped McNeil inside the Everton half and the Toffees used this as an excuse to pile everyone forward. Pickford took the free-kick and picked out James Tarkowski just outside the box, who proceeded to head the ball inside the area. Michael Keane then won the next header, flicking it towards goal, where it was headed into the floor by Abdoulaye Doucouré, beating Navas and restoring Everton's lead. The ball didn't even touch the ground until Doucouré's effort, as Forest lost three headers in a row and found themselves in a losing position once again.

The first missed header was from Felipe, the second from a mixture of Worrall and Shelvey and the third was from Freuler. A polite way to describe the defending would be diabolical and once again, stupid mistakes were hampering the Reds. Everton made it to half-time with their lead intact and did their best to dig in for the second half, frustrating Forest. With 20 to play, Cooper made a triple change as Yates, Ayew and Dennis came on for Freuler, Colback and Wood, again switching to the 4-2-3-1 in an attempt to salvage something.

This time though, it was much more effective. With Everton happy to camp, it made no sense to have an extra midfielder for protection as Forest were chasing the game, so the extra attacker gave the Reds added impetus and not even 10 minutes after the changes were made, they paid off. Felipe tackled Doucouré near the halfway line and immediately gave it to Johnson, who pushed it to the right for Yates to chase down. Rather than cross, Yates calmly pulled it back for Johnson, who, after taking a touch, expertly placed it into the top corner, giving Pickford no chance.

That goal gave Forest confidence and they aggressively hunted down a winner that would put them seven clear of the drop zone. Johnson came so close to getting a hat-trick when an Ayew shot was parried back into open play by Pickford, but he just couldn't get to the ball in time. Right at the end, Johnson swung a teasing ball in, but Worrall couldn't quite reach it. In the end, a point would have to do. Forest's unbeaten run at home was now at nine games, but there was a sense of frustration that defensive errors had cost them two points.

As much as Cooper deserved criticism for his tactical switch in the West Ham game, he deserved plaudits for how his tweaks ensured Forest left with something all the same. The gap to 18th stayed at four points, but the Reds did have a game in hand on Everton. Weirdly, it felt like positions didn't really matter that much, given that between 12th and 20th, there was a gap of just six points. So long as Forest had at least three teams beneath them after 38 matches, fans weren't going to care too much what position they finished in and they had 13 more games to make sure that became a reality.

The next match was always going to be very difficult though, as Forest made the trip to the new Tottenham Hotspur Stadium, with Spurs looking to strengthen their grip on fourth in the league. However, all was not rosy at Tottenham, who in addition to going three games without a win in all competitions, had exited the Champions League at the last-16 stage a few days earlier. In addition, manager Antonio Conte was at war with just about everyone associated with Spurs, taking swipes at his own players and claiming that the fans lacked patience and understanding, while insisting the club weren't ready to win trophies.

Throw in the fact that Forest had dumped Spurs out of the Carabao Cup a few months earlier and there was faint optimism that the Reds had caught Tottenham at a good time. Forest would need to be at their best to get even a point, but a home win was far from a guarantee. Cooper shuffled his pack to accommodate the returning Lingard, with Forest going for the false nine approach once again, while Mangala came in for Colback in midfield. Going back to the false nine was bold, but it did cause Spurs issues in the league match earlier on in the season, so the logic was sound.

After just three minutes, Oliver Skipp caught the entire Forest defence out with a lofted through ball, which Richarlison ran onto and promptly smashed passed Navas, but VAR took a closer look and ruled that Richarlison was marginally offside. 15 minutes later though, Richarlison muscled his way past Shelvey down the right and while his cross was poor, Forest were unable to clear and Pedro Porro promptly swung a ball in for Harry Kane to head home from. 15 minutes after the goal, Kane was picked out and played a ball inside the box for Richarlison to run onto, but as he got there, Worrall clattered into him from the side and needlessly gave a penalty away.

It was a reckless, late challenge that was nowhere near the ball and unlike at The City Ground, Kane didn't miss from the spot. Half-time couldn't come soon enough for Forest and when it came, Cooper was ruthless. Off came Lingard and Mangala, with Dennis and Ayew replacing them as Cooper also abandoned the false nine formation, switching to a 4-2-3-1 instead. The early signs were promising and Forest made goalkeeper Fraser Forster work when

Gibbs-White picked out Johnson, but as Forest were throwing caution to the wind, they were leaving notable gaps in behind.

Just after the hour mark, these gaps were exploited when a Forest attack broke down and Spurs immediately sent the ball down the right wing for Richarlison. His cross to Kane was brilliantly halted by an acrobatic Worrall block, but the ball fell back for Richarlison and his second cross found Son Heung-min, whose first touch took him away from Aurier, allowing him to fire a shot through Shelvey's legs and past Navas to make it 3-0 Spurs. In response, Cooper took Freuler and a limping Johnson off for Wood and Yates, who was back from a spell on the sidelines.

However, only seven minutes after coming on, Wood had to come off with an injury of his own, so Williams entered the fray. At this point, Forest reverted back to the 3-4-1-2 formation that had seen them get promoted, with Williams at wing back, Aurier at centre back and Dennis and Ayew as the two forwards. With nine minutes to play, a Gibbs-White corner was flicked to the back post by Felipe, allowing Worrall to head into an empty net. Suddenly, Spurs started to look a bit panicked and Forest began to dream of a very unlikely comeback.

Halfway through stoppage time, Dejan Kulusevski basically punched a ball away while trying to clear and after VAR intervention, Forest had a penalty. Suddenly, the prospect of a draw looked much more likely – if they could convert it. Spurs would have to ride out three minutes of relentless pressure and given they'd already started to fold, it was very much on. Ayew stepped up to take it, but in an anti-climactic fashion, Forster guessed correctly, kicking it away and just like that, any hopes of a draw were extinguished. 3-1 Tottenham, the final score.

Elsewhere, results were not kind for Forest. Bournemouth and Everton both won, while Leeds, West Ham and Southampton all drew. The only team beneath Forest to lose was Leicester and as such, the gap to the relegation zone was now just two points. In fact, Forest were now only four points from bottom. The good news was that Forest were on home soil next, but the bad news was that they were facing high-flying Newcastle United, who were fifth – four points behind Spurs with two games in hand on the North London side.

Before the game, Cooper was given a colossal boost as Niakhaté – some seven months after his injury against West Ham – was finally ready for selection again. There was further good news for Forest fans too, as Johnson was fit to start. Worrall was straight out of the side to make way for Niakhaté and Cooper made some tactical changes from Tottenham, starting with a 4-2-3-1 outright with Dennis on the left with Yates and Shelvey operating as a midfield duo, with Ayew leading the line on his own.

Much like before with the 4-2-3-1 though, Forest were quickly overran and Newcastle were finding space very easily. They should've taken the lead when Jacob Murphy drilled a ball across the penalty box for Joe Willock, but Willock fired over with the goal gaping. Soon after, a clever free-kick from Kieran Trippier put Alexander Isak in one-on-one and his effort beat Navas, but it deflected off Lodi and onto the bar, before eventually falling safely into the goalkeeper's arms.

With 25 on the clock, Shelvey banged a ball down the right wing for Ayew to chase after, but Dan Burn got there first and passed back to goalkeeper Nick Pope. However, Burn's pass was weak and Dennis intercepted it inside the box, although he was being forced away from goal. Despite this, Dennis delicately chipped Pope with such precision that it nestled in the back of the net, despite Trippier's best attempts to keep it out and completely against the run of play, Forest had a valuable lead. The shot required outrageous technique from Dennis, with a chip that Tiger Woods would've been proud of at Augusta, but he made it look easy.

Newcastle didn't take going a goal down very well and didn't let it disturb their rhythm. After getting the better of Lodi, Murphy pulled a ball back to the edge of the box for Sean Longstaff, whose effort deflected off Felipe and onto the crossbar, as the Magpies searched for an equaliser. Moments before half-time, Ayew seemed to be fouled on halfway, but the ref didn't give anything and from that, Newcastle worked it down the right clinically before Willock crossed for Isak, whose incredible acrobatic effort hit the inside of the post and went in.

On the one hand, it was a huge sucker punch as not only should it have been a foul on Ayew, but it was literally seconds before the interval. On the other, it was very much deserved and Forest had a job on their hands to contain Newcastle for another 45 minutes. The Reds were much more defensive minded in the second half, with

Newcastle having a lot of the ball, but doing little with it. After an hour, Yates had to come off injured and was replaced by Freuler and a few minutes later, a dangerous Isak ball was half cleared back to the striker in bizarre fashion, allowing him to jink past Lodi and cross to the back post for Elliot Anderson to head home.

It was a deserved lead for Newcastle, but VAR took a look at it and after a lengthy check, ruled that in the process of the ball coming back to Isak, Niakhaté tried to clear it and it deflected off an offisde Longstaff back into Isak's path. It was a ridiculously harsh decision – Longstaff couldn't really do anything and as such, there was no clear or obvious error with it at all. The decision massively benefitted Forest and gave them 25 minutes to hang onto a draw. Call it even after the Ayew foul not being called for the Isak equaliser, I guess.

Newcastle huffed and puffed, but couldn't find a way through. Wave after wave of pressure amounted to nothing and as the game went into its dying embers, it seemed Forest were set for a hugely valuable point. With the game in stoppage time, a Willock cross found Isak, whose header was beaten away by Niakhaté – the only issue was that it was beaten away with Niakhaté's arm, giving the referee no option but to award a penalty. It was a tired action from a physically exhausted Niakhaté and it would likely cost Forest dearly.

Navas and Shelvey were both booked before the penalty could be taken, with Navas doing all he could to put Trippier off before he could take it. Once Navas was sent away though, Trippier stepped out of the box and allowed Isak to take it instead. Isak very calmly put the penalty away to give Newcastle a 2-1 lead and while Cooper threw Scarpa on for Shelvey to try and make something happen, it was too little too late. Forest had lost and it was the sort of result where you feel hopelessly deflated in the aftermath.

It also ended Forest's impressive unbeaten home run, which was proving the bedrock of any survival plan. The Premier League is the best in the world, but when results go against you, it's a hugely bruising experience. There's no hiding place and the limelight burns. Would Forest have deserved a point from that game? Probably not. Yes, they defended brilliantly for large parts of the second half, but Newcastle could've been 5-1 up at half-time. Would it have been invaluable to the Reds' survival cause? Absolutely.

Forest had dropped down to 16th following the defeat, but were still two points clear of the drop zone due to results elsewhere. It was also time for an international break, meaning fans had to stew on that late Isak dagger for two weeks. Lodi's impressive form had seen him return to the Brazil fold, but other stories emerging from Brazil were of concern to Forest and in particular, Scarpa. It had emerged that the attacking midfielder had been subject to a cryptocurrency scam and lost around £1m according to The Guardian, so he'd been taking some time in his home country to sort it all out.

The club had pledged its full support to Scarpa while he dealt with the matter, which can't have been easy to deal with when adapting to a new country. To make matters worse for Scarpa, during the break, he suffered a calf injury. That wasn't even the worst news from an injury perspective though, as Aurier also picked up a knock on international duty, while Wood was ruled out for the remainder of the season with a thigh injury. The Wood signing, up until this point, had mostly been a very costly failure – though it wasn't always his fault.

There were times where he looked off the pace, which was to be expected given he barely played for Newcastle before signing, but it was more in the manner he was being played. Wood is and has always been a striker who needs the ball worked into him, be it on the floor or in the air. Making him chase the ball down the wing made no sense, as it just wasn't his game – he isn't a Keinan Davis for example, who thrives off doing that. The one time Forest had actually worked the ball to him, he scored against Manchester City.

Wood's absence represented a blow, even though the dye was already cast with the vast majority of the fanbase regarding his use to the side. There was a positive though, namely regarding O'Brien. While Blackburn's appeal to loan him was rejected during the break, Major League Soccer side DC United – managed by Wayne Rooney, of all people – signed O'Brien on loan until July. It was a good resolution to the clown show that took place at Blackburn and finally, O'Brien could try and get back to the level he was at before.

Forest faced Wolves on April Fool's Day for their first game after the break and the game promised to be a spicy affair after the Carabao Cup quarter-final earlier that season. Perhaps as a result of the injuries, Cooper went for the false nine again, with Dennis and Johnson either side of Gibbs-White, while Toffolo and Williams came in for Lodi and Aurier. Danilo also returned to the team, taking Shelvey's place and forming a midfield three with Mangala and

Freuler. Predictably, it was a very hard-fought encounter between the two sides.

Wolves came close to taking the lead when a dangerous Matheus Nunes cross was inadvertently headed onto his own bar by Niakhaté, but otherwise, Forest were mostly on top. Seven minutes before half-time, Gibbs-White and Danilo shared some exquisite interplay as they made serious inroads towards the Wolves box, before Danilo chipped a ball over for Johnson at the back post, who side footed it through José Sá's legs and into the back of the net. Johnson did Gibbs-White's celebration, much to the annoyance of Wolves fans and Forest went into the break looking on course for three vital points.

Wolves were much better after half-time and had a half penalty claim when Felipe tangled with Adama Traoré, sending the winger crashing to the floor. Felipe had put his hand on Traoré's shoulder, but it didn't warrant that kind of reaction and the referee promptly told the attacker to get up. This didn't go down well on the touchline, with the Wolves bench furious and sparking a melee with their Forest counterparts as a result, leading to Forest's Alan Tate and Wolves' Pablo Sanz both being sent off by the referee.

After an hour, Lodi came on for Toffolo and immediately got involved, winning the ball back and passing it to Freuler, who found Gibbs-White in space and in a prime area to launch a counter-attack. With his first touch, Gibbs-White sent the ball right towards Dennis with the outside of his boot and suddenly Forest were on a two-on-two with Gibbs-White available to square it to. Instead however,

Dennis went solo and his shot was saved by Sá, while the rebound was put wide by Johnson. Gibbs-White was exasperated with the decision and rightfully so – a pass over to him and he scores an open goal.

Shortly after, Worrall came on for Dennis as Forest switched to a 3-4-1-2 formation, which was more a 5-3-2 out of possession as Forest looked to shut down the game. With just seven minutes left to play, Diego Costa got to a cross before Worrall and played it back to Pedro Neto, whose shot was blocked by a combination of Worrall and Mangala. However, the ball pinged into Daniel Podence's path, who sold Williams a dummy before planting the ball into the top corner. The celebration tit for tat continued as Podence mimicked Gibbs-White's celebration, but Forest had shot themselves in the foot again.

In response, Forest brought on Kouyaté and Awoniyi, both of whom had returned from injury and it didn't take long for Kouyaté to get involved. The midfielder was unceremoniously barged over by Costa when challenging for a ball and tangled with Costa's legs while on the floor, sending the forward to the turf with him. When both players got up, they were both fine about it, but Podence got himself involved and as he was being moved away, he clearly gestured to spit at Johnson. Johnson put his hand on his face immediately as if he felt something, but despite checking several times, VAR didn't intervene.

In the end, it finished 1-1 and a point didn't really help either team – as both West Ham and Bournemouth won, Forest were now down to 16th – one point clear of the drop zone, with Wolves a point and three places above them. After the game, Cooper highlighted the increase of ill-discipline on the touchline since Julen Lopetegui took over as Wolves manager and claimed Forest were prepared for a flare-up, while stating he had trust in the authorities they'd deal with Podence after seeing the incident back.

The FA opened an investigation pretty much straight after the game, eventually taking no action as they found the evidence unconvincing. In truth, the controversy had taken away from the fact Forest had drawn a game they should've won and maybe went too defensive too quickly, allowing Wolves time to build momentum and eventually punish the Reds. Still, Forest couldn't dwell on it for too long as they had another massive game just a few days later as they'd finally be playing their rescheduled Leeds away fixture.

In the immediate aftermath of Forest's 1-0 win over Leeds back in February, the Whites sacked Jesse Marsch and replaced him with Javi Gracia, who had previously managed Watford, Valencia and Olympiacos. Of his five league games so far, Leeds had won two and drawn one, so they'd certainly picked up a bit of a bounce under the new man. Cooper went with an unchanged side for the game, which was something of a rarity and again enabled him to go with the false nine formation.

Forest started firmly on the front foot and almost silenced the home support very quickly when a Gibbs-White corner was flicked on by Felipe and ricocheted into Dennis' path, who swivelled quickly and was desperately unlucky to hit the post with his effort. Minutes later,

Dennis picked out Danilo, who played it back down the left for Dennis to run onto. Upon receiving it, Dennis picked out Mangala on the edge of the box, whose first touch was a deft one to take him away from Luis Sinisterra, while his second was a caressed effort straight into the bottom corner.

With the goal advantage though, Forest began to drop off and Leeds upped the ante significantly. Jack Harrison was making a nuisance of himself and despite being sized up by Toffolo, he managed to get away and find Weston McKennie on the edge of the box, who quickly played it to Marc Roca, with Roca firing towards goal. Navas saved his effort, but parried it straight into the path of Harrison, who'd escaped Toffolo's attention and swept home. It was a rare error from Navas, but he'd also been sold short badly by his defence.

Forest's lead lasted just eight minutes and Leeds now smelt blood. After applying serious pressure, with the ball barely leaving Forest's half, Leeds got their breakthrough just before half-time. Sinisterra was faced up by Williams and after feigning to go one way, went the other and found the bottom corner with a brilliant effort. A promising start up in smoke and really, down to a negative approach. Worryingly, despite the urgency for Forest to equalise, in the second half, they didn't really offer much.

If anything, Leeds looked the more likely to score again – Sinisterra curled one just wide and when Felipe and Williams went for the same ball, the ricochet ended up at Patrick Bamford's feet, but the striker's effort was wayward. When the full-time whistle went, it marked four straight defeats on the road and meant that Forest were without a win in eight. They were now only out of the relegation on goal difference and if the alarm bells weren't ringing before, they certainly were now.

Cooper was asked about his future after the game and reiterated that the club would always come first, but that he really believed in the players to turn it around, as much as he bemoaned the level of performance. He also claimed he felt he'd let the fans down and despite the rumours swirling about Cooper's future again, the fans rallied behind him once more. He was serenaded despite the defeat at Elland Road and the peril the club found themselves in. The connection Cooper had with the fans couldn't be underestimated – even despite the recent run, there were still no calls for his head or anything like that.

Patrick Vieira, who'd recently been sacked as manager of Crystal Palace, had been mooted as a replacement and eyebrows were raised when the Daily Mail reported that after the Wolves game, Marinakis spoke to the players and expressed his dissatisfaction with their second half performance and Cooper's tactics. It seemed inevitable a change was coming, so much so that The Athletic reported someone high up at Forest described Cooper as a "dead man walking" after the Leeds defeat, but for the second time in a season, Marinakis relented.

Instead, he publicly backed Cooper via a statement on the club website. "No-one denies that our Club is in a difficult position in the Premier League, but we wish to end the speculation and the false and disruptive reporting in the media to confirm that Steve Cooper remains our manager," it read. "We have all been disappointed with recent performances and it is very clear that a lot of hard work needs to be done to address this urgently. Results and performances must improve immediately."

As far as backing the manager goes, that was some statement, although the underlying message was crystal clear and this was strike two for Cooper. There wouldn't be a third reprieve and in the event results didn't pick up, it looked likely Cooper wouldn't be there much longer – although this would be very silly, given he'd proved he'd be perfect to take Forest up from the Championship. Much like earlier on in the season however, it felt like if Marinakis couldn't sack Cooper, he would make other changes to the club's structure.

Before anything of that nature could take place however, Forest had a trip across the Midlands to Aston Villa, who were a very different Aston Villa to the one they played earlier that season. Steven Gerrard was sacked and Unai Emery had taken over, with Villa flying under his management – Villa were seventh going into the match with eyes very firmly locked in on a European place. Cooper effectively went to a 5-3-2, with Williams, Worrall, Felipe, Niakhaté and Toffolo as a back five, Shelvey, Danilo and Kouyaté in midfield with Gibbs-White and Johnson as forward options who would drop in to help out.

The gameplan worked brilliantly – Villa offered nothing of any substance in the first half, while Forest carried a threat on the counter. The home side got in behind just once, where Leon Bailey picked out Ollie Watkins, but it was a difficult chance and Watkins put it out for a goal kick. The only negative was that Kouyaté had to come off with a knock after 25 minutes for Freuler, but otherwise, the half-time message would've been to do the exact same as Forest looked very good value for at least a point.

Straight after half-time, Ashley Young sent Bertrand Traoré down the right wing and his low cross was beaten away by Navas, straight to Shelvey. Without looking, Shelvey played a blind pass to Niakhaté across the six yard box, but it was weak and nowhere near Niakhaté, allowing Traoré to run straight onto it and finish first time. As mistakes go, that was by far the worst of the season and one of the worst I can ever remember a Forest player making. It was a pass devoid of any footballing intelligence whatsoever and it proved to be immensely costly.

To make things worse, Shelvey showed no desire whatsoever to atone for his error. He just sort of moped about until he was hooked after 65 for Mangala, with Awoniyi coming on for Worrall at the same time as Cooper reverted to the normal 4-3-1-2 in an attempt to get something out the game. Just before the subs, Danilo had Forest's best chance of the game as he picked the ball up near the edge of the box and let fly, but it wasn't hit with any real conviction and goalkeeper Emiliano Martínez saved it comfortably.

With the added space, Villa started to go up a few gears to kill the game off. Jacob Ramsey was given space and time to pick out Alex Moreno down the left – the same Moreno who turned Forest down in the summer – and the left back sped past Williams before cutting it back for Emiliano Buendia, but his effort went wide. Forest didn't heed the warning however and in stoppage time, Watkins found

Ramsey in the box but rather than shoot, Ramsey gave it back to Watkins, who took it past Toffolo before slotting home to wrap the game up.

As a result of West Ham and Bournemouth's victories elsewhere, Forest were now in the relegation zone on goal difference. Cooper was spared the fans' anger and was given a warm reception when he came over, but the players weren't – with Johnson in particular taken aback by the rage shown from the away end. This was naivety from Johnson as ultimately, Forest had gone nine without a win and games were running out fast. The fans were coming to the realisation that something they craved for 23 years was slipping away at a rapid pace, so of course they were going to be upset.

The good news was, as it was so tight, just one result could swing momentum – Forest were only four points behind Wolves in 13th, so there was still belief Cooper could pull a rabbit out of a hat from somewhere. One person who wouldn't be there to see if he could though was Giraldi, who was sacked after just six months in the role of Sporting Director. Given it came straight after the Villa game, one wonders whether Shelvey's error was the final straw as on the whole, the January recruitment that Giraldi would've overseen had been mixed.

Wood had scored one in seven, didn't seem a tactical fit and was now injured for the rest of the campaign. Ayew was – to be polite – ineffective and while Shelvey started promisingly, his form had fallen off a cliff and it was very easy to see why Newcastle had moved him on. Every single time, Shelvey would just look for a long ball forward and the way he played was hampering the other midfielders too, especially Freuler and Gibbs-White, who were nowhere near as effective after Shelvey was brought into the side.

Scarpa was another one who hadn't quite fully fit, be it for injuries, personal issues or not really having a run in the team and while Danilo had shown glimpses of serious potential, it was clear patience was needed with him while he adapted to his new surroundings. The only signings that could be called standout successes at that moment in time were Navas and Felipe, both of whom had showed their class and given their all for the cause. The thing was, Cooper had pushed for Ayew, Wood and Shelvey, so Giraldi taking the can for that seemed harsh.

Forest were quick to move on as Ross Wilson, then at Rangers, was brought in as Giraldi's replacement. The Rangers fans were hardly sad to see him go, which wasn't exactly a ringing endorsement, but he still had a very good reputation in the game. As for Giraldi, he later expressed his anger at the decision, though he did praise the Marinakis family for their care for the club. He also told The Athletic that he frequently went into bat for Cooper and was dismayed about the Vieira links in the media, while stating that as much as it hurt, he realised Marinakis wanted to change something and preferred it to be him than Cooper.

That did say a lot about Giraldi's character, but the main thing for Forest now was to club together and to try and find a positive resolution to the situation they found themselves in. That meant winning games, although the next one was a rather daunting encounter with Manchester United. It was at The City Ground at least, but even before a ball was kicked, it felt like Forest would likely need some positive results elsewhere. There was a Forza display for the game, celebrating 50 years of the tricky tree that is the Forest badge, which was – as always – impeccable.

Somewhat boldly, Cooper returned to the 3-4-1-2, with a returning McKenna coming in for Worrall, Lodi replacing Toffolo and with Awoniyi leading the line. Tellingly, there was no Shelvey after his error in the Villa game, with Freuler partnering Danilo as a midfield pair. While the ambition was there in theory, in practice it was a very different story. United swarmed Forest from the get-go and should've gone a goal up when Bruno Fernandes drilled a ball across and forced Navas into pushing it away, but the ball fell as far as Jadon Sancho, whose effort was cleared off the line by Felipe.

United were coming through at will and Navas had to be on hand again when a clearance sat up on the volley for Fernandes, making a brilliant stop to keep the scores level. A rare forage into the United half saw Forest win a corner and from that, Gibbs-White picked out McKenna, whose effort hit the post and bounced clear. A few minutes later from another corner, Harry Maguire punched the ball behind and out of play, sparking vociferous appeals for a penalty by Forest players and fans alike, but neither the ref or VAR were interested.

In truth, this was nothing short of a scandal. According to VAR, they felt that despite Maguire leading with his arm and beating the ball away off his arm, it was a "congested area" and therefore unintentional. Never in my life, before or after, have I seen a blatant handball like that dismissed due to a 'congested area'. It's the sort of decision you get when you can't buy a win and it's also the sort of decision Sky Six sides like Manchester United seem to get on a regular basis. Had the roles been reversed, it felt like the ref wouldn't have been able to blow quick enough for a penalty.

That decision proved decisive as with 32 played, Danilo was robbed in possession by Anthony Martial and the ball fell to Fernandes, who promptly put Martial through one-on-one. Navas made a brilliant save to stop Martial, but the rebound fell for Antony, who tapped in at the back post. With the lead, United saw the game out until half-time, but the overriding feeling was that Forest had been hard done by from a frankly outrageous call from the officials. The game was 0-0 at that point, if Forest score the penalty, it's a completely different game. Instead, they went in at half-time a goal down.

The message from United boss Erik ten Hag seemed to be that they'd got away with one and to kill the game off. As such, United flew out of the proverbial blocks and Navas had to roll back the years when Fernandes lashed a curling effort towards him, getting fingertips on the ball and pushing it onto the bar in the process. It was a sensational save and Navas was becoming something of a one-man wall. Fernandes tried again from outside the box and Navas showed lightning quick reflexes to tip it round the post for a corner, despite seemingly seeing it late.

Martial then went close after Casemiro picked him out, but his header went just wide of the post as Forest struggled to do anything with the ball at all. The pressure told when Antony cut inside and slipped a lovely ball into the box for Diogo Dalot to run onto, who calmly slotted past Navas to make it 2-0. Cooper brought on Lingard and Dennis in response, but United closed the game out comfortably. The boos at full time were not a surprise as Forest didn't manage a single shot on target. On home soil, that's abject. I know it was Man United, but that's what teams who deserve to go down do.

Cooper was enraged with the officials after the game and laid into them, telling BBC Sport that, "At this level, they should be doing better." Of course, he wasn't wrong, but I won't lie, driving back after the game, I thought Cooper was done. Forest had lost their last three games, had gone 10 league games without a victory, had just failed to manage a single shot on target in a game of football – at home – and were 18th with just seven games left to play.

The only saving grace was that Leeds got smacked 6-1 by Liverpool and Everton lost 3-1 at home to Fulham, so the Reds were only in the drop zone on goal difference and Leeds were only two points ahead. Ultimately, the only person that could arrest the slump was Cooper, but time was running out in order for him to do so. The wave of positivity after the City draw and the momentum generated from a very successful January were just a distant memory at this point.

After the game, Niakhaté took to Twitter to make a statement, where he posted: "To the fans: we know we have to do better and we will fight for every point available until the final whistle blows. It's a big challenge but we are ready for it. I am completely convinced that together we will pull this off" and signed off with a hashtag, #TimeToShowNow. He was right, too. It was time to show up, stand up and be counted, leave it all out there and to get the points needed to get over the line.

It's like the Rocky quote – "It ain't about how hard you hit. It's about how hard you can get hit and keep moving forward." Right now, Forest were up against the ropes taking a proper beating. But nobody was throwing in the towel just yet, no matter how much the blows kept landing. Could they find a way to push through? Was there a counter punch in there to swing momentum back their way? Time would tell, but if they were going to do so, they needed to hurry up.

CHAPTER TWELVE – WAKA WAKA

The saying goes that sometimes, things get worse before they can get better and those at Forest must've been thinking the same thing when after a 10 game winless run, they checked the fixture list to see that their next match was Liverpool away. Fans had been waiting 23 years for a return to Anfield and it came at a point where Forest's status as a Premier League club hung in the balance, with only a handful of games remaining.

Much like at Villa, Cooper elected to go for what was 3-4-1-2 on paper, but effectively a 5-3-2 – Felipe, Niakhaté and McKenna made up a back three, Lodi and Williams (against his former side) were wing backs with Freuler and Mangala as central midfielders, while Danilo and Gibbs-White would be supporting Awoniyi. It turned into more of a 3-6-1 with Danilo and Gibbs-White dropping in to help contain Liverpool, while Awoniyi (also against his former side) would try to hold it up and relieve some of the pressure.

In the first half, the tactics largely worked. Liverpool weren't doing much from open play, but instead, looked incredibly menacing from set-pieces taken from Trent Alexander-Arnold. Liverpool fashioned three chances from Alexander-Arnold set-pieces that should've led to goals – the first saw Virgil van Dijk force Navas into a fingertip save after the centre back powerfully met a free-kick, the second saw Cody Gakpo actually beat Navas from an Alexander-Arnold corner, but Williams was on hand to clear off the line, while the third saw Diogo Jota miss a free header from inside the six-yard box after Alexander-Arnold expertly picked him out from another free-kick.

Forest meanwhile, offered nothing in response and were very happy to go in at half-time level – especially as McKenna had to go off with an injury after 30 minutes. The only contribution of note from a Forest perspective came from the fans, when a banner referring to the Hillsborough disaster was unfurled in the away end that read, 'Respect the 97. Solidarity with survivors – no to tragedy chanting.' This was greeted with widespread applause from the Liverpool fans, who sadly have had their fair share of opposition fans singing vile and reprehensible chants about a catastrophe that ultimately connects both clubs forever.

In the second half, Alexander-Arnold's right foot was continuing to cause havoc for Forest and straight after half-time, a corner from the England international was unintentionally headed back towards the six-yard box by Niakhaté into Fabinho's path, who nodded it across goal to Jota, who headed home. There was a feeling that the goal effectively ended the game as a contest, but just four minutes later, Forest found themselves on a rare counter attack that saw Gibbs-White about 25 yards outside the Liverpool box. Gibbs-White sprayed it right for Williams on the edge of the box, whose shot took a deflection and beat Alisson in the Liverpool goal to give Forest an equaliser.

It's fair to say that wasn't in the script and suddenly, Forest had something to fight for. Williams didn't celebrate out of respect for his former club, but those in the away end certainly did as the Reds had chalked up only their sixth away goal all season. Four minutes after that, an Andrew Robertson free-kick found a bizarrely unmarked Jota, who had time to take it down on his chest, turn and shoot past Navas to restore Liverpool's lead. The Forest defence were all at sea, with two Liverpool players (including Jota) totally unmarked. It was like half the team just stopped and ball watched.

The inquest had barely finished when Ibrahima Konaté pinged a glorious ball over Williams and Worrall for Jota to get a header on goal, but Navas expertly denied him a hat-trick with a great save. Forest were back at square one, but had a secret weapon up their sleeve. Niakhaté's long throw was causing chaos in the Liverpool box and 12 minutes after Jota made it 2-1, another Niakhaté throw was poorly cleared by Liverpool and fell for Gibbs-White on the penalty spot, who leathered it towards goal and courtesy of a couple of deflections, made its way into the bottom corner.

Incredibly, it was 2-2 and once again, Forest again had something to defend – with only 25 minutes left, too. Three minutes after the equaliser though, another Alexander-Arnold free-kick caught Forest unaware and Mohammed Salah read the situation better than Freuler, getting to the ball first and giving Navas no chance. Again, Forest had folded pretty much immediately after scoring and now time was running out – but, unlike in previous games, there seemed to be a belief that they could snatch something. Another Niakhaté throw sparked carnage in the Liverpool area and after a brief game of head tennis, Worrall flicked it goalwards and Awoniyi attempted an audacious overhead kick, which narrowly went over.

It was so strange – Forest would get a throw and you could sense the panic reverberating around Anfield. Niakhaté's technique was surreal too, as he had no run-up; he just stood by the line, launched in an absolute rocket and for some reason, Liverpool couldn't defend it. Yet another Niakhaté throw was put into the box and again, Liverpool couldn't clear their lines and this time, it was nodded into substitute Johnson's path by Mangala, who successfully dinked an effort over Alisson. Agonisingly for Forest, his effort hit the bar. That was as close as Forest got and Liverpool – under instruction from a bewildered Jürgen Klopp – shut the game down, securing a 3-2 victory for his side.

Despite the defeat, the immediate reaction from a Forest perspective was very positive. Ultimately, there are ways of losing games and the manner in which Forest lost this one was admirable. They went toe to toe with one of the best sides in the country and but for the crossbar, would've left Anfield with a draw. The performance rekindled hope that survival was possible and while the result knocked Forest down a place to 19th – one point from safety – there was still a lot of football to be played yet.

They would be without McKenna for the remaining games however, as it emerged that he'd fractured his collarbone at Liverpool. This was a blow to Forest, but with a fit Niakhaté – and his long throw – in the side, they were more than covered to deal with that. They would also likely be without Shelvey, although for very, very different reasons than an injury and reasons that saw the fanbase completely turn against the former Newcastle man, to the point his Forest career was effectively over there and then.

The Telegraph reported that Shelvey had angrily confronted Cooper after being told he would be on the bench for the trip to Liverpool – one of Shelvey's former sides – on the basis that he had a calf injury and wasn't fully fit to start. As such, Cooper – who the same report highlighted was already unhappy with the six-time England international's performances in training – banished him from the matchday squad completely and told him to stay at home that weekend, rather than travel with the team to Anfield.

At a time where everyone needed to pull together, at a time where team spirit needed to be as high as possible given what was at stake, Shelvey behaved childishly and took it upon himself to openly challenge the manager – all whilst being injured. It beggared belief and Cooper was completely right to do what he did. How arrogant do you have to be to behave in such a manner? Forest were yet to win a game in which Shelvey had participated in and he's acting like that?

I suppose it shouldn't be too much of a surprise as self-awareness or humility are hardly traits associated with Shelvey. One example of this came when Shelvey publicly expressed his bewilderment that singer John Legend rejected a staggering £50k offer to perform at his wedding. Another came when Shelvey, on a night out with Lingard and Wood, met a girl and took her back to his residence, sat her down in front of a TV and showed her his highlight reel on YouTube. Yes, really.

He really doesn't do the footballer stereotype many favours and the incident with Cooper further proved it. To get anything from Liverpool, you have to hope they have a bad day and that all of your players are at 100%. You can't afford to carry any passengers or have any weaknesses out on that pitch. The fact his ego couldn't get out the way of stone cold logic – pretending like his appalling error at Villa didn't happen in the process – says everything you need to know about him.

If anything though, Shelvey's hubris further galvanised the fanbase and brought everyone closer together. As fans, the mentality was if you aren't with us, you're against us and we'll back those who are with us until the end. After all, fans knew it was them against the world before a ball was even kicked – even before the team was dismembered and pieced back together with new parts, the odds were heavily stacked against Forest. But now there were just six games left to play and the team were going to need the support from the stands more than ever for the home straight of the 2022/23 Premier League season, if the Reds were to survive.

As such, it made the midweek fixture against Brighton tantalising. A night under The City Ground lights with a rejuvenated fanbase beckoned and while the Seagulls were in great form, to the point they were only four points off fifth going into the game, no-one was writing Forest off. Especially after Brighton had just lost an FA Cup semi-final in heartbreaking fashion, going out on penalties to Manchester United after 120 gruelling minutes of football. Changes were made by Cooper, with Johnson being restored to the starting XI in place of Freuler, allowing Danilo to drop into midfield with Mangala, while Aurier came in at centre half alongside Felipe and Niakhaté.

Forest started intently and after just 10 minutes, Gibbs-White's cross was poorly dealt with by Brighton defender Pervis Estupiñán and allowed Williams to sneak in, resulting in Estupiñán tangling with the Forest defender and flooring him. Penalty given, but Johnson's effort was read brilliantly by goalkeeper Jason Steele, who dived correctly and kept it out. In a double blow, Niakhaté came off shortly afterwards with an injury, being replaced by Worrall. That save woke Brighton up and Kaoru Mitoma took it upon himself to break the deadlock when he sped down the right hand side before cutting it back for Julio Enciso about eight yards out, who connected with it excellently.

Somehow, Navas' reflexes were quick enough for him to get a glove to it and to tip it over, making a save that defied all belief. Normal goalkeepers just don't make saves like that. However, just before half-time, Navas was defying all belief once again. A Solly March effort from outside the box was pushed straight into Facundo Buonanotte's path by Navas, giving him a tap in in front of the Trent End to give Brighton the lead. The life of a goalkeeper – making save of the season and error of the season contenders in the same half of football.

The goal was yet another kick in the balls for Forest, but seconds before the break, Danilo found Awoniyi in the box, who held off his man and played it left for Lodi. Without hesitating, Lodi lashed it across the six-yard box, where it deflected off Pascal Groß and found its way past Steele. Lodi celebrated emphatically, punching the air and pulling at the Forest badge and suddenly, momentum had shifted Forest's way again. Finally, a slice of luck had gone their way and it was their turn for once to inflict a sucker punch.

After the break, they got another slice. A rapid Brighton counter attack ended up with Forest defenders sprinting helplessly towards their own goal as Buonanotte put Mitoma in one-on-one, but Mitoma – with time to pick his spot – somehow fired past the post. From that goal kick, Forest went straight up the other end and had a chance when Gibbs-White hung a cross into the box and Williams flung himself at it, but his header went wide. Unfortunately for Williams, Johnson also went for Gibbs-White's cross and accidentally booted Williams in the face, leaving him stricken on the turf.

Following a lengthy delay, Williams had to come off and was replaced by Kouyaté, as Forest switched to a 4-3-1-2 with Aurier at right back and Kouyaté as part of a three-man midfield with Danilo and Mangala. Just four minutes after the switch, Danilo won the ball on the halfway line and quickly fed Awoniyi, who laid the ball off for Danilo to run onto. After entering the box, Danilo arrowed an effort into the bottom corner, sparking huge celebrations in the ground and from Danilo himself, who celebrated his first goal in

English football by running behind the goal and pointing his fingers at the crowd.

The crowd were in full voice and aside from giving Danilo a new chant – to the tune of Spandau Ballet's 'Gold' – another chant started to ring around The City Ground with sincerity:

"30 signings, who gives a fuck?

Nottingham Forest, are staying up"

The next 20 minutes were very tense from a Forest perspective, evoking memories of Fulham away in the promotion season. As a fan, you just wanted to press fast forward and see the result, preserving some of your life expectancy in the process. In the 88th minute, a Gibbs-White corner was smashed away by Lewis Dunk's arm and unlike in the Manchester United game when Maguire did similar, VAR stepped in and for the second time in the match, the referee pointed to the spot for the home side. This time, Gibbs-White stepped up and sent Steele the wrong way, securing a 3-1 win for the Reds.

After 14 minutes of stoppage time, the roar at full time was one as much of relief as it was unbridled joy, but the blissful reaction to both 'Just Can't Get Enough' and Cooper's fist pumps told its own story. It was the first time all season that Forest had come from behind to win a game of football and after going 11 matches without a win, some must've forgotten what victory tasted like. Better yet, due to results elsewhere, the win lifted Forest out of the bottom three, leaving them one point above the drop zone.

Following the match, Cooper heaped praise on the fans and The City Ground itself, stating that, "This place oozes football soul and when it comes together on a matchday and things go well, it's such a brilliant place to be." It certainly was after that result, but out of Forest's five remaining games, three would be on the road. Simply put, in order for the Reds to survive, they would need to figure out a way to get results – even draws – away from Trentside.

First up was Brentford, who still had an outside chance of making Europe as they were only five points off fifth. Cooper only made one player change from the Brighton win, with Worrall coming in for the injured Williams, who was now out for the rest of the season with a broken jaw, allowing Aurier going to right wing back. Thankfully for Forest, Niakhaté was fine to start. The first half was very slow, with Brentford's only chance coming when Ethan Pinnock got a shot off following a poorly dealt with long throw, which Navas dealt with brilliantly.

A few minutes later and with the last action of the half pretty much, another long throw – this time from Niakhaté – was dealt with horribly, allowing Gibbs-White a shot from outside the box. The shot was blocked, but fell sweetly into Danilo's path about six yards out, with the Brazilian midfielder making no mistake to make it two goals in two games for him. For the second game running, Forest had got in a sucker punch just before the half-time whistle and had something valuable to protect.

The second half was just as cagey as the first, although Forest nearly doubled their lead in bizarre fashion. A deep Lodi free kick was headed into the sky by Niakhaté and no-one challenged the loose aerial ball and sort of stood still and watched it, so with his back to goal, Niakhaté connected with an overhead kick and forced David Raya into a smart stop. Brentford still weren't really offering much and as the game went on, it seemed like Forest were on course to make it back-to-back wins.

The Reds had very much gone into protect the lead mode, with Cooper withdrawing both Awoniyi and Johnson for Ayew and Kouyaté, sacrificing one forward for an extra defensive midfielder. With nine left to play, Kouyaté conceded a free-kick about 25 yards out and Brentford striker Ivan Toney stepped up, but rather that stand firm and block it, the wall defending the free-kick jumped out the way. Navas saw the ball late as a result and while he got a glove to it, he sort of pushed it in. Somewhat undeservedly, Brentford were level and now had their tails up with just minutes left to play.

Smelling blood, Brentford started to throw bodies forward, safe in the knowledge that Forest couldn't really hit back with what they had on the pitch. Navas immediately atoned for his half error by pulling off another miraculous save when Frank Onyeka's effort from the edge of the box deflected off Toney, as despite being wrong footed, Navas managed to get to ground quickly and prevent it going in. In the 94th minute though, Josh DaSilva cut inside of Lodi and through a sea of bodies, fired a goalbound effort that crept in at Navas' near post.

It was a cruel, cruel way to lose a game that Forest deserved a point from and really, it harked back to that defensive wall for the free-kick. It was Kouyaté who jumped out the way of it, and if he stands strong, there's no way Brentford generate the momentum to win that game 2-1. There was some criticism for Navas as well for reacting too slow for the first and being done at his near post for the second, but it wasn't entirely on him. In any case, Henderson wasn't coming back – The Independent reported that after yet another setback in his rehab, he had to go under the knife for surgery, ending his season.

It was a real shame for Henderson, who had really been taken to by the fans, but despite the surgery, the England international stopper was sticking around to see out the rest of the season. That merely highlighted his commitment to Forest, as he could've very easily just returned to Manchester United for the final few games of the campaign. Regardless of injury, there was hope among the fanbase that Forest could still find a way to bring him back to The City Ground in the summer, as he had performed admirably at times.

As a result of Leicester's draw with Everton, Forest dropped back into the bottom three on goal difference, with just four games left. Cooper was reluctant to single out individuals after the game, stating to BBC Sport that the conceded goals were, "really disappointing," but with heads inevitably dropping after the manner of that defeat, he was likely aware he'd have to do his bit to eradicate lingering disappointment by the time Forest's next game came about. With four games to go and with survival on the line, in theory all of them were huge, but this one was especially huge as 20th placed Southampton rocked up on Trentside.

Nathan Jones was long gone and instead came Rubén Sellés, who was former manager Ralph Hasenhüttl's assistant before he was axed for Jones earlier in the season. Sellés had instigated a slight fightback, with Saints notably securing a 1-0 win away at Chelsea in addition to draws against Tottenham and Arsenal, but going into the match, they were six points off safety and knew that a defeat would realistically send them down. As such, the game gave Forest the opportunity to take away one of those three relegation spots and as it was moved to a Monday night for Sky, the potential of another magical night under the City Ground lights beckoned.

Before the game, Forest had received a boost as Leicester had lost 5-3 at Fulham, so given that Leeds had already lost that weekend to Manchester City, a victory for Forest would take them above both teams and back out the relegation zone. Everton had also done their bit as well, incredibly winning 5-1 away at Brighton, but again, Forest would leapfrog them with victory. Cooper went back to the 4-3-1-2, with Yates making up a midfield three with Mangala and Danilo, while naming a very strong back four of Aurier, Felipe, Niakhaté and Lodi. Awoniyi also kept his place in the starting XI with Johnson alongside him, with Gibbs-White behind them.

There was a different feel about the game and Forest instantly made life incredibly difficult for Southampton. After 18 minutes, a rare Southampton attack broke down and Danilo pinged over a ball for Johnson, who squared it across goal for Awoniyi to finish first time. Goalkeeper Alex McCarthy was slow to react to it and maybe should've done better, but Forest weren't complaining and the roof came off. Three minutes after that, Southampton cleared a shot as far as Yates outside the box, who nodded it out left for Lodi. Lodi put a low ball in and found Danilo, who flicked it up for Awoniyi. Despite having Armel Bella-Kotchap yanking his shirt, Awoniyi span him and volleyed past McCarthy.

After conceding in quick succession so often during the season, it was now Forest inflicting the damage. Four minutes after the goal though, Gibbs-White played a loose ball back to Danilo and Southampton pounced, putting them in a three-on-two situation. Che Adams found Carlos Alcaraz, who in turn squared it for Stuart Armstrong, who made no mistake and Saints were back in the game. After that goal, the contest became more of a midfield battle – both teams had blocked shots, but nothing really clear cut in terms of chances.

Then, before half-time, Aurier threw to Gibbs-White inside the box, who flicked it for Johnson. Ainsley Maitland-Niles intercepted it, but made a pig's ear of his touch and subsequently allowed Johnson a chance to steal the ball. Before Johnson could, Maitland-Niles went to clear, but kicked Johnson instead, who was too quick for him and the referee gave a penalty for Forest. Gibbs-White stepped up, at the same end where he missed that crucial one for Sheffield United and smacked it straight down the middle, giving Forest a 3-1 lead after a breathless opening period.

Just seven minutes into the second half and with the rain lashing down, a James Ward-Prowse corner found Lyanco's head and just like that, Saints were back in the game again. For whatever reason, Forest were just incapable of making life easy for themselves. Aurier and Yates both picked up knocks so were replaced by Worrall and Kouyaté, with Worrall taking to the unfamiliar role of right back given Williams' unavailability, but much like before when Saints got a goal back, the game just became a midfield battle instead of any team gaining the upper hand and creating chances.

With 73 on the clock, Kouyaté fortuitously slipped in Johnson down the right, who fired a low ball over. Gibbs-White met it first and carefully flicked it with his right foot onto his left heel, caressing it into Danilo's path in the process with a velvet touch, who slammed home to make it 4-2 in an extraordinary game of football. It's undoubtedly one of Forest's best ever assists, as the skill levels required to pull that off, in a game of such vital importance with all the pressure surrounding it as well, are beyond the mere mortal.

It's also worth checking out the Sky Sports highlights of the game, just for Seb Hutchinson's commentary for the goal. "In it goes to Gibbs-White, DANILOOOOOOOOO" is as iconic a piece of Premier League commentary you'll get for a Forest game, potentially ever. With the two goal lead restored, Forest could breathe again and it felt like Southampton knew their race was done. Forest even had the ball in the net again when a Gibbs-White free-kick was nodded in by Felipe, who celebrated with an acrobatic side flip, but alas VAR ruled he was offside.

Four minutes into stoppage time, Navas punched it clear and Romeo Lavia challenged for the loose ball inside the box with sub Surridge, before dropping to the floor instantly as the two went for it. Surridge had faintly caught the top of Lavia's boot, which in no way warranted his dramatic fall, but the referee bought the reaction and gave a penalty. The drama wasn't over yet. Ward-Prowse stepped up and put it down the middle to make it 4-3, with just a few minutes left to play.

Five agonisingly tense minutes after the penalty, the ref blew for full time. Forest had managed to hold on and the outpour of joy and relief at full-time was palpable. They'd come out the right side of a Premier League classic and with three games to go, Forest were three points clear of the drop zone – although the reaction of the forlorn Southampton players and fans was a stark reminder that Forest couldn't get carried away. It would only take a couple of bad results for them to be feeling the same way, knowing that Championship football was calling them next season.

With three games to go, the situation was this. Southampton were on 24 points, bottom of the league and surely dead and buried given they were eight points off safety with nine points left to play for. Leeds, who had gone on an awful run since beating Forest, were 19th on 30 points – two points off safety. Leicester also had 30 points, but the Foxes were in 18th above Leeds on goal difference. Outside the relegation zone in 17th was Everton, who were two points clear sitting on 32 points, with Forest 16th, three clear on 33 points.

Wolves, West Ham and Bournemouth had all been in notable danger of going down at various points during the season, but with the finish line in sight, all three were either mathematically or realistically safe. If Forest were to join them, a lot would hinge on their away form. The last 12 points they'd taken had all been on home soil and with two out of their last three games away, something had to change. There are certainly easier places to choose for that to change than Stamford Bridge, the home of Chelsea Football Club, but that was the task ahead of Cooper and his side.

Thankfully for Forest, this wasn't the trophy guzzling Chelsea of old, but one very much in transition and one as low as 11th, which no-one had predicted going into the season. Things had gotten so bad that club legend Frank Lampard had returned as manager on an interim basis having been sacked by Everton earlier on in the season, making him Chelsea's third gaffer of the campaign. Lampard was in charge of Everton when the Reds left Goodison Park with a point back in August, so fans – including England cricket icon Stuart Broad, who was in the away end that day – were hopeful lightning could strike twice.

Forest went back to the 5-3-2 formation that served them well at Liverpool and Villa, with Johnson coming out for Worrall and despite Chelsea's riches of talent, they were finding it very difficult to create anything meaningful against a stubborn and well drilled Forest. In fact, Forest had a good chance to score when a Lodi corner found Felipe, but he headed wide. With a quarter of an hour played, Mangala brilliantly dispossessed Mateo Kovačić and the loose ball fell to Danilo, who immediately sprayed it left for Lodi. Lodi swung a ball into the box for Awoniyi, who despite being sandwiched in-between Thiago Silva and Benoît Badiashile while having goalkeeper Édouard Mendy running at him, got his head on the ball first and sent it into an empty net.

By scoring that goal, Awoniyi became the first Forest player since Bryan Roy in 1995 to score in consecutive Premier League games and while conceding that goal gave Chelsea a kick up the arse, they still couldn't fashion much. The closest they came was when Lewis Hall skipped past Aurier and put an inviting ball in for João Felix, but his header from the edge of the box was easily saved by Navas and Forest went in at half-time fully deserving their one goal lead. Straight after the break, it was almost a two goal lead as another Lodi corner found Felipe, whose flick on just evaded Niakhaté's outstretched boot at the back post.

A few minutes after that Niakhaté chance, Chelsea pushed forwards with Trevor Chalobah, who gave it to Noni Madueke on the right wing, before passing it back to Chalobah in the box. Chalobah, who hadn't been tracked by Mangala, then pinged it across goal, where it deflected kindly into Raheem Sterling's path on the penalty spot, who blasted home to equalise. One mistake is all it takes to be punished against the top sides, even when they're struggling. Chelsea now had life and five minutes after the equaliser, Ruben Loftus-Cheek ran through the midfield and fed Sterling inside the box, who sat Felipe down with a deft touch inside, before curling one into the top corner. Bang, bang.

Within a five minute period of the game, Forest had gone from limiting Chelsea to nothing and leading 1-0 to being 2-1 down. They'd picked a pretty awful time to have another implosion, but they had to dust themselves down quickly and that's exactly what they did. Just four minutes after Sterling's second, a Niakhaté throw was poorly cleared to Mangala on the edge of the box, who simply chipped a ball in for an unmarked Awoniyi to head past Mendy. VAR had a look while the celebrations were ongoing to see if Awoniyi was offside, but they adjudged that he was onside and the goal stood.

With about half an hour to play, it felt like another high-scoring thriller was on the cards, but weirdly, that didn't transpire. Instead, the rest of the game became a rather anticlimactic midfield battle, with Chelsea having a lot of the ball and doing nothing with it. By the time the ref blew for full-time, there was acceptance from all corners of the ground that a draw was a fair result and importantly for Forest, they'd managed to claim a point on the road at a crucial time in the season and elsewhere, results were kind to Forest.

Southampton had their relegation confirmed with a 2-0 home defeat to Fulham, while Everton and Leicester both suffered 3-0 defeats to Manchester City and Liverpool respectively. Given Leeds' draw with Newcastle, the Whites were now in 18th, overtaking Leicester, but still three points behind 16th placed Forest, who themselves were now two points clear of 17th placed Everton. Awoniyi stated after the Chelsea draw that the Reds had, "two cup finals left," but Forest could mathematically secure Premier League survival in front of their own fans in the penultimate gameweek. All that stood in their way was...Arsenal.

As daunting as the task seemed, it was arguable that the dreaded phrase of, "it's a good time to play them" very much applied to Arsenal. Having spent a Premier League record 248 days at the top of the league, desperately seeking to win their first title since the

2003/04 season, Arsenal had crumbled at the worst possible time. Three consecutive draws – including a draw at West Ham when they were 2-0 up and a draw at home to Southampton – had seen their lead eaten into by Manchester City, who since drawing with Forest, had won 11 league games in a row, one of which was against Arsenal.

As such, Arsenal were in a position where they had to win all of their remaining games and hoped City slipped up somewhere, but their title aspirations took a huge dent when they lost 3-0 at home to Brighton on the same weekend Forest drew at Chelsea. That defeat meant that anything but a victory at The City Ground for the Gunners and City would win the title, so with the pressure on and with their form all over the place, the prospect of Forest away – where Forest could secure survival with a win – wasn't exactly an appealing fixture.

Forest were unchanged from the draw at Chelsea, but as it was a 5:30 kick-off, fans were eagerly checking the Wolves-Everton game elsewhere. Everton drew 1-1 at Molineux, so Forest knew victory would mathematically secure survival, as neither Leicester nor Everton could reach 37 points. A huge roar greeted the players as they walked out the tunnel, with the loudest 'Mull of Kintrye' of the season yet. It felt like a final and with the sun shining and a Forza display of Giuseppe Garibaldi and a banner reading, 'Our Redshirts, you have given us your all and once more, we give you ours in return', the stage was set.

From kick-off, Arsenal had pretty much total control of the ball. They had a chance early from a corner when a headed Aurier

319

clearance went to the back post for Gabriel Jesus, but the Brazil international nodded over. Otherwise, Arsenal were toiling. Forest's 5-3-2 formation had completely restricted all space between the lines, so Arsenal were just passing it about in front of Forest with no cutting edge. After 19 minutes, Martin Ødegaard tried passing it back to the centre circle but his pass was read by Gibbs-White, who latched onto it immediately and suddenly Forest were three-on-two. Approaching the box, Gibbs-White went right to Awoniyi, who slotted past goalkeeper Aaron Ramsdale to make it 1-0.

The noise when that goal went in was off the charts. Suddenly, the prospect of survival seemed very, very real. Forest now needed to be composed and that's exactly what they were – they stuck to their gameplan and half-time came around with Arsenal still struggling for ideas. This was not the swashbuckling Arsenal that put five past Forest earlier in the season, but one mentally spent and waiting to be put out of their misery. Forest nearly did so in the second half when a Gibbs-White free-kick was nodded across goal, but after not being cleared properly, the ball fell for Felipe, whose shot was blocked behind for a corner.

Arsenal just offered nothing. Bukayo Saka had a shot on target from an angle he was never going to score from after being picked out by Ben White, but they just looked completely devoid of ideas. If anything, Forest looked more likely to score again. Gibbs-White hit the side netting after pouncing on a poor White first touch inside the box, while he also went close again in the 90th minute after dancing round half the Arsenal team before getting a shot off, but Ramsdale saved it comfortably. From Ramsdale's throw out, Gibbs-White harried it down relentlessly, eventually sending the ball out for a throw, before screaming at A Block in celebration. Forest had one hand on top of the mountain now.

There was one slight twist in the tale yet, as right at the end of the game, Navas went down with an injury and had to be subbed for Hennessey. It was like déjà vu from the play-off final, where Samba had very little to do all game and ended up needing to be replaced right at the end. Just like the play-off final, the final action of the game was a sub goalkeeper smacking the ball up the field. Forest had done it. Against all odds, against all logic and belief, against what felt like the whole world against them – they'd done it. A 1-0 win against Arsenal, with their first clean sheet in 16 games in the process, had secured Premier League survival.

The outpouring of emotion told its own story. Awoniyi dropped to his knees, arms outstretched with a huge smile on his face. Lodi – a loan player – burst into tears. Lingard, who wasn't even on the bench, was sprinting onto the pitch with Biancone, both bouncing around in jubilation, while Henderson was banging his crutches against the floor in celebration. As for Cooper, you could see the relief on his face. You could see the happiness in his eyes as 'Just Can't Get Enough' boomed around the ground. This was the hardest challenge of his career by a country mile and he'd accomplished it with a game to spare.

All of the players made their way onto the pitch for their lap of appreciation for the fans, with all of them embracing each other. Even a very awkward looking Shelvey got a cuddle from Cooper before he did his fist pumps, which were met with roars so loud, it was like a goal had been scored. Marinakis also made his way pitchside to soak it all in, before giving Sky Sports a rare interview, in which he stated that he, "took a wise decision" in keeping Cooper and said that, "To change a coach, you need to bring someone better and to be available at the time."

It was a bit bold of him to praise himself for sticking with Cooper when the club reportedly actively sought out replacements at two different points in the season, but ultimately, Marinakis was right. It was a wise decision, there wasn't anyone better to replace him and the proof was in the pudding. No-one else would've had that bond with his players, no-one else would've kept the supporters onside amidst the turbulence, no-one else would've galvanised a bunch of strangers and turned them into a band of brothers. This success was on Cooper and he deserved every bit of adulation he received.

In typical Cooper fashion though, he didn't want the onus to be on him. Speaking to Sky Sports immediately after the game, he said that it was a day for the supporters and a day for the players, while saying that he was just pleased that staying up gives Forest a chance to keep building and to keep working towards getting the club back into a bracket where it belongs. When pressed on a personal level, he found the positives in having a rough season by saying that you need to suffer in order to get to where you want to be.

Not long after that interview, Niakhaté was doing his press duties, only for Cooper to gatecrash them. What came next was very touching and perhaps epitomises the importance of overcoming adversity and of course, togetherness. The two cuddled, before Cooper praised Niakhaté's attitude to recovering from his injury and the mentality he showed when he was back in the side, then declared how proud he was of him. In return, Niakhaté thanked Cooper for his confidence in him, to which Cooper quipped, "We did this together."

Being together also helps shut out the outside noise and with Forest that season, there had been an awful lot of it. Straight after the game, fans were making sure journalists and experts were made to eat their words and took great glee in doing so. Some took this much better than others. For example, Luke Edwards at The Telegraph – who went on a tirade after Forest lost at Manchester United – had his words put back to him, to which he replied, "Steve Cooper deserves a huge amount of credit for making it work. Really happy Forest have stayed up. Proper football club," which was rather magnanimous of him.

By contrast, Adam Crafton at The Athletic was not so happy his prediction of Forest becoming QPR 2012 didn't come to fruition. "Leeds, Southampton and Leicester all going down would be quite a thumping rebuke to the model of cashing in on talent and recruiting largely young potential. Wonder if it'll make other clubs think more short-term," he tweeted. "Be more Forest. Sign everyone." You could feel the sarcasm and anguish dripping off the page and seeing those with egg on their face was just as satisfying as seeing Forest get over the line.

Back in the changing room, it was a full blown party. It wasn't quite the carnage from a year earlier, but the happiness and joy was off the scale. At some point, someone put 'Waka Waka' by Shakira on and the whole team was filmed belting it out in unison, which fans didn't take long to pick up on. "30 signings, who gives a fuck, Nottingham Forest, are staying up" was revamped to, "Tsamina mina, eh eh, Waka Waka eh eh, 30 signings who gives a fuck, the Reds are staying up!"

There was still one game to go, in the form of Crystal Palace away, but everyone was at ease about it. There were eyes on who out of Leeds, Everton or Leicester would join Southampton in being relegated, but as the Forest fans couldn't join the players for their party in the changing room, the plan was to bring the party to the away end at Selhurst Park. Fans ventured down to Croydon in fancy dress, Cooper masks and bearing inflatables, chanting their version of 'Waka Waka' non-stop, as fans sought to enjoy a stress free game of Premier League football for the first time all season.

Cooper made two changes, with Hennessey coming in for the injured Navas and Johnson coming in for Danilo, who picked up a knock in the Arsenal win. As such, Forest went back to their 3-4-1-2 formation, as they sought to get on the front foot a bit more. Palace started very well and should've scored when Michael Olise swung a ball in for Eberechi Eze, who took it down brilliantly before firing goalwards, but it hit his own player in Jordan Ayew on the line. The rebound fell straight for Will Hughes, but his rasping drive was well saved by Hennessey.

With half an hour on the clock, Odsonne Édouard tried to play a safe ball back, but gave it straight to Gibbs-White who, with the outside of his boot, pinged a raking pass straight into Awoniyi's path. Despite that pass playing him in one-on-one, Awoniyi seemed to stumble over the ball, but kept his footing, twisted past a recovering Joachim Andersen and belted home with his left foot, making it 10 league goals for him in his debut season and making him the first Forest player since Stan Collymore in 1995 to score in four consecutive Premier League matches.

If the away end's 'Waka Waka' rendition wasn't loud enough before, it certainly was now. It was literally all you could hear until the half-time whistle, with a celebratory mood very much on the menu at Selhurst Park. After the break though, Palace stepped up the pressure and got their rewards with 25 to play, as an Olise cross was flicked in by Hughes via a Boly deflection. This must've meant a lot to the former Derby man, as in addition to his allegiances towards Forest's enemy, the away end were gleefully on his case whenever he touched the ball.

After that, bar one Eze volley that stung Hennessey's palms, both teams seemed pretty content with a point and saw the game out with little incident. The result meant that Forest finished 16th on 38 points – four points clear of 18th placed Leicester and seven clear of 19th placed Leeds, both of whom joined Southampton in being relegated. At full-time, the players joined in with the away end party, singing 'Waka Waka' with them and being serenaded by the Forest faithful, while letting their hair down – as shown by Johnson holding up an inflatable sex doll like it was a trophy.

It had been a bruising year, but against all odds, it ended in all smiles. Marinakis and his entourage made their way over to join in too, with the owner hugging Cooper before a group photo was taken in front of the away end. After 23 years away, all fans wanted was for their return to not be a flying visit and that's exactly what Cooper, with Marinakis' financial backing, delivered. Cooper's second miracle on Trentside was complete and now, the task would be to build from this platform and establish Forest as a steady, midtable side. It would be another big challenge for Forest, but who could write them off now?

CHAPTER THIRTEEN – ANOTHER BUSY SUMMER

With survival secured, Forest could look at where to improve in order to become a more established Premier League side and really, there was quite a bit to improve upon. In fact, looking at the stats, it was a miracle in its own right that Forest survived. With 38 goals scored, only four teams scored less than the Reds, while with 68 conceded, only three teams conceded more. Their goal difference of -30 was the third worst in the league, while their form on the road was simply appalling. With 11 goals, no team scored fewer away from home than Forest, who won just once on their travels – also a league worst.

Forest had also conceded three goals or more on 10 separate occasions in the league, while in seven different games, Forest conceded at least two goals within a 10 minute spell. However, it wasn't all doom and gloom and there was ample evidence to suggest Forest belonged at Premier League level – namely at home. Forest had the 10th best home record in the league, taking 30 of their 38 points on home soil. Had Forest replicated their home form on the road, they would've finished with 60 points – the same total as 8th placed Tottenham. Clearly, there was something there for Cooper to work with.

That was, of course, if Cooper remained. Despite Forest fans claiming he should've been in the Manager of the Year conversations, the Daily Mail reported that Crystal Palace were keen to appoint him as their manager that summer, in the event Roy Hodgson returned to retirement. In addition, The Athletic reported that Leeds United – despite relegation to the Championship – seriously toyed with the idea of approaching Cooper, as they felt he could be prised away from Forest due to the intense working environment Marinakis encourages. In the end, Palace stuck with Hodgson and Leeds opted for Daniel Farke, with Cooper happy to kick on at Forest.

Ultimately for Cooper, the way Forest played in the 2022/23 season was very much against how he felt a football team should play in an ideal world. but he was hardly given ideal circumstances. As such, he set Forest up that way in order to survive. It worked and now the challenge would be for Forest to build on that and to start playing the type of front foot football that Cooper cherished on a more regular basis, which meant that despite signing so many players the previous summer, recruitment would again be a key factor as Forest sought to fix their issues.

One early recruit would help with that, as coach Steven Reid returned to the Forest set-up. This was a huge boost for Cooper, with Reid playing a key role in the promotion season, but from a player perspective, there were question marks over just how much Forest could spend. Forest had spent at least £150m in the 2022/23 season, as Marinakis put his money where his mouth was when it came to backing up his ambition. The downside though was that that spree would've put Forest very close to their PSR limit, which was determined over a three-year period. According to The Athletic, chairman Nicholas Randall QC had assured everyone that Forest were fine, but that still didn't stop teams from testing the waters for players – namely Johnson.

On the PSR deadline day of June 30, the final day clubs can include transfers in their accounts for the three-year period, 90min reported that Atlético Madrid submitted a bid of around £43m for the Wales forward, but The Athletic added that any move was dependent on Atlético selling first. On that basis, negotiations with Forest – who pushed their luck and asked for £55m – ceased. Despite Randall's confidence, it did seem that without a major sale, Forest wouldn't be able to strengthen in the way they'd like to for fear of breaching their PSR limit.

There were still notable outgoings though, with Lingard, Ayew, Colback, Cafu and Lyle Taylor all departing at the expiration of their contracts, while Will Swan was sold to Mansfield. In addition, Lodi, Navas and Henderson all returned to their parent clubs. Kanurić was also let go, making his signing very bizarre, while Jordan Smith was released. The Lingard experiment didn't work – his last appearance for Forest was the 2-0 loss against his former club Manchester United, but despite not always playing, he seemed a genuinely good addition to the dressing room and a key component in the squad's harmony.

It's also arguable signing Lingard raised the profile of the club sufficiently to attract some of the other signings – including Lodi and Navas. Navas' situation was straightforward as he would be returning to PSG, but there was initially hope that Forest could keep Lodi, who had become an integral part of the side. However, there were complications. According to Marca, the option to buy Lodi was only valid until March – which Forest couldn't activate as they had no idea what league they'd be in – while they also found Atletico's suggested fee of £26m too high and wanted to renegotiate.

Unfortunately for Forest, in the summer break, Lodi's agent spoke to GE Globo and said that the Brazil international wanted to compete at the highest level and return to the Champions League, which naturally put Forest at a bit of a disadvantage. In the end, Lodi moved to French giants Marseille, which was a huge shame and meant that Forest had to buy another left back with some rather big shoes to fill. As for Henderson, despite returning to Manchester United, the England goalkeeper was still very much an active target, so it remained to be seen whether his departure was a temporary or a permanent one.

Really though, the saddest departure was Colback, who'd been a fantastic servant for the club and was a key player in the promotion season, in addition to more than playing his part helping the club staying up. Though many were upset to see him leave – and Cafu for that matter – these felt like the kind of decisions the club needed to take in order to try and reach that next step. As for Ayew and Taylor, those departures made sense. Ayew hadn't shown anything to warrant an extended deal and while all fans will be forever grateful for Bristol City away, it was the right time for Taylor to go.

Behind the scenes, there were changes too. Lee Charnley had departed the club after a year, which perhaps wasn't a great shock given he wasn't made CEO when Murphy left, but more shockingly, Gary Brazil departed. Brazil had given the club 10 years of service and his exit didn't please supporters. Forest had so much to be grateful for when it came to Brazil, whose development of players had helped them massively from a financial aspect. Under Brazil's tutelage, players like Oliver Burke, Ben Brereton Díaz, Matty Cash, Ben Osborn, Arvin Appiah and Anel Ahmedhodžić had come through and been sold, earning Forest at least £50m in transfer fees.

In addition to those players, Johnson, Worrall and Yates had all come through and were now first team regulars, while players like Mighten and Smith made big contributions to the first team after stepping up from academy level. The Athletic reported the board debated not renewing his services and that in itself made his situation untenable, leaving a bitter taste in the mouth as someone who had done so much for the club – and was still able to offer a significant amount – shouldn't have been moved on at all, let alone that ruthlessly.

Helping to replace Brazil's input would be Craig Mulholland, who was previously academy director at Rangers, while assistant academy manager Chris McGuane would also have a more hands-on role as a result. Brazil would be a loss for the club, but otherwise from an incoming perspective, things were very slow. Wood was formally announced as a permanent signing, as per the obligation in his loan, while Aurier signed a year extension, which was celebrated among the fans. The 30-year-old's form at right back was instrumental in keeping the Reds afloat, so it felt very sensible to give him another year.

In fact, things were so slow that Forest began their pre-season without any new signings. This was less than ideal for Cooper, especially with an early injury to Felipe and an attempt to woo Fulham winger Willian ending in a last second change of heart from the Brazilian, but while The Athletic reported that the plan was for five or six quality signings, it seemed clear that Forest had to sell before they could buy. That sale would likely be Johnson, given he was Forest's most sellable asset and as he was an academy graduate, all monies banked from his transfer would count towards PSR.

Johnson registered eight goals and three assists in his debut Premier League campaign, so the thought of losing one of Forest's most potent attackers – with all of his best years still to come – wouldn't have exactly been something for Cooper to celebrate. Things weren't exactly getting easier for Cooper, either. To celebrate Forest leaving kit manufacturer Macron for adidas in the biggest sponsorship deal in the club's history, also as per The Athletic, the club did a special kit release at Nottingham Castle.

It was quite the event, with all three kits being unveiled and with Cooper, Danilo, Worrall and Awoniyi in attendance. Switching to adidas made a lot of sense and not just from a commercial level – the brand is synonymous with Forest as they were kit manufacturer during Brian Clough's glory days, so the event generated a lot of excitement and chairman Randall was there too. Rather embarrassingly though, Randall got hold of a microphone for a speech and during said speech, proceeded to joke about Cooper's clothing choices and about Worrall's footballing ability.

According to The Athletic, Cooper laughed off the quip about his clothes. However, he was absolutely livid Randall went for Worrall. The chairman told the audience, made up of sponsors, guests and fans, that Worrall had dreams of becoming a professional cricketer as a child, before saying that halfway through the season, everyone from a Forest perspective wished he'd became one, too. Cooper didn't see the funny side and felt Randall had mortified his captain in a public setting, which caused a lot of friction behind the scenes.

The new kits would get a runout for the first time in Nottingham, although not at The City Ground. Forest hopped over the River Trent for a friendly with Notts County, which they won 1-0 thanks to a Hwang Ui-Jo goal, before jetting off to Spain for a pre-season camp. Prior to the Notts game, Forest had lodged a bid for Ibrahim Sangaré of PSV Eindhoven, which was rejected. Forest had wanted Sangaré a year earlier, but couldn't finance a move for the defensive midfielder. According to ESPN, the player would need some convincing to sign, but there was clearly optimism that a move could be done from a Forest perspective.

In Spain, the Reds lost 1-0 to Valencia before beating Levante 2-1, with Yates and Danilo getting on the scoresheet – although Awoniyi was sent off, which takes some doing in a friendly. The trip to Spain had come at a cost, though. During the Valencia game, Niakhaté went off injured and it turned out to be a dislocated elbow, which would rule him out for at least a month. With Felipe still injured, Cooper now had his best centre back pairing on the sidelines, which added yet another hurdle to his pre-season.

Upon their return from Spain though, the transfer wheels started turning. 26-year-old Nigeria international full back Ola Aina signed on a free transfer from Torino, while a few days later, winger Anthony Elanga checked in from Manchester United for a £15m fee, as per the BBC. The Guardian had reported that Forest had beaten off heavy competition from Everton for the 21-year-old Sweden international and both players were renowned for their speed, making them valuable assets to the Forest squad, while Elanga's potential was very exciting for fans.

Forest were optimistic that Elanga wouldn't be the only arrival from United, as the clubs were still trying to get Henderson back. This had become complicated according to the Manchester Evening News due to the Red Devils surprisingly releasing David De Gea, meaning Henderson was just one of two goalkeepers at the club and as such, was needed for the early stages of pre-season. However, with United signing goalkeeper Andre Onana from Inter Milan, there was hope that a deal could be struck, with Henderson especially keen to return to The City Ground.

Aina at least partially solved the left back issue as despite preferring to play as a right back, he was very comfortable playing on the left, but the goalkeeper issue was something of a major concern for Forest. The Reds' current goalkeeping pool was Hennessey, George

Shelvey from the academy and Horvath – who despite helping Luton Town to promotion via the play-offs had returned, with the Hatters looking elsewhere for a goalkeeper. In effect, this was two backups and a kid. As such, so Henderson's arrival would be very timely, if Forest could get it over the line.

One person who wouldn't be there to see whether that happened or not though was Surridge, who was sold to MLS side Nashville SC for around £5m, according to The Tennessean. It was hard not to feel sorry for Surridge, who would've likely offered more than Ayew towards the back end of the season, but it's equally true that he seemed to struggle with Premier League football. A move was therefore maybe best for all parties, but it was still a sad departure and Surridge's contribution to promotion will remain part of Forest folklore forever.

Prior to Forest's next friendly against Leeds, Forest were rocked when news emerged that former players Trevor Francis and Chris Bart-Williams had passed away on the same day. Both had left their mark on the club, with England international Francis a Miracle Man who scored the winning goal for Forest in the 1979 European Cup final, while Bart-Williams played 245 games for the Reds and was a beloved character in addition to being a fantastic footballer. Both were devastatingly sad losses, with the club wearing black armbands in their honour for the friendly.

The friendly itself didn't go to plan, with Forest losing 2-0 and the day after, Brentford tested Forest's resolve again with a bid of over £35m for Johnson, which was rejected as Forest valued Johnson at

£50m, according to The Guardian. The Telegraph later expanded on this bid, which strangely was submitted via WhatsApp, claiming that it was £35m up front, £5m in add-ons and a 10% sell on fee. The same report also stated that Cooper had informed Johnson he may well be sold, which suggested the Wales forward's days were numbered.

Soon after, Forest were back in action and interestingly given the Sangaré story, away at PSV Eindhoven. Forest lost 1-0, but clips on social media emerged of Sangare's car being mobbed by Forest fans asking him to sign and you'd suspect it was a topic of conversation between the two clubs after the match. There were more outgoings as Bowler and Laryea went on loans to Cardiff City and Vancouver Whitecaps respectively, while Ojeda's temporary spell at Real Salt Lake proved successful as the MLS side signed him for £3m, as per The Telegraph.

Next up for Forest in pre-season was Rennes, which was a debacle. Cooper went with an experimental side and the French side ran out 5-0 winners, with Horvath in particular looking very ropey. Pre-season results are mostly irrelevant, given that they're fundamentally about fitness and tactics, but some fans were growing very concerned. The Reds' final pre-season friendly was away at Eintracht Frankfurt and in a game Forest clearly took a lot more seriously, they drew 0-0. Really, they should've won 1-0 after a McKenna header was inexplicably ruled out, but despite the result, it was clear Forest had work to do.

Forest went with a 5-2-2-1 formation, with Danilo and Gibbs-White – deservedly voted as the club's 2022/23 Player of the Season – on the wings with Johnson up front, which didn't really seem to get the best out of any of the three. While George Shelvey played in goal and delivered a hell of a performance, Forest badly needed a goalkeeper. With a week to go before the season started, it was fast becoming a critical situation and it wasn't helped by the fact the Henderson deal was becoming a transfer saga in its own right. The Sun had reported that Manchester United were reluctant to let Henderson go for a medical at Forest, as they felt there was a genuine threat he could reaggravate his injury during it.

Forest were willing to wait until the end of the window when his injury had fully healed, but still needed a goalkeeper. As such, they turned to Arsenal's Matt Turner, with the 29-year-old United States of America international joining for a £7m fee, as per the Daily Mail. Signing Turner highlighted just how desperate Forest were for a goalkeeper, especially for that fee. A year earlier, Arsenal signed him for £5.5m according to talkSPORT and in that year, he didn't play a single Premier League game and repeatedly looked dodgy in the Europa League games he featured in, costing them several goals in the process.

Despite all of this, according to The Athletic, Cooper had personally told Turner that he would be his number one. That in itself raised doubts over Henderson's move, but at least in the short term, Forest had a goalkeeper that Cooper was happy with. For Cooper's sake though, Turner needed to be good – especially after Shelvey, Ayew and Wood, all players he wanted, failed to make an impact after signing in January. Meanwhile, on the same day Turner signed, Cook departed for QPR for an undisclosed fee. Much like Colback and

Surridge, it was sad to see another prominent promotion hero leave, especially one as likeable as Cook, but like the others, it was the right decision.

Ironically for Turner, his first game would be away at Arsenal, with Forest given a particularly rough start to the 2023/24 season. Superstitious fans would have noted that in the 1998/99 season, Forest's last in the Premier League before Cooper took them back, they opened that campaign with an away day at Arsenal too, which ended in defeat. Prior to the game, Cooper revealed that in addition to Niakhaté and Felipe being out, Awoniyi had picked up an ankle knock and would also be out, which also explained his absence for the Eintracht Frankfurt game.

Cooper also told the media that, "We're in a position with our squad where we would like it to be a bit different," which was quite telling. Thankfully for Cooper, there were still a few weeks left of the window, but bedding in any new signings would be done without the comfort blanket of pre-season, which made life more difficult. Pre-season in itself had been a very challenging one, but with Forest the other side of it now, all eyes were on Arsenal and Cooper lined up with the same 5-2-2-1 formation on display in Frankfurt, with Aurier, Boly, Worrall, McKenna and Aina making up a back five, Mangala and Yates starting as deeper midfielders and with Gibbs-White and Danilo supporting Johnson up front.

In a huge boost for Forest, both Niakhaté and Awoniyi were on the bench. Whether either would play would be another matter, but with new signing Elanga on the bench also, the substitutes looked notably stronger than they did a year earlier for the trip to Newcastle. As expected, Arsenal had a lot of the ball early on, but Forest were stubborn and after 10 minutes, a Boly header near halfway found its way through the Arsenal defence and left Johnson one-on-one with the goalkeeper, but with the goal at his mercy, Johnson failed to even hit the target.

15 minutes later, that miss proved very costly. Gabriel Martinelli managed to squeeze a ball through Danilo and Aurier to Eddie Nketiah inside the box, who moved inside and got a shot away, with his effort deflecting off Worrall and going in. Six minutes later, Gibbs-White lost the ball cheaply in a defensive area, allowing Ben White to feed Bukayo Saka on the edge of the box, with the England international proceeding to rifle one in the top corner. Once again, Forest had conceded two goals in quick succession and once again, they'd conceded a goal from outside the area.

In the second half, chances were more at a premium for both teams. Turner tipped a deflected Declan Rice effort from outside the box onto the post, while Boly fluffed a free header from a corner, but otherwise, not much happened. Forest made changes, bringing on both Awoniyi and Elanga and immediately, they had an impact. An Arsenal corner was headed away into Awoniyi's path and he burst forwards, before playing it left into space for Elanga to run onto. Elanga shot up the pitch down the left hand side, with Arsenal defenders trailing in his wake unable to catch him, before he cut it back for Awoniyi to score.

The Emirates went deathly silent. It was a superb counter attacking goal and all of a sudden, Forest had momentum. Immediately after the goal, Elanga zipped down the left wing again and cut it back to Gibbs-White on the edge of the box, whose powerful first-time effort flashed just over. After that scare, Arsenal got their heads together and saw the game out, but it was a brilliant response from Forest and a huge improvement from many of the away displays Forest had conjured up the year before. Despite showing familiar frailties, it seemed very much a step in the right direction – especially against an elite side.

Forest's next match would be a lot easier, at least on paper, as they hosted newly promoted Sheffield United. It was the first meeting between the two sides since that dramatic play-off semi-final and pantomime villains Paul Heckingbottom and Jack Robinson were both still there, which added to the occasion. Forest found themselves in a rare position where they went into a Premier League match as favourites and it would, in theory, allow Cooper to try and play some of that front foot football he craved.

Going into the game though, Cooper's focus was on matters more important than football. A few months prior, when Forest were in their off-season, the city of Nottingham suffered a period of darkness. Three residents were stabbed to death; two 19-year-old students named Barnaby Weller and Grace O'Malley-Kumar and a 65-year-old named Ian Coates. Straight away, Marinakis and Cooper wanted to make sure Forest would do whatever they could to help the community recover from an awful tragedy and when it became clear that Coates was a Forest fan, Cooper took it upon himself to get involved.

According to The Athletic, Cooper got hold of Worrall and world featherweight boxing champion Leigh Wood, another Nottingham lad who is frequently seen at Forest games, before arranging for the pair to come to his training ground office and meet Coates' three sons in James, Lee and Darren. There, the three relatives spoke about their father at length for an hour, explaining how he was at both European Cup finals and had a tattoo of the club's badge on his leg, before Worrall took Coates' three grandchildren out for a kickabout.

"We just wanted to let the family know we were there for them and find out if there was anything we could do," Cooper told The Athletic. "If they feel they were supported and that it has helped them, that gives me a lot of joy personally." Forest's involvement didn't stop there, as Yates and Cook both donated generously to an online appeal to help cover funeral expenses, while two days after the tragedy, a vigil was held at Old Market Square. There, James, Lee and Darren all wore Forest shirts, while many of the 7000 in attendance were also wearing Forest shirts, at Lee's behest.

For the Sheffield United game, James, Lee and Darren would be watching from the director's box, with Cooper keen to stress to them that their visit to the training ground wasn't a one-time thing – he genuinely wanted them to feel that their involvement was everlasting. Cooper's actions told their own story as to what he was like as a person, with one of Nottingham's favourite adopted sons no doubt hoping the trio's visit went as well as it possibly could do amidst the circumstances.

Much like the games in the Championship, Forest lined up with a 3-4-1-2 formation, with Yates making way for Awoniyi and Williams coming in for Aina to play left wing back. This enabled Danilo to drop into a midfield two and pretty much straight from kick-off, Forest surged forwards and Danilo nodded a ball towards Johnson, which promotion hero Max Lowe – back at Sheffied United – missed completely, allowing Johnson to dart into the box. Johnson then passed back to Aurier, who swung in a superb cross for Awoniyi to head in and to become only the second Forest player after Stan Collymore to score in six consecutive Premier League games. 124 seconds after kick-off and Forest were 1-0 up.

For the next 30 minutes, Forest looked every bit an established Premier League side. They were faster, stronger and frankly, much better than their opponents, who looked hopelessly out of their depth. However, Forest couldn't quite get that second goal and towards the end of the first half, Sheffield United started to gain confidence and dig in a bit – if they could take it to half time at only 1-0, they at least had something to build from. And that's exactly what happened. Three minutes after half-time, a Sheffield United corner was cleared to the outside the box for Gustavo Hamer, no-one closed him down and he whipped an absolute beauty into the top right corner.

For the second game running, Forest had conceded a goal from outside the box. Much like Saka's goal, it was an excellent hit from

Hamer, but again, a familiar problem was exploited and suddenly, it was Sheffield United who looked more likely to snatch a winner. They nearly did when a hopeful punt forwards saw both McKenna and Worrall challenge for the same ball with neither getting it and instead, allowing Bénie Traoré to run through on goal. Thankfully for Forest, Turner kept Traoré's effort out well, but it was very alarming how they'd just fallen to bits against a side that were expected to be cannon fodder that season.

With just six minutes left to play, Cooper took Awoniyi off for Wood and five minutes after his introduction, Aurier picked him out with an inch perfect cross that Wood simply steered home with his head. Somewhat fortuitously, Forest had snatched a winner. The reaction at full time – even to 'Just Can't Get Enough' – was more relief than joy, as Forest had very much gotten away with one. Afterwards, Cooper stressed the importance of the win and said Forest were the only team who, "played the real football in the game," which he wasn't exactly wrong about, but equally, he'd surely be concerned by Forest's second half display.

Before Forest's next match, there was some activity on the transfer front as Scarpa and Richards were both sent on loan to Olympiacos. It was clear that Scarpa wasn't Cooper's choice, so that made sense, but it was great to see Richards finally had a chance to play some football again, after a frankly horrendous injury ordeal. Initially, Cooper claimed Richards wouldn't be out for "months and months and months", but unfortunately for both Richards and Forest, that's exactly what happened and the challenges Richards had to overcome were remarkable.

Richards took to his Instagram to explain that five months after his fracture, one of the metal pins in his leg needed removing as it was causing him discomfort and when he recovered from that, he tried to get back to fitness a bit too hard and after a scan, found out he had a hernia on both sides, ruling him out for the 2022/23 season. A fresh start to play some football away from the Premier League glare was exactly what he needed, so that deal worked well for everyone.

Elsewhere, Dräger was sold to FC Basel on an undisclosed fee, ending that chapter, while in a transfer that highlighted just how much ground there now was between the two rivals, Fornah crossed the A52 to sign for League One Derby. One minute, both clubs were jostling for East Midlands supremacy in the Championship, the next, Forest were sending Derby their academy graduates they didn't think would make the cut at Premier League level. How times change. There were incomings too, as World Cup winning right back Gonzalo Montiel checked in on loan from Sevilla, with an option to make the deal permanent.

While there was excitement a World Cup winner had signed for Forest, other fans were uneasy from a moral standpoint. The 26-year-old Argentina defender, who scored the winning penalty in the 2022 World Cup final penalty shootout, was under investigation by Argentinian authorities for alleged rape. While no charges had been brought against him, some fans were uncomfortable that Forest had signed a player with that hanging over him. The Athletic reached out to Forest for comment, to which they responded, "The club has conducted due diligence and we are fully satisfied following conversations with his representatives."

In addition to Montiel, Forest also signed Brazil U20 captain Andrey Santos on loan from Chelsea, with big things expected of the midfielder. There was one slight problem, however. According to The Athletic, Cooper had no idea Forest had signed Santos until he showed up at the training ground. While it's true a head coach in modern football will have less say on the players that come in, it's quite an ask to just sign someone and not tell them about it. One thing Cooper was aware of however, was that Syrianos was back in a consultancy role, with Marinakis presumably accepting he was too hasty to dispense of Syrianos' services less than a year earlier.

This was a huge boost for Forest as really, Syrianos shouldn't have been axed to begin with and with the recruitment mastermind back in the picture, the Reds could really focus on getting in the quality required to kick on. Next up for Forest was another difficult away game in the shape of Manchester United, with Cooper boldly sticking to the 3-4-2-1 formation and only making one change, with Aina coming in for Williams at left wing back. Montiel was on the bench for the occasion, while on the opposing bench was Henderson, who got a warm reception from the away end.

Pretty much from kick-off, United won a corner, but from that corner, the ball was cleared out and headed forwards by Gibbs-White into Awoniyi's path. Awoniyi knocked it beyond Marcus Rashford and two other United defenders, before sprinting onto it and somehow finding himself one-on-one with Andre Onana. The striker composed himself, sat Onana down and rolled the ball into the corner to give Forest a very unlikely lead and to become the first Forest player to score in seven consecutive Premier League games.

Two minutes later, a Gibbs-White free kick out wide deflected off Lisandro Martínez and onto Boly's head, giving Onana no chance. With four minutes gone at Old Trafford, Forest were 2-0 up.

Being in the away end, it was like a 'someone pinch me, this can't be real' moment. Weirdly though, after the second goal, there was a sense of unease among the away end that this was likely going to be as good as it got and 13 minutes later, those fears rang true. A Bruno Fernandes shot from distance was parried back into play by Turner and straight to Anthony Martial, who quickly gave it to Rashford. The England international then got past Aurier and fizzed a low ball across for Christian Eriksen to tap in from.

Otherwise though, Forest held United off well. They could've gone 3-1 up when Johnson burst into the box and cut it back for Gibbs-White, but his goalbound shot struck Awoniyi and United cleared. However, the overriding feeling was that by hook or by crook, United would find a way to restore order. Just seven minutes after half-time, Fernandes caught everyone out with a free-kick as he went sideways to Rashford, who under no pressure, chipped it to the back post for Fernandes to run onto. Fernandes, who'd escaped Johnson's attention, simply nodded it across the six-yard box for Casemiro, who couldn't miss.

United now had their tails up and Turner had to be on red alert to keep out a curling Antony effort, but with 25 to play, the game changed drastically. A long ball caught the Forest backline out and Worrall hauled down Fernandes, which referee Stuart Attwell – officiating his first Forest match since his assistant referee's howler at

Bournemouth arguably cost the Reds automatic promotion – brandished a red card, deeming Worrall to be the last man. However, replays showed that Worrall wasn't the last man and that there was a covering defender, so it should've been downgraded to a yellow.

It wasn't and nine minutes later, Forest had more reason to be furious with Attwell. Rashford knocked the ball past Danilo and the midfielder half dangled a leg out, which Rashford promptly jumped into. Attwell couldn't wait to give a penalty and VAR had no interest in overturning it, allowing Fernandes to step up and give United a 3-2 lead. Right at the death, there was still time for one more twist when Elanga, who'd come on as a sub, rampaged down the left and pulled a ball across goal for another sub in Wood, but it was just fractionally ahead of Wood's outstretched leg and the chance for a 3-3 draw went.

Forest's mood at full time was not pleasant. Cooper told Sky Sports he had to bite his tongue over his thoughts on the officials, but The Telegraph reported that the club went one step further and lodged an official complaint with PGMOL over Attwell's officiating. To make matters worse, United had agreed to sell Henderson to Crystal Palace. Despite Forest seeking several types of deals for Henderson, including loans as there were concerns over his injury according to The Athletic, United eventually sold to Palace for a £15m fee. For the second year running, Forest had complicated dealings with United that led to a player seemingly keen to sign moving elsewhere.

Next up was a Carabao Cup game against Burnley and after reaching the semi-finals the year before, optimism was high that Forest could embark on another cup run. Montiel, Elanga and Andrey Santos all made their first starts for the club, while Niakhaté was also fit to start after his injury. There was no Worrall however, after he received awful news that his uncle, Sergeant George Saville, had sadly passed away after being hit by a train while helping a man in distress on the tracks.

Cooper told ITV that they were giving Worrall their unconditional support behind the scenes and that the club were ready to help with whatever he needed, stressing that family comes first and football second. There was a minute's applause for Sergeant Saville ahead of the Burnley game, with Worrall in the stands watching on. The game itself was far from a classic, with neither side creating much of note. Forest's best chance came when Santos sent Elanga down the wing brilliantly and his cross found Yates, but his header went wide.

In the 90th minute, with penalties seemingly a guarantee, Yates and Aurier both let Sander Berge run past them, as Berge moved towards the area before picking out Jóhann Berg Gudmundsson out wide. Gudmundsson's ball across was blocked by Santos, but looped up in the air and allowed Josh Brownhill to head it into the six-yard box. Boly missed the header completely, with the ball falling for Zeki Amdouni, who couldn't miss. Just like that, Forest's Carabao Cup venture was over before it started.

Johnson came on as a sub in the game, suggesting that no exit for him was imminent, but the next day, in addition to finally securing a front of shirt sponsor in Asian betting company Kaiyun Sports, Forest signed 21-year-old Brazilian defender Murillo from

Corinthians for around £15m, as per the BBC. Murillo, a left-footed centre back, was very highly thought of in Brazil, but signing him did suggest that someone was on their way out. In addition, BBC also reported that Arsenal left wing back Nuno Tavares was very close to signing on loan, with The Athletic reporting that he was a Cooper target, as he wanted pace down both sides with Tavares and Aina.

Where this left Williams was another matter entirely. Effectively a year after signing for £17m, he was now fourth choice right back, behind Aina, Montiel and Aurier. According to The Telegraph, Leeds were interested, but as of yet, there was nothing doing. The day after that was deadline day and suddenly, everything starting to happen – and happen very, very quickly. Tavares was announced early on in the morning, but the headlines were that Forest had accepted a bid of £47.5m from Tottenham for Johnson, as per The Telegraph. The Telegraph also reported that Brentford had bid again, this time £40m, but it got to a point where Forest had point blank refused to sell to them.

Whether Johnson would've even gone to Brentford anyway is another matter, as it didn't really signify a forward step – Spurs however, did. Johnson was training as normal when the bid was accepted, before being taken out of training to head down to London to complete a move. The deal was bittersweet. On the one hand, Forest had got a club record sale by some distance for quite possibly their best ever modern day academy graduate – on the other, they were losing not only a promotion hero, but someone so integral to the team.

It was very sad, but ultimately, with where Forest were in the food chain, they were always liable to their best players being poached by the elite sides. Replacing him would be a very tough task, but at least Forest had the money to try and do so – and become a better team in the process. Joining Johnson in departing the club would be O'Brien, Panzo, Hwang and Mbe Soh, who went to Middlesbrough, Coventry, Norwich City and Almere City respectively, all on a temporary basis, as Forest made room for a number of incomings.

First was Argentina international midfielder Nicolás Dominguez from Bologna, who Fabrizio Romano claimed signed for around £8.5m. The deal was interesting as it saw Freuler going the other way on an initial loan, with an option to buy for around £4.25m, as per Gazetta dello Sport. Dominguez was renowned for his pressing, tenacity and his ability on the ball, which made him a very exciting fit. Unfortunately for Freuler, the move for him just didn't work. It felt like a case of a good player just not clicking in a certain environment, as had he come into a more stable Premier League side than Forest, he probably would've been fine.

It also felt like Cooper didn't know how to get the best out of him. Freuler was instrumental in the nine-game unbeaten home run, but was notably out of the side towards the end of the season. Speaking to the media after he was presented as a Bologna player, Freuler found the situation strange as Cooper made him captain for some games, then didn't explain what went wrong as he was taken out of the side, before saying, "By the end, I think we were on slightly different wavelengths." In the end, a move was best for all parties and Forest seemingly had a very able replacement in Dominguez.

An hour later, Forest signed winger Callum Hudson-Odoi from Chelsea, with The Telegraph reporting that they'd secured his services for an initial fee of just £3m, while the BBC added that Forest had beaten Fulham to his signature. Hudson-Odoi was part of Cooper's U17 World Cup winning squad, so Cooper no doubt swayed his decision and suddenly, Forest had a very exciting potential Johnson replacement. A few years earlier, Hudson-Odoi – a three-time England international – was linked with £70m moves to German giants Bayern Munich, but injuries hampered his progress. If Cooper could unlock that potential, Forest would have a hell of a player on their hands and for an outstanding fee, too.

Next, Forest finally signed another goalkeeper, as 29-year-old Odysseas Vlachodimos signed from Benfica for around £4m, as per Jornal de Notícas. According to Radar, Marinakis was very keen on signing a Greek international for Forest and now he had one with the Greece number one. Interestingly though, The Athletic had reported that the club had told Vlachodimos he would be their number one, which immediately gave Cooper a problem, given he'd told Turner the same thing. Before much thought could be given to that though, Forest were still going and their next signing was a big one.

At long last, they'd got their man in Sangaré. The Daily Mail reported that a £30m fee had been agreed and Forest now had a Syrianos approved defensive midfielder who they felt could help unlock their attacking players even further. It was a huge coup for the club, with the 25-year-old being linked with Bayern Munich, PSG and Liverpool at various points of the window and the hope was that

Sangaré alone could transform Forest from a relegation battler into something much more competitive.

Forest still weren't done and next through the door was Norwich City centre back Andrew Omobamidele, with the 20-year-old signing for £11m, as per The Athletic. The Athletic also reported that Omobamidele wasn't their first choice, as the Reds lodged a £25m bid for Chelsea defender Trevor Chalobah, but Chalobah didn't want to move. Thankfully for Forest, despite it being late in the day, the Republic of Ireland international wasn't too far away from Nottingham as Norwich were away at Rotherham United, so everything was signed off in an orderly manner.

Amazingly, there was still space for one more. According to The Athletic, Marinakis Jnr yet again wanted striker Michy Batshuayi, but instead opted to sign AC Milan striker Divock Origi on loan, with an option to buy for around £4m. It was difficult to see where the 28-year-old would fit and frankly, it felt like a signing for the sake of making a signing, but it was another option for Cooper. What was meant to be five or six key signings turned into 13 new additions, seven of which came on deadline day.

Doing the bulk of your business on deadline day isn't ideal, however, it was better late than never. Forest had a much better squad at end of the window than they had at the start of pre-season, despite losing one of their best players in Johnson. Ultimately, that has to be the aim of every summer window and it was one that the club eventually achieved. As Forest had a game the day after deadline day, it would likely be too soon for the majority of the deadline day signings to feature in the matchday squad, but there was a keen sense of excitement as Forest made the trip down to Chelsea for the last game before the first international break.

Cooper went back to the 5-3-2 that worked so well towards the end of the last season, with Aina and Aurier starting as wing backs, a back three of Boly, McKenna and a returning Worrall, a midfield three of Yates, Mangala and Danilo and with Gibbs-White behind Awoniyi. Felipe was fit enough to be on the bench, while of the deadline day signings, Tavares was the only one in the matchday squad. Chelsea had all of the ball from kick-off and almost took the lead when a Ben Chilwell low cross found Raheem Sterling inside the six-yard box, but an outstanding Aina block prevented any goal and Forest survived.

Aside from that, at a very hot and sunny Stamford Bridge, Chelsea didn't really do anything. They had a lot of the ball, but seemingly with no idea of how to pick the lock. Also, whenever they did fashion half an opening, an inspired Worrall was on hand to thwart them. It was like there were three of him on the pitch, although he did make a hash of Forest's best chance in the half. A Gibbs-White free-kick was atrociously dealt with by Chelsea and a loose ball fell in the box for Awoniyi, but Worrall swung for it as well and proceeded to smash it into orbit.

Just before half-time, Danilo went off with a hamstring injury and was replaced by Elanga and after the break, it only took a few minutes for him to make his mark. Yates pickpocketed Chelsea's new £115m signing Moises Caicedo on halfway and gave it to Awoniyi, who immediately passed it through the middle for Elanga to run onto, coolly slotting past goalkeeper Robert Sánchez to give Forest the lead. Despite going a goal down, Chelsea still had no real ideas on how to get through – striker Nicolas Jackson was denied by a brilliant Boly challenge, but otherwise, they seemed clueless.

Montiel and Tavares both came on to help see the game out and the plan seemed to be working, up until the 84th minute. Cole Palmer expertly picked out Sterling down the right, who burst to the byline and cut it back for Jackson. Inexplicably however, Jackson – with the goal gaping – got underneath it and poked the ball over the bar. The season was not even four games old yet and we'd already had a miss of the season contender. 10 minutes later, with Forest fans whistling loudly for the full-time whistle, the ref called time and the cheers from the away end told their own story.

A very sweaty Cooper – who misjudged the weather by opting for a jumper and needed a towel all game to wipe himself down, eventually afraid to put it down out of superstition because Forest were playing well – delivered his fist pumps to loud roars. When the players came over to celebrate, the away end serenaded Worrall, who after going through so much adversity off the field, had comfortably put in his best ever performance in a Forest shirt. It had taken Forest half a season to register an away win the previous season, but this time, they'd registered one on just their third attempt and at a Sky Six club, no less. It had been another busy summer, but with six points on the board already and with new players now in, things were looking up for both Cooper and Forest.

What Forza do is amazing. Above: Leeds (H). Below: Celebrating 50 years
of the Tricky Tree before Man Utd (H)

Two huge goals. Above: Taiwo celebrating v Chelsea (A). Below: Gibbs-White celebrating v Southampton (H)

Above: Forest in Frankfurt. Below: Awoniyi scores at Old Trafford. Taiwo, you've no idea the carnage you caused in that away end

The end. Above: Luton (H). Below: Fulham (A)

CHAPTER FOURTEEN – THE DIFFICULT SECOND SEASON

The afterglow of the Chelsea win was magnificent. Cooper said in the immediate aftermath that to win away, "against the modern Chelsea is something that can really help us going forward" and it genuinely felt like that. And with Awoniyi too, Forest had a centre forward who was the envy of the league. While the Nigeria international couldn't score in an eighth consecutive game (although he did get an assist), to even get to seven meant that he was tied with Emmanuel Adebayor and Mohammed Salah as the only Africans to score in seven consecutive Premier League matches.

His form hadn't gone unnoticed and ironically, just before the window shut according to The Athletic, Chelsea made an enquiry about him, which was swiftly dismissed. Ultimately, Forest had decided they were only going to sanction one major sale, which was Johnson. Marinakis put out a club statement where, among other things, he stated that there is, "something special continuing to grow within our club", gave Johnson a glowing reference and revealed the news that Randall had been replaced as chairman by season ticket holder Tom Cartledge, who was CEO of Handley House.

Interestingly, Handley House included architectural company Benoy and Marinakis confirmed that Cartledge, "will reignite plans to redevelop our famous home." It was no secret that Forest had long mooted plans to renovate The Peter Taylor Stand, so Cartledge's arrival suggested those plans were finally about to ramp up. Randall was kept on as a board member, but it really felt at that moment in time that the pieces were falling into place, both on and off the pitch, with Forest seemingly well placed to avoid the dreaded 'second season syndrome'.

For those unaware, this is where a team gets promoted and has a successful season, only to be caught out in their second season and end up massively struggling as a result, normally resulting in relegation. A prime example are Forest's good friends, Sheffield United. After promotion in the 2018/19 season, the Blades defied expectation and ended up in the mix for a European place, finishing the 2019/20 season in ninth on 54 points. Fast forward 12 months and they were relegated, bottom of the league and embarrassing themselves with just 23 points.

With two wins on the board already though, Forest were in a good place. The September international break allowed Cooper time with some of the new recruits, though not all of them. One of the realities of being a Premier League side is that the majority of the signings you make tend to be internationals, but Cooper did get time with Hudson-Odoi, Tavares, Murillo, Origi and Dominguez ahead of Forest's next outing. There was still squad trimming to be done too, as not all of the European transfer windows had closed and Forest used this to their advantage.

Mighten and Dennis were loaned out to KV Kortijk and Istanbul Basaksehir respectively, while Biancone and Jonjo Shelvey were moved on permanently. Biancone went to Olympiacos for an undisclosed fee, while Shelvey went to Turkish outfit Caykur Rizespor. There was some conjecture about Shelvey's departure, however. Forest announced that they'd loaned Shelvey for the season, but this breached FIFA rules, as you can only loan seven players out to continental leagues. Shelvey would've been the eighth, so it seemed that upon being made aware of this, Forest terminated Shelvey's contract and got him off the books that way.

It was a strange incident, but few among the Forest fanbase cared – they were just happy Shelvey was off the books. As for Biancone, it was a case of what could've been and unfortunately for him, injuries derailed what might've been a promising Forest career. Both loans made sense too, as Mighten was never going to play and Dennis was evidently out of favour. While Cooper now had a squad on paper that he could really work with, in addition to bedding the newbies in, one of the challenges would be from a fitness perspective. Nearly all of the new signings wouldn't have had a sufficient Premier League ready pre-season, which was certain to cause issues later down the line.

For now though, all focus was on facing Burnley again, with the newly promoted side visiting The City Ground for a league match this time. Cooper lined up with a 4-2-3-1 formation, with Montiel, Sangaré and Hudson-Odoi all making their first league starts for the club, while Worrall, fresh from signing a new contract, started at centre back alongside McKenna. Turner remained in goal, which made sense as he hadn't done anything to warrant being dropped, but he was now in the knowledge that the slightest mistake could see his place at threat.

Much like the Sheffield United match, Forest were expected to win and much like that game, Forest started well. A chance came early when Awoniyi dispossessed Jordan Beyer on the edge of his own box and fed Hudson-Odoi, but Burnley keeper James Trafford denied him with a smart stop. However, like the Sheffield United fixture, Forest fizzled out in the first half and Burnley grew into the game. Turner made a good save to deny Zeki Amdouni from distance, but five minutes before half-time, Luca Koleosho skipped down the left wing and got into the penalty area, before cutting it back for Lyle Foster. Foster shanked his effort, but the ball fell for Amdouni on the edge of the box, who rifled it into the bottom corner.

It was a great hit and Turner was powerless to keep it out, but again questions would be asked about Forest's in-game management. With an hour gone though, Sangaré whipped a peach of a cross to the back post for Awoniyi, who took it down on his chest and laid it off for Hudson-Odoi, who checked inside, wrapped his foot around the ball and curled an exquisite effort off the inside of the far post and in, leaving Trafford clutching at air. It was an outstanding strike and as first impressions go for Hudson-Odoi, scoring one of Forest's best ever Premier League goals was a pretty good way to introduce yourself.

Despite getting the equaliser, Forest couldn't really kick on and with 12 to go, a hopeful long ball found Sander Berge, who ran past

McKenna and pulled it back for Foster, who tapped into an empty net. When the celebrations died down though, VAR got involved and after a lengthy check, decreed that Berge had taken the ball down with his arm. It was incredibly harsh on Burnley and frankly, Forest had a huge let off – it certainly didn't seem a clear or obvious error and it felt like a case of VAR getting involved for the sake of it. The drama didn't stop there either as in injury time, Foster was sent off for violent conduct after another VAR check, which saw him elbow Yates off the ball.

In the end, Forest were somewhat fortunate to get a 1-1 draw and after the game, Cooper did highlight how with new players coming in and with a change in formation, it would be difficult to get into a rhythm off the bat. He wasn't wrong to say that, however, but for a very contentious VAR call, Forest would've lost at home against a newly promoted side – a game that would've been earmarked by just about every fan as a must win in order to survive in the league, let alone kick on. Rightly or wrongly, the expectation had increased among the fanbase and results like that would be scrutinised a lot more than before.

It was a mixed game for the newbies, too. Hudson-Odoi stole the headlines with his incredible goal and Sangaré looked tidy in midfield, but Montiel was very rash and ended up coming off early in the second half. Tavares and Origi both came off the bench, but neither added a tremendous deal and while it was only one game, it felt again like Cooper was going to have to perform something special to get everyone singing from the same hymn sheet. With a trip to Manchester City next, it wasn't going to get much easier, either.

Since Forest last played City, they went on to win the treble – the Premier League, FA Cup and Champions League – and did so in breathtaking fashion. The only other English team to have won the treble was Manchester United in 1999 and much to the glee of the light blue side of Manchester, City won it in a much more convincing manner. There was no doubt that City were the best team in the world at this point, so Forest would need to be at their very best to get anything out of the match.

Perhaps unsurprisingly, Cooper changed formation to a 5-4-1 as Forest sought to contain City as best they could. Niakhaté, Boly and Aurier played as centre backs, with Tavares and Aina as full backs, while Dominguez and Gibbs-White started on the wings, with Mangala and Sangaré in central positions and Awoniyi up front on his own. After just seven minutes though, Kyle Walker had peeled away from Tavares and Rodri picked out his run into the box with a raking pass, allowing Walker to cut it back for Phil Foden, who finished emphatically.

Seven minutes later, a poor Tavares clearance was picked up by new City signing Matheus Nunes, who sprayed it wide right to Julián Álvarez, who played it inside for Foden. Nunes had made an overlapping run and Foden picked that out brilliantly, allowing Nunes to cross for Erling Haaland, who powered a header past Turner. With Forest 2-0 down inside 15 minutes, flashbacks to the previous season where City hit six began to become more prominent. It could've been three when Jeremy Doku picked out Álvarez inside the box, but an excellent block from Boly denied the Argentina international a certain goal.

Forest survived until the break and immediately after it, the game swivelled on its head. Gibbs-White tussled with Rodri for the ball by the corner flag and Rodri didn't take too kindly to it, squaring up to Gibbs-White. After some handbags, Rodri twice put both his hands around Gibbs-White's throat and on the second occasion, Gibbs-White went down, giving the ref no choice but to send Rodri off. It was a total headloss moment from one of the best midfielders to ever play the sport and suddenly, Forest had half a chance to get back into the game.

Almost immediately, Forest forced a corner and from that, substitute Montiel picked out Mangala on the edge of the box, but his effort was high and wide. Boly then picked out Awoniyi with a dinked pass that caught the entire City backline out, but while Awoniyi took it down sublimely, his shot on goal was all wrong and went miles over. Right at the end, Gibbs-White picked out another substitute in Elanga with a good ball and the Sweden international unleashed a venomous volley towards goal, but City goalkeeper Ederson kept it out excellently and in the end, Forest fell to a 2-0 defeat.

The feeling at full-time was strange. On the one hand, as defeatist as it sounds, a 2-0 loss at Manchester City is something of a let off, as City are just that good. On the other, Forest played 10 men for 45 minutes and despite City not having their most important player on the pitch, only managed to force the goalkeeper into one meaningful save. Cooper felt the same way and told BBC Sport that he was unsure how to feel really, but in any case, it was a damn sight better than what happened a year earlier and that alone represented significant progress.

Behind the scenes though, a different story was brewing. The Telegraph reported that McKenna was training away from the first team after a contract dispute, with the Scotland international being informed that he wouldn't be getting a new deal and seemingly not reacting well to the news. The Athletic expanded on this, stating that following discussions, both Cooper and Marinakis were in agreement that McKenna's priority wasn't Nottingham Forest and as such, he'd have no further part to play.

The whole thing was odd. Reading between the lines, what could have possibly been said that led both Cooper and Marinakis to the conclusion that McKenna would effectively down tools? It was such a shame. McKenna was a promotion hero, Player of the Match at Wembley and Forest's Player of the Season for that blissful campaign. He also played a solid part in keeping Forest in the league. For his time at the club to effectively be over in such scandal seemed sad, frankly. It also left Forest a centre back down and without perhaps their best aerial option too, with McKenna renowned for dominating his aerial duels.

Kicking off October, Brentford were next for Forest and sure enough, McKenna was nowhere to be seen in the matchday squad. That wasn't the only talking point from the matchday squad, though. Cooper boldly went for a 4-3-3 formation, with no Gibbs-White in the starting XI. There was also no Aina or Yates, while Niakhaté was in the somewhat unusual position of left back. Making up the midfield three was Sangaré, Mangala and Dominguez, while in defence, Murillo made his debut, being partnered with Boly. Up front, Hudson-Odoi and Elanga were either side of Awoniyi in a front three.

Speaking to Sky, Cooper explained that it was a tactical decision, but dropping Gibbs-White was a huge call. Forest started well in his absence though and had the ball in the net when a Hudson-Odoi corner was flicked to the back post by Murillo into Awoniyi's path for a tap in, but the official's flag went up immediately for offside. However, like previous home games, Forest couldn't maintain that intensity and the opposition grew into the match as a result. A very well worked Brentford free-kick found Vitaly Janelt alone in the box, but while Turner kept out his strong effort, the rebound caused pinball in the Forest six-yard box. The ball eventually pinged towards Yoann Wissa, but it was just ahead of him and he couldn't turn it in.

The scores were level at the break, but just after it, Turner miscontrolled a routine pass outside the six-yard box and that allowed Wissa to poke the ball towards an open goal, being wiped out by Turner in the process. As the ball slowly rolled towards an empty net, Boly sprinted back to clear off the line and somehow, Turner wasn't pulled up by VAR for his infringement. This was another huge reprieve for Forest, but a few minutes later, they weren't so lucky. Niakhaté – already on a yellow card and struggling at left back – was late into a challenge on Wissa and ended up raking his studs down the Brentford attacker's calf, resulting in a second yellow and subsequently, a red card.

From that free-kick, Mathias Jensen clipped it in for an unmarked Christian Nørgaard to get a soft header on goal, but the ball seemed to go through Turner and in. From the marking to the goalkeeping, it was a terrible goal to concede and Forest had half an hour to salvage something from the game, despite being a man down. Cooper retaliated instantly and on came Gibbs-White and Toffolo, as Forest set about putting things right. Five minutes later, Gibbs-White found Toffolo running down the left in space, Toffolo whipped a ball in for Dominguez and the Argentina international's header looped over a surprised Mark Flekken and in.

Just like that, Forest were level and both subs combined tremendously for the goal, but with the man advantage, Brentford started to boss possession and suddenly, a point looked like the best possible outcome for Cooper's side. Forest managed to contain Brentford until stoppage time, when Michael Olakigbe danced his way into the box and beat Turner with his goalbound effort, but Murillo was standing behind Turner to clear the ball away. Shortly afterwards, the ref blew for full-time and Cooper had a lot to reflect on after a very eventful match.

The last two home games felt like Cooper throwing things at a wall and hoping some of it stuck, which was in complete contrast to the start of the season. The 5-2-2-1 maybe didn't do Danilo any favours, but the team at least looked settled and knew what they were doing – even when there were formation changes. It was little wonder that The Telegraph reported that Cooper was frustrated with so many new signings coming in on deadline day, as he was up against the clock to get them familiar with his tactics. Ultimately, trying to squeeze the newbies in ended was likely leading to disjointed performances like that.

Perhaps that's why Forest were starting so brightly, but unable to maintain it. However, what wasn't down to the new players were strange tactical choices. For example, Brentford full-back Aaron Hickey was booked after just two minutes, but Elanga never really got at him for the rest of the game, despite Hickey being in peril. By contrast, Brentford targeted Niakhaté as soon as he was booked and got their reward for that. In hindsight as well, not starting Gibbs-White or a natural left back in Toffolo was an error, although Cooper at least deserved credit for solving that within the game itself.

Next was a trip to Crystal Palace and it was another case of the dreaded phrase, 'a good time to play them'. Palace were without star players Eberechi Eze, Michael Olise, Jefferson Lerma, Cheick Doucoure and a certain Dean Henderson, so there was optimism Forest could get at least a point. According to The Athletic, Cooper had reassured Turner he still had faith in him after his display against Brentford and was true to his word, keeping him in the XI. In addition, he stuck with the 4-3-3, but this time started Gibbs-White – albeit out on the right wing. Toffolo also came in at left back for the suspended Niakhate, while Wood was chosen to lead the line ahead of Awoniyi, who'd worryingly picked up a recurrence of his groin injury and would be ruled out for a month.

Forest took control of the game early and almost scored from an unlikely source as a Gibbs-White corner was cleared to Toffolo some 30 yards out, who unleashed a rocket of a shot that goalkeeper Sam

Johnstone parried away well. Soon after, Murillo clipped a sublime diagonal ball over the Palace defence for Gibbs-White, who chipped Johnstone with his first touch, but was desperately unlucky to see the ball hit the base of the post and bounce back into Johnstone's very grateful arms. It was a superb ball from Murillo, but he wasn't finished showing what he could do yet.

After receiving the ball midway through the Palace half, Murillo charged towards goal, slalomed his way past three players, rolled his left foot across the ball and sat Marc Guehi down, before firing off an effort with his right, which was well saved by Johnstone. The ball came back to Murillo, but the Brazilian defender's second attempt on his weaker foot was much tamer and Johnstone clutched the ball to his chest. It was a truly sensational piece of play – it's not often you see a centre back beating four players and testing the goalkeeper.

In the second half, Palace should've scored when Odsonne Édouard laid it across the box for Jean-Philippe Mateta, but his effort went wide. That proved to be their only meaningful attack of the game, but Forest were still struggling to break through. An acrobatic effort from sub Montiel from outside the box was deflected over when it looked like it was creeping in and right at the end, a Dominguez curler forced Johnstone into a very good save, but that was as good as it got. Forest had secured a clean sheet (much to Turner's relief after his haphazard performance against Brentford) and a point on the road, but the feeling was that it could and should've been more.

However, despite having an incredibly rough away run to start the season, Forest now had two clean sheets on the road – as many as they managed in the entirety of the 2022/23 season. "I guess this is a sign of the progress we are making that we come to a side like Crystal Palace and we're disappointed in just getting a point," Cooper told BBC Sport after the game. That was the important takeaway, as while the Brentford and Burnley draws were frustrating, the club were making strides. This time the previous season, Forest had four points and had just lost five games in a row, conceding 18 goals in those five fixtures alone.

This time around, they were on nine points and despite playing several big hitters, had only conceded 10 goals. The only concern was that the club may end up viewing Brentford, Burnley and Palace as missed opportunities further down the line, but when you took a step back and compared, it was undeniable that progress was being made – and that's with Cooper bedding in new players during the season again. If Forest could beat newly promoted Luton Town after another international break, which they'd be expected to as they'd be on home soil, a lot of nerves would be calmed.

Since Forest's last meeting with Luton, a lot had changed for them. Out went Nathan Jones after he jumped ship to Southampton and in came Rob Edwards, who despite joining mid-season, took them up via the play-offs. Everyone had expected Luton to be smacked every week and initially that looked to be the case, with the Hatters conceding seven in their first two games, but Edwards shored things up defensively and they instantly became much more competitive, beating Everton away and only losing to Tottenham, West Ham and Fulham by just one goal. It certainly wouldn't be an easy task, but really, it was a game that Forest should win.

Cooper only made one change from the team at Palace, with Elanga coming in for Hudson-Odoi, who pulled his hamstring in the build-up to the match – again highlighting the risk of signing players who hadn't had a proper pre-season, as The Telegraph reported Hudson-Odoi was training away from the main Chelsea group before his move. From kick-off, you could clearly see Forest were the better side – it was like watching a Premier League side play a Championship one in the cup, with it feeling like a matter of time until the deadlock was eventually broken.

Wood had an early sight of goal when Toffolo picked him out, but his volley into the ground was held by Luton goalkeeper Thomas Kaminski. Soon after, a Gibbs-White cross caused chaos in the Luton box and nearly allowed Toffolo to score, but Tom Lockyer scooped away at the last second. Just before the break, Boly found Gibbs-White down the right again, whose cross was kicked away by Kaminski straight to Sangaré, but despite having an open goal, Sangaré put the ball wide. Incredibly at the break, it was still 0-0, but Luton had barely been allowed out of their own half.

Three minutes after the restart, Gibbs-White played in Elanga, who put the ball into Wood's path, who made no mistake. Forest finally had their goal and were hungry for more – soon after, Elanga again found Wood, this time from a cross out wide, but Wood narrowly headed over. With 14 to go, Elanga again found Wood with a cross, but this time the New Zealand international steered his header past Kaminski and in. It was a deserved goal and one that reflected Forest's superiority in the game, as Luton had been no match for them at all.

After the goal, Cooper made a triple sub, as Yates, Worrall and Kouyaté came on for Sangaré, Boly and Dominguez. Immediately after the subs, it felt like Forest were on the back foot and unable to keep the ball in midfield, resulting in fouls. Gibbs-White was booked for cleaning out Ross Barkley out wide and from that free-kick, Andros Townsend mishit his delivery straight to Aurier, but Aurier bizarrely ducked under it trying to head it clear and the ball bounced off an unassuming Toffolo into the path of Chiedozie Ogbene, who slammed his effort past Turner.

Despite being in total control of the game for 80 minutes, Forest now looked nervy and Luton had momentum. The Reds had gone from looking like a midtable Premier League side to a Sunday league one. Everything was desperate and it seemed outrageous that Forest were in this backs against the wall position. Cooper brought on Aina and Williams to stem the tide, withdrawing Elanga and Aurier and going to a back five and Forest seemed to be riding out the storm, albeit unconvincingly, as the board went up to indicate nine minutes of injury time.

Two minutes in, Lockyer pinged a diagonal ball into Elijah Adebayo's direction, who was marked by Worrall. Rather than try and go for the ball, Worrall instead tangled with Adebayo, who shrugged him aside, took the ball down on his chest and squeezed it past Turner at his near post. Unfathomably, Luton were level in a game they'd turned up for 10 minutes in. There was still one last twist as a Williams ball found Wood inside the box and the striker fired home, but the flag went up for offside. Full-time, 2-2.

Boos louder than Mull of Kintrye before a game rained down from stands. This was the first time in Cooper's tenure that there was a notable crack in his relationship with the fans, who were furious at what they'd witnessed. As a manager, you live and die by your decisions and the decision to make that triple sub cost Forest the game. The subs reeked of complacency and in a league where you can't take anything for granted, that was incredibly naïve. It felt like, "we've won this, let's get some minutes into legs for you three." Had Forest won, of course no-one bats an eyelid, but they didn't.

In total, Kouyaté and Yates completed just four of the 10 passes they attempted in the time they spent together on the pitch. All four were by Yates, with Kouyaté looking incredibly rusty. Forest's inability to control the ball saw them retreat and the mistake by Worrall was a by-product of that. That being said, the players needed to take accountability too and Worrall's mistake was exceptionally poor. It emerged after the game that Boly asked to come off as he was exhausted from international duty, but Cooper still had a choice of Worrall or Niakhaté. Knowing Adebayo was on the field and given Worrall had tended to struggle against big target men strikers, not choosing Niakhaté was bizarre.

The real shame was that for 80 minutes, that was the most complete performance Forest had managed in the top flight since their return. Unfortunately for Forest, games don't stop after 80 minutes and with a trip to Liverpool next, those two dropped points suddenly felt very damaging. You're only ever three games away from a crisis in the Premier League and having failed to beat Brentford, Burnley, Palace and now Luton – three of those being on home soil, the bedrock for survival the previous season – alarm bells were certainly starting to ring.

Taking the positives from the game, if Forest were to perform at the level they played at for 80 minutes at Anfield, they might have a chance of causing some issues for the home side. However, they'd have to do so without Wood, who'd picked up a hamstring injury. As such, Cooper opted for a 5-4-1 formation, with Aurier and Aina as full backs, Murillo, Niakhaté and Boly as centre backs. Ahead of them were Dominguez and Gibbs-White down the wings, Sangaré and Mangala in centre midfield and Elanga up front on his own. Interestingly, Awoniyi was back on the bench and seemingly ahead of schedule, though whether he actually was or whether he was rushed back because of Wood's absence was another matter.

The Forest containment job was going relatively well and 30 minutes passed without incident, until Murillo decided to weave his way around two Liverpool players just inside the Liverpool half. The centre back was halted by Alexis Mac Allister and with Murillo miles out of position, Mac Allister promptly played the ball into the exposed space for Mohammed Salah, who quickly fed Darwin Núñez, whose shot was parried by Turner straight into Diogo Jota's path for his seemingly customary goal against Forest. Four minutes later, Salah popped a ball behind the Forest defence for Dominik Szoboszlai to run onto, who pulled it across the six-yard box for Núñez to put away with ease. Just like that, it was pretty much game over for Forest.

It wasn't for Liverpool though, who kept coming forwards. Ryan Gravenberch and Szoboszlai both had efforts outside the box well saved by Turner, as despite sitting deep, Forest couldn't find a way to handle Liverpool. Forest rode it out until half-time and in the second half, the Reds improved as Liverpool took their foot off the pedal a bit. Cooper's side should've had a goal back when Murillo picked out Gibbs-White down the right, who put a lovely weighted ball across the penalty box for Dominguez to run onto, but Dominguez seemed to lose his footing at the crucial moment and instead, fell over the ball.

With about 13 minutes to go. Niakhaté fired in one of his trademark long throws and Forest won the flick-on, but Liverpool were able to clear as far as Szoboszlai outside the box, who proceeded to ping a ball over the top for Salah to latch onto. Inexplicably, Turner sprinted miles out of his goal to try and get there ahead of Toffolo, only to get in Toffolo's way, misjudge the bounce and allow Salah an open goal to pass into, which he could scarcely believe he was presented. To say it was a diabolical piece of goalkeeping would be polite.

Just before full-time, Yates whipped in a ball and Elanga latched onto it first time with a thunderous volley that thumped the Liverpool crossbar, but that was as close as Forest got as Liverpool ran out 3-0 winners. The only talking point after the game though was Turner's antics. Turner didn't start playing football until he was 14 and whenever the ball came to his feet, it showed. In every game, whenever the ball was played back to him, it was like he treated it like a grenade – Turner would just smash it away with no real direction, with the ball frequently going out of play or finding an opposing player rather than a Forest shirt.

It was a clear weakness in his game and you could see the panic amongst the Forest defence when given a choice to play it back to him. That largely went under the radar when he was making saves, but even his shot-stopping abilities were being questioned after Brentford's goal and Liverpool's first. As for the third, well. No words can describe what went through Turner's head to possess him to do that. In any case, something had to give. Having two number one goalkeepers at the club with no hierarchy to differentiate them was an accident waiting to happen and it was showing in Turner's form.

Forest's next game was against high-flying Aston Villa and predictably, Cooper was asked about who his goalkeeper would be. As always, Cooper was very honest and said he felt sympathy for Turner as the reaction when a goalkeeper makes a mistake is understandably different to when an outfield player makes one, given it nearly always leads to a goal. He then stated to the Nottingham Post that, "We want to be a team and a coaching staff that when people make mistakes, we support each other and not criticise too much and isolate people," but despite saying this, he would've known he had a big decision to make – especially with Forest on a six-game winless run.

In the end, Cooper twisted. Vlachodimos came in for his Forest debut against a Villa side who would've gone third with a win, with Cooper sticking to the 4-3-3. Murillo and Niakhaté became Cooper's sixth different centre back selection in 11 Premier League games, while Awoniyi was back to lead the line with Gibbs-White and Elanga either side of him. Interestingly, there was no Worrall anywhere, with Cooper dropping him completely from the matchday squad – a move which, according to The Telegraph, the Forest captain didn't respond well to. In fact, Worrall was so angry about his exclusion that he refused to attend the game, citing that he wasn't in the right frame of mind.

It was hardly an ideal reaction from the club captain, but nevertheless, that could wait as Forest had a job to do on a chilly November afternoon. After just five minutes, some lovely interplay between Elanga and Dominguez sent Elanga storming down the wing and into the Villa box, where he hit something of a brick wall and had to turn back and pass to Toffolo. Upon receiving the ball, Toffolo feigned to cross and instead passed it back across the edge of the box, where Aina ran onto it and drilled an effort into the bottom corner. It was a dream start for Forest, with Aina getting his first for the club in emphatic fashion.

Villa didn't take too kindly to that and soon after found themselves in a three-on-three, with Moussa Diaby finding Nicolò Zaniolo inside the box, but his effort was well kept out by Vlachodimos. Otherwise though, Forest – like they were at Villa Park the previous season, before Shelvey gifted a goal away – were looking very solid and made it through to half-time without any major problems. Villa had a lot of the ball, but couldn't seem to find a way through as Forest's midfield of Sangaré, Mangala and Dominguez were shutting them down at any opportunity.

Two minutes after half-time, Toffolo found himself in a good crossing position, but instead opted to play it to Mangala outside the box, who let one fly. Villa keeper Emiliano Martínez sprung across his line and got a hand to it, but pushed the ball up into the sky, where it bounced down behind him and over the line. It was a freakish goal, but Forest weren't in a mood to complain as against all odds, the Reds were 2-0 up. It was nearly three when Awoniyi caused havoc inside the box and the ball fell to Dominguez, but his effort was saved.

Villa came to life a bit late on and fashioned a great opening when John McGinn crossed for Ollie Watkins, but Watkins planted his header wide. Diaby also had a chance when the ball was worked to him inside the box, but his curling effort was seen all the way by Vlachodimos. In the end, it was made to look fairly comfortable by Forest and when the ref blew for full-time, the roar that came from the fans was one of pure euphoria. Forest had done it the hard way – if you'd said Forest would take four points from Luton and Villa, most would've predicted a draw with Villa and beating Luton, but typically, the Reds had done it the other way around.

The jubilation during 'Just Can't Get Enough' was infectious and Cooper's customary fist pumps, which hadn't been seen in a while, were a very welcome sight for supporters. Much like in the Luton game, Cooper was judged on his decisions and this time, he made the right calls. Vlachodimos was a safe pair of hands in goal, while all 10 starting outfielders put an immense shift in. There was even a welcome return for Danilo off the bench and after a rough few weeks, it felt like Cooper had found a successful formula again.

Navigating the second season was always going to be difficult, especially with the influx of new players, but by beating a very competitive Villa side, things were looking up again.

CHAPTER FIFTEEN – ALL GOOD THINGS...

In theory, there should've been a huge lift after beating Villa. There was amongst the fans, with people realising Forest were closer to seventh than they were to the bottom three as a result of that win, but on the Forest training ground, it was a different story entirely. The Telegraph reported that upon returning to training, Worrall had a blazing row with Cooper that subsequently saw him isolated from the rest of group, with the Forest captain joining his centre back partner McKenna in first-team exile as a result.

When the news broke, people were in two camps – one was that an academy boy in Worrall, who'd captained Forest to success at Wembley, had more than enough credit in the bank to effectively be put in a bomb squad. The other were in disbelief a Forest captain could act that childishly, defy the manager like that and felt Worrall's actions were arguably worse than Shelvey's in the previous season. Cooper's popularity was such that the latter camp were much more prominent and vocal, with Worrall getting the moniker 'Wobbler' on social media because of it.

No matter which way you looked at it, it was far from a good situation. There was no doubt Worrall had been inconsistent at Premier League level, but your captain is meant to be a beacon of leadership, not a lightning rod for division. Still, the show had to go on and Forest – minus Worrall – looked to build on their very impressive performance against Villa with a trip to West Ham, in what would be Cooper's 50th Premier League game in charge of the Reds – making him only the second Forest manager after Frank Clark to hit that milestone.

Cooper named an unchanged team for the occasion, but after just three minutes, Dominguez tried to clip a ball to Aina and instead hit the back of Sangaré, with the ball falling for Lucas Paquetá, putting West Ham in a three-on-two situation just outside Forest's penalty box. With options either side, Paquetá instead rifled an effort into the bottom corner to give West Ham the lead and to give Forest a mountain to climb. If anything though, the goal kicked Forest into life and they nearly had an equaliser when Toffolo picked out Awoniyi with a cross, whose header was brilliantly kept out by West Ham stopper Alphonse Areola.

With Forest much the better team, it felt like something was coming and just before half-time, Sangaré robbed Mohammed Kudus by the halfway line and sprayed a superb ball for Gibbs-White down the right that allowed him to burst into the penalty box and get an effort on goal, which was saved by Areola. However, the rebound fell for Awoniyi, who bundled in a well-deserved equaliser just before the break. Forest had given West Ham a head start, but were playing well and were good value to get something more than a point.

After the restart, Forest kept the pressure on and with 63 on the clock, Sangaré released Aina down the right wing, who intelligently drilled the ball to an unmarked Elanga on the penalty spot, who found the bottom corner with a first time effort. With 25 to go, it felt like Forest were on course for a rare away win. Just two minutes later however, West Ham went up the other end and forced a corner, from which James Ward-Prowse expertly picked out an unmarked Jarrod Bowen, who headed in an equaliser.

Once again, Forest had been the architects of their own downfall and now it was West Ham who had momentum. Another Ward-Prowse set piece delivery caught Forest out and Tomás Soucek escaped his marker to get a header on goal, but this time, Vlachodimos was on hand with a brilliant save to keep the score level. Forest were now very much on the ropes and West Ham were gifted another chance to lead when Aina attempted a back header rather than clear his lines, inadvertently passing straight to Soucek, but he hit the bar with his shot.

Approaching the 90th minute, fans would've taken a draw despite the earlier dominance and that would've been a fair result, but there was still one more twist. Yet another Ward-Prowse corner had the Forest defence tied up in knots and at the third attempt, an unmarked Soucek beat Vlachodimos with a bullet header into the corner. There wasn't enough time for Forest to rally back and in a match where they were the better side for two thirds of the game, they'd come away with nothing.

Cooper wasn't happy after the game and it was very easy to see why. West Ham hadn't had to work for their win – they'd been given a gift for the first goal and their other two had come from set pieces. "We've lost the game on our own actions," Cooper bemoaned to BBC Sport. What made it more frustrating, the result aside, was that it was very clear Forest had a competitive Premier League team, but for whatever reason, the Reds weren't doing everything needed to win a game consistently.

For example, in that West Ham game – bar the one Dominguez error – Forest's open play defending was brilliant. The Reds were also very good on the ball, made good chances and showed a ruthless touch in front of goal. All things considered, West Ham's only other notable chance from open play came from Aina's mistake. Forest's set-piece defending on the other hand, was atrocious. To score two goals in a game and not win is galling at the best of times, but shooting yourself in the foot like that is particularly annoying.

Brighton were up next for Forest, but before that was the last international break of 2023 and an especially important one for Forest's African contingent, as it was the last break before the African Cup of Nations (AFCON), which would take place in January. As such, Niakhaté, Kouyaté, Sangaré, Aurier, Boly, Aina and Awoniyi all went away, although there was a lot of trepidation with Awoniyi jetting off for a friendly when there were still question marks over his fitness, even if he had played – and scored – in the West Ham game.

Sadly, those fears were confirmed pretty swiftly. Awoniyi played for Nigeria in a friendly against Lesotho and afterwards, withdrew from the squad immediately after feeling serious discomfort. Ahead of the Brighton game, Cooper confirmed that Awoniyi would have to undergo groin surgery once more, keeping him on the sidelines for "months" and also ruling him out of AFCON. Injuries are of course unfortunate, but once again, it felt like Forest had more than a bit to answer for – especially when Awoniyi had clearly been feeling that injury since October, as he had no part to play in the Palace draw.

It was no secret that it felt like Awoniyi was rushed back to deal with Wood's absence, but naturally as fans, you want your best players on the field so you don't question it too much – until it goes wrong. If Forest knew Awoniyi was potentially one over exerted stretch for a ball away from needing surgery, why on earth was he allowed to go on international duty for a friendly? It's easy to see both sides as from Awoniyi's perspective, playing for Nigeria is no doubt one of his greatest honours in the sport and there's no way he'd willingly turn that invitation down, even if he was carrying a knock – especially ahead of an international tournament. Surely though, common sense should have prevailed in that situation.

In addition, Sangaré would also be unavailable. The official line was that he'd picked up an illness on international duty, but The Athletic later reported that Sangaré had in fact contracted malaria, which had seen him drastically lose weight. This was a blow as while the jury was still out for Sangaré among the fanbase, statistically, he was doing what he was brought in to do – win tackles and get blocks in. Weirdly though, Cooper had been playing him in a more advanced midfield role instead of the defensive midfield position he was signed to fill.

The Athletic shed some light on this and explained that while Sangaré was adapting to the league, Cooper didn't want him making mistakes in areas of the pitch where Forest could be punished, but that kind of defied the point in signing him to begin with. It was proving effective though as after a fair bit of chopping and changing, the midfield Cooper had settled on of Sangaré, Dominguez and especially Mangala had really started to bear fruit, so the Ivory Coast international's injury wasn't good news at all.

Accommodating for Sangaré's absence, Cooper switched formation to a 4-1-4-1 for the Brighton game, who were without a win in six and missing six key players, with Danilo coming in for Sangaré and with Mangala taking a deeper role in midfield. The only other change from the West Ham game was up front, as a fully fit Wood came in for the injured Awoniyi, while Origi was on the bench. After just three minutes, Brighton bizarrely allowed Gibbs-White to carry the ball 40 yards down the right flank unopposed, allowing him to cross the ball straight onto Elanga's head, who planted his header across the goalkeeper and in to give Forest a sensational start.

After conceding though, Brighton stepped up several gears as they sought to get back into the match and after 25 minutes, Pascal Groß found Evan Ferguson just inside the penalty box, where the Republic of Ireland international used Niakhaté as a goalkeeper screen and magnificently curled the ball into the far corner to level the scores. Forest looked all at sea and were clinging on for half-time, but in the fourth minute of first half stoppage time, Groß was allowed the freedom of Nottingham to put a cross onto João Pedro's head on the penalty spot, where his powerful effort gave Vlachodimos no chance.

Forest were slightly improved after the restart, but with half an hour left to play, referee Anthony Taylor awarded Brighton a penalty after seeing João Pedro go down very softly from a Wood tussle. Wood did have his arm around João Pedro, but the way the Brighton forward went down was very theatrical and unfortunately for Forest, the referee bought it. João Pedro stepped up to take the spot kick and sent Vlachodimos the wrong way, giving the Seagulls a 3-1 lead. Suddenly, things started to look very, very bleak.

Cooper threw Origi and Yates on to try and get a goal back, but referee Taylor was in the spotlight again when Murillo clipped a ball into the box and sub Hudson-Odoi was clearly tripped by Jack Hinshelwood, but no foul was given. While Forest protested furiously, Brighton went straight up the other end and fashioned a scoring chance of their own, which they spurned, sparking furore among the fans. Eventually, VAR took a look at the incident and ruled that Forest should have a penalty. Before it could be taken, Brighton skipper Lewis Dunk was booked for dissent immediately after the decision, didn't stop mouthing off after he was booked and was then sent off for "personally abusive language," according to the Daily Mail.

Gibbs-White stepped up and sent the keeper the wrong way to make it 3-2, making for an enthralling final 20 minutes of play. With a man advantage, the crowd onside and with momentum, it was very possible Forest could dig themselves out of the mess they'd made for themselves and still even win the game. Toffolo went close with a deflected shot from distance and Gibbs-White had a great chance to level when a ball was whipped in for him, but he timed his jump wrong and ended up hitting the ball with his shoulder, rather than his head.

With Forest pouring men forwards, Brighton were hoping for a counter to kill the game off and got it when Mangala was caught in possession by João Pedro, who ran towards the Forest goal. As soon as he got into the box though, Murillo – out of nowhere – found a burst of speed, got back and won the ball back cleanly with a crunching tackle, leaving João Pedro in a heap in the process. There was still time for one more chance and right at the death, Hudson-Odoi picked out Elanga at the far post, who headed into the six-yard box for Yates, but Yates' header was at a comfortable height for the goalkeeper and the moment was gone.

Shortly after, the full-time whistle blew. Brighton manager Roberto De Zerbi sprinted onto the pitch celebrating wildly, so much so that he didn't even shake Cooper's hand as is customary for managers after a game, as his side ended a six-game winless run with half a team out injured. Once again, Forest had deserved at least a draw but once again, had only themselves to blame for defeat. It was now three wins in 13 for Forest and it felt like the pressure was ramping up on Cooper again – this time though, it felt very different to the previous season.

For a start, in those 13 games, Forest had taken the lead six times and only won three of them. Then, The Athletic reported that while the mood in the boardroom was calm, Julen Lopetegui – who had left

Wolves before the season started – was someone that the club respected. Personally, media outlets finding out and reporting that another manager is liked seems the pretty opposite of calm to me. The feeling Cooper was under pressure only intensified further when The Telegraph ran an exclusive stating that Marinakis was furious Forest hadn't hired a set-piece coach and had wanted one for the start of the season.

The report highlighted that Gianni Vio, Tottenham's former set-piece coach and a well-regarded one in the game at that, was set to sign for the club, but the move fell through. The Athletic expanded on this, saying that Cooper had personally vetoed the move. It was no secret that Forest were poor from set-pieces, both from a defensive and an attacking standpoint, so it did feel a bit strange there wasn't one at the club. The Telegraph report also stated that Marinakis was frustrated with results and performances, with the Greek owner feeling that he wasn't seeing a return on his investment, which since promotion, was around the £250m mark.

After the Brighton loss, Forest were 15th – eight points from safety, but had they held onto their leads, they'd be 10th, which is perhaps where Marinakis was expecting Forest to be. It had gotten to a point now though that the relationship between Cooper and Marinakis had pretty much ground to a halt. The Athletic had reported that it had grown fractious between the pair after a turbulent last two months on the field, while The Telegraph went one further and said that the two were barely speaking to each other and were actively ignoring each other's phone calls.

389

It wasn't a healthy situation and as the club entered December, it felt that things were at a pivotal point. Forest's next three games were Everton at home, Fulham away and Wolves away. For a team looking to kick on in the top flight and be a steady lower half/midtable side, the very minimum target would be five points from that run – Fulham and Wolves were both two points ahead and Everton would've been three points ahead, but were instead seven points behind due to receiving a 10-point deduction for breaching PSR limits. Failure to win any would be a disaster and one that would likely mean the end for Cooper.

The rise in fan expectancy had seen things change for Cooper, too. There were boos again after the Brighton defeat and online, for the first time in Cooper's tenure, there was a noticeable shift towards those who were openly looking for a change. There had been some murmurs of discontent among the fanbase, exacerbated by the Luton implosion, but they were calmed by the Villa win. However, back-to-back 3-2 defeats had seen them spike again, with some of the belief that Cooper had the tools to turn Forest into a steady midtable side and wasn't using them properly, instead leaving the club in danger of a relegation fight again.

Of course, it wasn't quite as simple as that, but there was still a fair degree of nervous energy around the ground when Everton came to town, which wasn't helped when Forza were badly let down with one of their displays. Incorporating Cooper's "This place oozes football soul" comment about The City Ground, they'd put together a special display based around that, but before kick-off, the music for 'Mull of Kintyre' didn't play. Imagine someone forgetting to play 'You'll Never Walk Alone' at Anfield, it just wouldn't happen and really, that set the tone for what was to come.

Cooper, who'd told BBC Sport that, "You'll have to drag me out of this place...hands and feet" when asked about his future, went back to a 4-3-3 as Sangaré and Yates returned to the midfield for Danilo and Dominguez, while Boly came in for Niakhaté in defence. Those selections suggested Cooper felt his team were in for a fight and he was right. The game descended into a full on scrap and neither side seemed able to complete three passes, but the frenetic nature of the match – caused by the numerous mistakes – suited Everton far more than it did Forest.

Chances weren't coming frequently as a result, but the Toffees – with James Garner on his return to Forest in the heart of their midfield – were having the better of them. They should've scored when a booming long ball into the box from James Tarkowski was spilled by Vlachodimos after Boly accidentally barged into him and fell straight at Beto's feet, but the Everton forward skied over with pretty much an open goal to shoot at. Later in the half, Toffolo lost possession inside his own half and Everton sprung quickly, with Abdoulaye Doucouré finding Dwight McNeil in space inside the box, but while his effort beat Vlachodimos, Murillo read the situation perfectly and was on hand to clear off the line.

At half-time, Cooper hauled Boly off and put Felipe on and after the restart, a Toffolo corner found Elanga at the back post, who drilled a ball across goal for Felipe, whose effort hit the outside of the post. With all eyes on the ball though, everyone missed that Yates was dragged to the floor by Doucouré with the ball nowhere near him. VAR had a check and gave the all clear, but Forest had every right to feel hard done by as that could and should have been a penalty.

It was a decision Forest would soon regret going against them. An Everton free-kick into the box was poorly dealt with as Mangala headed it out for Jack Harrison on the wing, who after some neat interplay with Idrissa Gana Gueye, floated in a cross that found McNeil at the far post. McNeil then took it down and unleashed an excellently controlled half volley into the top corner, giving the goalkeeper no chance. Forest tried to rally, with Murillo forcing Jordan Pickford into a save and Elanga flashing one wide, but Everton held on pretty comfortably in the end.

For the second home game running, boos from the Forest fans greeted the final whistle. It was now three defeats on the spin – including two at home – and the Reds were now on a run of three wins in 14, just four points clear of a relegation zone inhabited by three teams fully expected to go down in Luton, Sheffield United and Burnley. It felt like Forest were sleepwalking into a relegation battle with sides much weaker than them and while Cooper correctly made the point that the Reds weren't losing games in the same manner as before, where there was a gulf in class between who they were facing, they were still losing games.

It also highlighted Awoniyi's importance to Cooper. Forest were now winless in the last 10 games he was unavailable to play in, losing six of those. There was also more than a tinge of envy seeing Garner dominate midfield in the way he did for Everton – the Forest promotion hero was outstanding on the night, as fans pondered what might have been if United didn't keep shifting the goalposts. However, the situation was still redeemable – it meant Forest doing something they'd not done under Cooper thus far in winning two Premier League away games on the bounce, but given their upcoming opponents, it was entirely possible.

One way to try and fix that was to play Gibbs-White in his more favoured central position. Forest's Player of the Year was doing a solid shift down the right wing, but he wasn't anywhere near as active in games as he was before and Forest were suffering as a result. Instead though, Cooper withdrew him from the side completely to face Fulham, in what was a huge shock. Forest went with a 4-3-3 again, with Hudson-Odoi taking Gibbs-White's place in the team, while Origi came in for Wood up front. There was a change at the back too, with Felipe coming in for Boly – making him and Murillo Forest's seventh centre back partnership in just 15 league games.

Forest started well enough and while Fulham's Andreas Pereira rattled the outside of the post with a free-kick, the Reds looked competitive. After half an hour, Fulham's Calvin Bassey moved upfield and gave it to Tom Cairney, who escaped Dominguez's press and played it left for Willian. A simple cross from Willian found Alex Iwobi at the back post for a tap in and just like that, Forest were 1-0 down. Four minutes later, Iwobi fed Pereira, who passed it into the box for former Wolves man Raúl Jiménez to make it 2-0.

The proverbial fat lady was very much on the stage now for Cooper and those in the away end knew it. Forest were a mess. The ease in which Fulham were playing through them was staggering, while there appeared to be no defensive structure whatsoever. Like at Leicester in that first Premier League season, Cooper was bombarded with supportive chants from the Forest fans, but it felt like the end. At half-time, Mangala and Sangaré were seen having a fierce row and had to be pulled apart by their own teammates, with the players showing more fight there than they had in the first half.

Up until that point, the players' desire and determination to succeed couldn't be questioned. They were losing to unlucky incidents and bad mistakes, but this was different. This felt like a performance that got the manager the sack and that was a huge concern. Sangaré and Dominguez were withdrawn at half-time, with Gibbs-White and Yates coming on, but Fulham smelt blood. Nine minutes after the restart, Pereira clipped a ball in-between Aina and Felipe for Jiménez, who got there first, outmuscled Aina, rounded Vlachodimos and backheeled it in.

For fans, I'm not sure what was worse. The fact it was 3-0 or the fact Felipe just gave up as soon as Jiménez got the ball. If Felipe – a warrior who'd put his body on the line for the club the previous season – had thrown in the towel, there were serious problems. Again the Cooper chants ramped up, but again Fulham came forwards. With 15 to go, Harry Wilson crossed to the back post for Iwobi, who again couldn't miss and made it 4-0. Still the Cooper chants kept going. One person who wasn't joining in with them though was Marinakis, who'd had enough and left after the fourth. Marinakis was so incensed that a Fulham native found his access all areas pass in their hedge, as the Forest owner launched it away in disgust on his way out the ground.

With four left and with Forest dying to be put out of their misery by a full-time whistle, Yates carelessly gave the ball away inside his own half and put Fulham in a four-on-one situation, which saw Pereira give it to Cairney, who slotted home to make it 5-0. Still the Cooper chants kept going. They were all you could hear. When the full-time whistle blew, that didn't change, although the attitude amongst the Forest camp was nothing short of a disgrace. Murillo was more interested in speaking to Willian, his former Corinthians teammate, while Mangala swapped shirts with fellow countryman Timothy Castagne and was wearing that as he came over to clap the fans off.

It just felt like none of them could read the room. Forest had just lost 5-0 to a midtable Fulham to make it three wins in 15 games. It was a totally unacceptable result and an even more unacceptable showing, yet they were acting like it wasn't that big of a deal. When Cooper came over, he just held his hands up to apologise, but the support for him wasn't subsiding by those in the away end. They had his back and he was loved regardless, but it felt like his time was very much up.

Speaking to BBC Sport after the game, Cooper seemed defeated and felt of the levels of adulation shown to him. "It means so much, but I'm personally embarrassed," he said. "I'm grateful, of course, but I don't deserve that. Regardless of who is playing, who the manager is, you can't let these people down like that – you just can't. We all let them down and we have to take responsibility." Walking back to the car, I fully expected to get a notification from Forest announcing a club statement with Cooper's departure. That was surely the end.

However, nothing came. Instead, Sky Sports reported that Cooper would get the Wolves game, but would be sacked if it ended in a defeat. They also stated that Marinakis was concerned about the direction Forest were heading in and felt Cooper was being worn down by the role. In addition, Sky reported there was a level of discontent amongst the players, with several players taking issue with his tactics. The Telegraph expanded on this, stating that others had taken issue with player selection too. It was easy to see why. Andrey Santos, Tavares, Origi and Montiel had all started one game each, while Omobamidele – despite all the defensive rejigging – was yet to make a single appearance for the club.

It was perhaps telling that all five of those signed either on deadline day or just before it and while The Telegraph didn't expand upon what players in particular had issue with Cooper's selections, it would hardly be a shock if all of them did. Whether it was with this in mind or not, Cooper hit the nuclear button for the trip to Wolves, switched to a 3-5-2 and made seven changes. Out came Vlachodimos, Felipe, Aina, Sangaré, Dominguez, Hudson-Odoi and Origi, in came Turner, Niakhaté, Boly, Williams Yates, Kouyaté and Gibbs-White, with Cooper seemingly going for the mindset of, 'if I'm leaving, I'm going out with a team I trust.'

Some of these could feel hard done by – Vlachodimos couldn't really do a lot about any of the goals he conceded, for instance – but mostly, the changes were fair game. And ultimately, the club came before any player's reputation. To show their support for Cooper further, the Forest fans displayed a banner of him in the away end and were chanting his name pretty much from kick-off and immediately, Forest showed more fight and belief than they had done at Fulham a few days earlier. After 14 minutes, they got their reward.

Kouyaté knocked it right for Williams, who after selling his marker by feigning to pass to Yates on the overlap, swung in a ball to the far post for Toffolo, who showed tremendous desire to win the header and put Forest ahead. About 15 minutes later though, Wolves benefitted from a throw-in wrongly being awarded to them and from that, Craig Dawson played a defence splitting pass the wrong side of Niakhaté for Pablo Sarabia, whose first time cut back for Matheus Cunha was gobbled up by the forward to level the scores. Forest had a great chance to regain the lead before half-time when Kouyaté – who was playing like a man on a mission – robbed Max Kilman and went through one-on-one, but his effort was saved well by José Sá.

After half-time, they had an even better chance when Williams – also playing like a man on a mission – retrieved the ball excellently in the corner before swinging in another peach for Toffolo, but despite having the goal at his mercy, the left back headed over. It was a golden chance and neither side could fashion a better one, with the game finishing 1-1. Forest were much improved, the players showed that they were still clearly fighting for their manager and but for the rub of the green going against them, would've won the game. That being said, they didn't win and were now on a run of three wins in 16.

At the end of the game, it seemed as if Cooper was waving goodbye to fans, although he insisted otherwise. Again though, it felt like the end of an era, but if it was, it was at least a more dignified ending than losing 5-0 at Fulham. However, much like before, it felt like he'd been given another stay of execution. That, or the club were yet to find a replacement. The Telegraph had reported that Forest had sounded out both Julen Lopetegui and former Eintracht Frankfurt manager Oliver Glasner, who won the Europa League in 2022 with the German outfit, but as of yet, there was nothing doing.

As such, Cooper would still be in charge for Forest's next fixture, which would be at home to Tottenham. The lack of clarity wasn't helpful for anyone and really, fans needed an answer one way or another. With Forest 17th and five clear of the relegation zone, it was fair to say this wasn't turning out to be the season the ownership or fans envisaged. For me personally, it had gotten to a point where I couldn't really defend Cooper anymore. Most managers get sacked after three wins in 16 and while many weren't actively pushing for him to get the chop, it felt inevitable. You were just hoping he could pull a rabbit out the hat to fix it.

Others weren't so pleasant and some of the stuff said by a select few on social media was getting nasty. One regular on a particular YouTube channel – who I will not name as I refuse to give them the engagement and recognition they so desperately crave – resorted to commenting on Cooper's physical features, referring to him as something along the lines of a "googly eyed monster." After fierce backlash from many angry Forest supporters, the channel took down the broadcast where it was said, but not before Twitter found it first, forcing said regular into issuing a grovelling apology.

There's no doubt fans were incredibly frustrated and angry, but to be that disrespectful and ungrateful to a man who had done so much for the club was outright wrong. Thankfully, it was a tiny minority, but still. The situation wasn't like that of many previous Forest managers, whose departures had been celebrated due to poor performance. This was a man who made dreams come true and as much as evolution and progression doesn't wait for anyone, it was desperately sad that the chapter of the club's best manager in over two decades was likely reaching its conclusion.

Whether or not it would against Tottenham was another matter, but it certainly felt like a win would be needed for Cooper – against a very difficult opponent, no less. Weirdly, before the game, Forest announced that former England U19s boss Simon Rusk had been announced as the club's first ever set-piece coach and The Athletic reported that Rusk was Cooper's pick for the role. Quite why the club allowed Cooper, potentially one loss from the sack, to pick a set-piece coach was baffling, to put it mildly, but the club at least filled that role at long last.

Armed with his new set-piece coach and knowing that defeat would likely spell the end to his time in the home dugout, Cooper named an unchanged side to the one who drew at Wolves, which wasn't much of a surprise really. Roars, chants and applause met him as he emerged from the tunnel, from fans not knowing whether this would be the last time he would do so while being in charge of

Nottingham Forest. What they'd have given for one more round of fist pumps with 'Just Can't Get Enough' blaring in the background.

Straight away though, it didn't look likely. It took just three minutes for Dejan Kulusevski to split the Forest defence wide open and to present Son Heung-min with a shooting opportunity, but he fired his effort straight at Turner. Not long after, former Forest man Brennan Johnson – on his return to The City Ground – forced Turner into another save, after Kulusevski picked him out inside the box. Johnson's involvement wouldn't last much longer however, as the forward picked up an injury and had to be replaced, departing the field to all four stands clapping him off and being serenaded with his 'one of our own' chant.

Just before half-time, Kulusevski was again allowed the opportunity to put a ball into the box and produced a sublime cross, which Richarlison met emphatically with his head to give Spurs a deserved lead. Cooper now effectively had 45 minutes to save his job, but it seemed like the players had his back. Not long after the restart, Elanga found Boly inside the box with a delightful ball, but the centre back wasn't the person you wanted on the end of it and he ballooned his effort over.

Shortly after, an even better delivery from Williams found Elanga inside the six-yard box, who fired home. However, VAR looked at it and Elanga was offside, so the goal was disallowed. Five minutes after that, Turner kicked a ball straight to Kulusevski, who moved into the box and despite having the angle against him, fired goalwards. Kulusevski's effort was straight at Turner, but the goalkeeper somehow couldn't keep it out. It felt like déjà vu from how the Hughton era ended – a night under the lights at The City Ground against a decent side and with an American goalkeeper gifting a goal to the opposition.

Forest lost all momentum after that howler, but five minutes later, they got a lifeline when Yves Bissouma planted his studs above Yates' shinpad and got a straight red card for his trouble. Forest now had 20 minutes against 10 men to get something out of the game and almost got one back when Gibbs-White's corner picked out Toffolo, but at point blank range, goalkeeper Guglielmo Vicario made an phenomenal stop to preserve his clean sheet. Forest came even closer when Elanga picked out Williams at the back post, whose effort hit the post and ricocheted onto Vicario before Spurs could clear, but once again, Forest couldn't make their man advantage count and ended up losing 2-0.

Speaking to the media after the game, while Cooper didn't say as much, it felt like he knew his time was up. "This job means the world to me – it always has done," he told the Nottingham Post. Again, the reception he got at full-time was one of pure love and affection, but it really did feel like a goodbye this time. Forest were now on a run of three wins in 17 and four days after the Spurs defeat, on December 19, 2023, the club officially relieved Cooper of his duties.

The statement was, compared to the majority of manager departures, very warm. "Everyone at Nottingham Forest would like to thank Steve for his superb contribution to our football club," Marinakis said. "Steve will always remain a friend of the Club and will forever be welcome at The City Ground." In addition, Marinakis Jnr took to his Twitter account and posted a picture of him with Cooper's team after the play-off final, with the caption, "Thank you for everything my friend."

As much as things got fractured between the ownership and Cooper and as demanding as they were with him, it did feel like they genuinely liked the bloke and appreciated what he'd done. It was maybe with this in mind that according to The Athletic, after Ross Wilson delivered the news to Cooper, he insisted on saying goodbye to Marinakis personally, where the two shook hands and had what was described as an amicable conversation. As for saying bye to his players, interestingly, journalist Daniel Taylor revealed that the first player waiting for Cooper to shake his hand and say goodbye was Worrall.

Some on Twitter have described the escalated situation between the two as a man grieving clashing with a man under intense pressure, which is probably right. It's a shame it went the way it did, but speaks volumes of Worrall's character that he was willing to do that. Meanwhile, The Athletic reported something that spoke volumes of Cooper's character. Before leaving the city to head back to Wales, Cooper went out of his way to see a terminally ill Forest fan he'd grown close to, gave him his Forest top and told him just how much he'd miss managing the club.

Classy doesn't do him justice. As is the case with modern football, Forest moved quickly to replace Cooper, but didn't end up with Lopetegui or Glasner. The Telegraph reported that Lopetegui was holding out for a bigger job, with half an eye on proceedings at both Manchester United and West Ham United. As for Glasner, he met with Marinakis to discuss the role and would likely have been a Syrianos choice given his Bundesliga background, but the Forest owner wasn't convinced.

Instead, Forest moved for Nuno Espírito Santo, who was in the frame to replace Cooper after that heavy defeat to Leicester. Since that link, the former Wolves and Tottenham boss had won the Saudi Pro League and the Saudi Super Cup with Al-Ittihad and got to work in Nottingham knowing he had huge shoes to fill and a precarious situation to get the club out of. It was all very real now. After two years, three months and 108 games in charge, the Steve Cooper era was officially over.

EPILOGUE

The days after the announcement were weird. It was like breaking up with a partner. I wasn't exactly overjoyed with Nuno arriving – it felt a bit like the scene in Harry Potter, where Harry shouts, "How dare you stand where he stood!" to Snape, but ultimately, football moves on. Nuno was very humble in his first press conference and gave Cooper a lot of credit for the work that he'd done, but it all felt very strange. Still, it didn't take long before fans were on Nuno's side, courtesy to quite possibly the single worst refereeing decision The City Ground has ever seen, when Boly was sent off for winning a slide tackle in Nuno's first game – a 3-2 defeat to Bournemouth at home.

After that, Nuno made his mark pretty quickly – and damningly for Cooper, with players he'd otherwise not utilised. On Boxing Day 2023, Forest trekked up to Newcastle and won 3-1, with Wood getting a hat-trick against his former side, while Montiel and Sangaré – in his natural position – were both outstanding. A few days later and despite another Turner howler, Forest beat Manchester United 2-1 on a very special night. Gone was 'Just Can't Get Enough' at full-time though, being replaced by Status Quo's 'Rockin' All Over The World.' It really was the end of an era.

Interestingly, in all three games, Forest looked much more structured and seemed to be more tactically aware, with a very evident gameplan. Unfortunately for Cooper, that wasn't always the case in the Premier League. In the first season, Forest were capable of being a defensively sound side who were blisteringly effective on the counter attack. In the second season, with another influx of new players, they were neither. It seemed like with Cooper trying to gel new players and be more expansive, Forest sort of became a bit of an inconsistent mess – they'd be good at things in patches, but would rarely perform all of the things you need to do to win a game.

This wasn't all on Cooper, really. It can be easier for someone to come in with a blank slate and go, "Right, this is what we're doing" than managing a situation for a while and trying to refit the pieces of a puzzle together. It was just one rebuild too far and there's no shame in that, as what Cooper was asked to deliver was incredibly difficult. Take Gian Piero Gasperini at Atalanta. At the end of the 2023/24 season, Gasperini – after eight years – finally won his first trophy there when his side won the Europa League, with his third rebuilt side. By contrast, Cooper was on his second rebuild in two years.

It just wasn't sustainable and inevitably, something was going to crack. Equally, you can't really fault Marinakis' ambition. It's not exactly an orthodox approach as he wants immediate success yesterday, but compared to previous owner Fawaz Al-Hasawi, whose totally disastrous reign had Forest one game away from being in League One again, he's a godsend. Fans – myself included – are forever indebted to his generosity and unrelenting drive to restore Forest to former glories. However, Marinakis' mentality was clearly at odds with Cooper's popularity and maybe there was an element of him underestimating the Premier League.

The Telegraph reported that his thought process was, "I've given you the players and spent the money, so deliver me results", but of course, it isn't as simple as that. Gelling teams takes time. Getting results in the toughest league in the world isn't easy. And with Cooper's immense popularity after taking the club back into the promised land after a two decade exile, fans were never really going to get on his back – something The Athletic reported that Marinakis couldn't quite understand and may explain some of his other tendencies during Cooper's reign.

The Athletic also reported that on several occasions, stories would be planted in the media that were designed to shift fan opinion on Cooper and whenever Marinakis was angry at results or tactics, that too would find its way out in the open. Cooper meanwhile, would feel undermined by these antics and probably pondered just what Marinakis knew about tactics and coaching more than he did. It even got so petty that the club's social accounts refrained from hyping up Cooper too much and wouldn't even wish him happy birthday, like they do for every other Forest player.

With all that in mind, it's perhaps little wonder The Athletic reported that after that brilliant day when Forest beat Arsenal 1-0 to secure Premier League survival, some of Cooper's allies were suggesting he take a pay-off and leave then, with his head held high and without having to deal with that working environment anymore. Ultimately, this was the man that took Forest from their worst start in over a century to a day at Wembley, won that match for promotion and kept them up despite losing his entire team and having to build a new one. And Marinakis questioned why fans still adored him amidst bad runs?

There's wanting to change the mindset of the club and its supporters and there's being realistic. Cooper's achievements made him an icon. The vast majority weren't going to run their hero out of the club as they still felt it was possible he could find a way to turn things around, even if factual evidence suggested it wasn't going to happen. In any case, Cooper's departure probably did him the world of good. A few weeks after, some fans clocked him roaming around Nottingham and got a picture with him. You could just see in his face that he looked so much healthier and the time with his family – something he values so dearly – had been a blessing.

As for Forest, well. Remember the "30 signings, who gives a fuck" chant? It turned out the Premier League did. Shortly after victory over Man United, it was revealed that Forest had breached their PSR limit – despite former chairman Randall insisting they wouldn't do so – and after months of waiting, were given a six-point deduction, reduced to four for the club's co-operation. The Reds had breached by £34.5m and tried to contest this by stating that this down to not being able to sell Johnson sooner, but to no avail.

In addition to dealing with that, Forest endured what can only be described as a series of atrocious refereeing decisions, each with severe ramifications. It got so bad that Forest ended up hiring former referee Mark Clattenburg as referee analyst, in an attempt to help them gauge when and when not to contest decisions with PGMOL and to try and build bridges with them, as opposed to frequently submitting complaints. Instead, Clattenburg's appointment only made things worse, as the decisions against Forest seemed to get even more bizarre.

Things came to a head when Forest went to Everton and lost 2-0, but were denied three penalties. Being objective, the first two claims were subjective and it was reasonable to see why they weren't given. The third one on the other hand, was a decision so bad that if anyone was doing their refereeing badges and said it wasn't a penalty, they'd be kicked off the course. Ashley Young scythed Hudson-Odoi down and got nowhere near the ball, but despite it being a clear and obvious error, it wasn't overturned by Stuart Attwell (him again) on VAR.

What incensed Forest was that Attwell is supposedly a Luton fan and with Luton directly beneath Forest at that point, it certainly benefitted them to see Forest lose. In the aftermath of the game, an explosive statement was released, where the club simply put, "Three extremely poor decisions – three penalties not given – which we simply cannot accept. We warned the PGMOL that the VAR is a Luton fan before the game but they didn't change him. Our patience has been tested multiple times. NFFC will now consider its options."

In fairness to Forest, they did have a point – a Luton fan should've been nowhere near that game. However, releasing such an inflammatory statement did not go down well with the media – or the authorities, with Forest later being issued a £750k fine for it – and it created its own storm, with Sky Sports in particular going ballistic at it. This led to Gary Neville accusing the Forest ownership of acting like they were in a "mafia gang", which promptly saw Marinakis sue Neville and Sky for defamation, leading to Sky issuing a cap in hand apology.

Soon after, Clattenburg resigned from his role and despite Marinakis revealing the Key Match Incidents panel admitted Forest had seven potentially match-altering decisions go against them, the Reds ended up doing what they needed to do to survive. Interestingly, Wood spearheaded Nuno's survival charge, scoring 11 goals in 16 games under his new manager and becoming a fan hero in the process. Speaking about his form to the New Zealand Herald, Wood said that it was down to feeling his manager's confidence in his abilities, which was very telling.

On top of all that, there was also a threat to leave the much beloved City Ground. Remember when Tom Cartledge came in as chairman and how it was hoped he'd move the redevelopment plans along? Instead, with the support of Conservative MP Ben Bradley, he openly explored a new stadium in Toton, which is closer to Derby's Pride Park than it is to The City Ground. Fans made their views very clear with chants of, "Toton's a shithole, I want to stay here" and eventually, the plans were shelved.

Nuno also waded in on the debate, insisting that The City Ground is special and publicly begged the ownership to keep the club at the ground. At time of writing, it seems like he has his wish as the club's focus is to extend The City Ground's capacity to at least 42,000. Things do seem to be heading in the right direction, with progress seemingly being made, but it's fair to say Cartledge – nicknamed 'Tory Tom' by some as a result of his actions – isn't exactly high on many Forest fans' Christmas card lists.

One wonders what Cooper made of it all. During hard times, he was seen as the glue holding everything together and I wonder how he'd have dealt with everything. He probably would've galvanised the fans, who were now booing the Premier League anthem they'd waited over two decades to hear. I suspect he would've encouraged togetherness and made the fans feel like everyone was in it together and together they'll find a way out, with The City Ground being the beacon for that. It does ooze football soul, after all.

As for Cooper, he didn't rush back into management. Crystal Palace parted ways with Roy Hodgson in February 2024, but while Football Insider stated that he was their first choice to replace him, Cooper didn't want to take a job midway through the season. Instead, Palace hired Oliver Glasner and by the summer, The Athletic reported that Cooper had interest from Sunderland, Burnley and Birmingham, but he dismissed all of them as he was holding out for a Premier League job.

That eventually came in the form of Leicester City, which was ideal for Cooper as he wouldn't have to leave his south Nottinghamshire home. What wasn't ideal for Cooper was the level of challenge he's undertaking. The Leicester fans were furious at his appointment given his Forest links (further proof it's an incredibly one sided rivalry) and the Foxes face a very serious threat of multiple points deductions in the 2024/25 season for previous PSR breaches. He certainly won't get the time he got at Forest to get results on the board.

Still though, if anyone can make the impossible possible, it's Cooper. I wish him luck. Not Leicester, as they're in the same league as Forest for the 24/25 season, but him. He deserved a Premier League opportunity and if he's still in charge by the time Leicester come to The City Ground, I've no doubt he'll get a rapturous reception. He'll still be Super Cooper to us, no matter what happens with the Foxes. In fact, I'm going to revisit that chant one last time, just for old time's sake.

"And it's Super, Cooper

Led the Garibaldi

Forest having fun

Cooper, you're the one

You took us back where we belong"

ACKNOWLEDGEMENTS

First off, I should probably thank my Dad. He had absolutely no idea I was writing this (keeping it a secret was difficult), but without all the sporting literature we've exchanged over the years, the concept of me writing a book wouldn't have seemed likely. The same thanks goes for my immediate family too and also my cats, who kept me company while I was typing away.

I'd also like to thank both Daniel Taylor and David Marples, both of whom were more than happy to answer any book related questions that I had, which was extremely helpful. This book would've been incredibly different had I not spoken to them for advice and for any Forest fans reading, I would thoroughly recommend you read their published works. 'I Believe In Miracles' by DT covers the Clough glory days perfectly, while 'Reds & Rams: The Story of the East Midlands Derby' is an excellent read from David. Also, a conversation with Nathan Joyes – founder of The Copa Club, which is superb – provided clarity on what I wanted for the book's appearance, so thank you for that!

On the topic of the book's appearance, a huge thanks to the brilliantly talented (and Forest through and through) photographer that is Ritchie Sumpter for allowing me to use his image of Cooper delivering his fist pumps after the Arsenal game. It captures everything so wonderfully and it's one of my favourite ever Forest images, so to be able to use it for this book is something I'm very grateful for. Ritchie's work for the club is phenomenal – if you've got a photo of a Forest player celebrating or in action as your phone wallpaper, there's a good chance Ritchie took it.

Otherwise, it was a very limited pool of people that actually knew what I was working on. A huge thanks to my partner Aimee for being so supportive and encouraging, while I'd like to give shoutouts to the Red Side of the Trent crew in Reiss, Lee and Adam, my uni housemates in Dave, Jamie and Lewi and two of my best mates in Ash and Jack for their backing. Fingers crossed you all like it.

Finally – and here's the long list – in addition to the Red Side of the Trent team, a very special thank you to Emma, Jess and Reiss, Chloe, Jethro and Amy, Georgia, Ruth, Tom Newton, Elliott, Emma-Louise and her husband Liam, Danny Tring, Robert, Ash and Sophie, Tom H, Charlie, Emma H, Gemma, Lauren and Beth, Rob and Ricky, James and Sal from B Block, Phil, Binit, Steve G, Dan S, Nathan S, Matt B, Vicky, Danny W, Brogan, Deb and everyone else who has made me or my dad (in many cases, both) feel welcomed at games or part of their group. It's not something we take for granted and to be a part of your extended Forest family is magic. See you all at a game, in the Nav or at Stratford Haven, soon. You Reds!

BIBLIOGRAPHY

CHAPTER ONE

Mariankis umming and ahhing re Lamouchi – The Athletic -
https://www.nytimes.com/athletic/2094888/2020/10/06/nottingh
am-forest-sabri-lamouchi-evangelos-marinakis-sacked/

Hughton not thinking Johnson was ready – The Athletic -
https://www.nytimes.com/athletic/3266381/2022/05/29/nottingha
m-forest-huddersfield-promotion-premier-league/

Hughton blaming Coventry defeat on tiredness/Covid situation –
Sky Sports -
https://www.skysports.com/football/news/11688/12375876/covent
ry-2-1-nottm-forest-captain-kyle-mcfadzean-gives-sky-blues-dream-
homecoming-with-last-minute-winner

Leaked WhatsApp message one – imgbb -
https://ibb.co/F8N7tbm

Leaked WhatsApp message two – imgbb -
https://ibb.co/F8N7tbm

https://ibb.co/1z9v1vN

Leaked WhatsApp messages being legit – The Athletic -
https://www.nytimes.com/athletic/2827694/2021/09/16/inside-hughtons-demise-at-forest-no-plan-b-leaked-whatsapp-messages-late-transfers/

Garner rejects Derby for Forest – Nottingham Post -
https://www.nottinghampost.com/sport/football/transfer-news/nottingham-forest-transfers-garner-derby-5840066

Forest's rejected Buchanan bids – The Sun (via Nottingham Forest News) - https://www.nottinghamforest.news/2021/07/25/report-forest-make-second-bid-for-derby-star-lee-buchanan/

Randall's Hughton comments – The Athletic -
https://www.nytimes.com/athletic/2781081/2021/08/20/the-big-issues-at-nottingham-forest-are-signings-good-enough-is-hughton-to-blame-how-can-it-get-better/

Maja deal falling through – Nottingham Post -
https://www.nottinghampost.com/sport/football/football-news/nottingham-forest-transfer-josh-maja-5869512

Ely injury – Transfermarkt -
https://www.transfermarkt.co.uk/rodrigo-ely/verletzungen/spieler/176140

Hughton claiming players were signed without his knowledge – talkSPORT (via YouTube) -

https://www.youtube.com/watch?v=LWCWdf8aOGo

Press being told Hughton was sacked while he was doing his post-match – BBC Nottingham/Nottingham Forest (via YouTube) -

https://www.youtube.com/watch?v=9mVSX3LL3UE

CHAPTER TWO

John Cross' tweet – Twitter/X -

https://x.com/johncrossmirror/status/1438417234054066180

John Terry distancing himself from Forest job – Metro -

https://metro.co.uk/2021/09/14/john-terry-breaks-silence-on-nottingham-forest-job-speculation-15255820/

Wilder linked and would want the job – Nottingham Post -

https://www.nottinghampost.com/sport/football/chris-wilder-nottingham-forest-manager-5928610

Cooper linked – The Guardian -

https://www.theguardian.com/football/2021/sep/16/nottingham-forest-sack-chris-hughton

Cooper at odds with Swansea direction – The Guardian -

https://www.theguardian.com/football/2021/jul/21/swansea-head-coach-steve-cooper-heading-for-exit-after-growing-unsettled#:~:text=Steve%20Cooper%20has%20departed%20Swans ea,season%20on%20a%20modest%20budget.

Cooper and Sterling + TAA – Swansea City - https://www.swanseacity.com/news/profile-steve-cooper

Ferdinand pushing Wilder – Twitter/X - https://x.com/rioferdy5/status/1438580330378768391

Ferdinand and Wilder on the same agency – New Era Global Sports - https://neweraglobalsports.com/news/2019/05/new-era-open-new-office-in-belfast

Palace overlooking Cooper for Vieira – The Athletic - https://www.nytimes.com/athletic/2688507/2021/07/04/exclusive -crystal-palace-finalise-appointment-of-patrick-vieira-as-new-manager/

Murphy pushing for Cooper – The Athletic - https://www.nytimes.com/athletic/3659616/2022/10/10/evangelos-marinakis-nottingham-forest-premier-league-olympiacos/?source=emp_shared_article

Forest compensation for Cooper – Sky Sports - https://www.skysports.com/football/news/11095/12410747/steve-cooper-nottingham-forest-set-to-appoint-ex-swansea-boss-after-gbp1-2m-compensation-agreed

Steven Reid in temporary charge – BBC Sport - https://www.bbc.co.uk/sport/football/58579227

Steven Reid's Huddersfield (A) post-match comments – BBC Sport - https://www.bbc.co.uk/sport/football/58525100

Cooper's statement – Nottingham Forest – https://www.nottinghamforest.co.uk/news/2021/september/Message-to-Forest-supporters-from-Steve-Cooper/

Forest 2015/16 season results – Soccerbase - https://www.soccerbase.com/teams/team.sd?team_id=1845&teamTabs=results

Cooper's Birmingham (A) post-match comments – BBC Sport - https://www.bbc.co.uk/sport/football/58687612

Lyle Taylor's Pink October – Nottingham Forest - https://www.nottinghamforest.co.uk/news/2020/october/lyle-taylor-launches-pink-october-for-cancer-research-uk/

Cooper post Bristol City (A) – BBC Sport - https://www.bbc.co.uk/sport/football/58879696

Grabban Forest fee – BBC Sport - https://www.bbc.co.uk/sport/football/44745167

Harry Wilson Fulham fee – Sky Sports - https://www.skysports.com/football/news/11681/12363317/harry-wilson-fulham-sign-liverpool-winger-for-gbp12m-on-long-term-contract-until-2026.

Mitrovic wages - https://talksport.com/football/1495527/al-hilal-bid-fulham-aleksandar-mitrovic/.

CHAPTER THREE

Cooper post Preston (H) – BBS Sport -
https://www.bbc.co.uk/sport/football/59099839

Reading six point deduction – Reading FC -
https://www.readingfc.co.uk/news/2021/november/17/club-statement---efl-confirm-points-deduction-penalty-/

David Johnson tweets – Football League World -
https://footballleagueworld.co.uk/david-johnson-delivers-scathing-verdict-on-nottingham-forest-star-following-reading-draw/

Jones and Cooper comments post Luton (H) – Sky Sports -
https://www.skysports.com/football/news/11688/12475833/nottingham-forest-0-0-luton-town-hatters-pay-for-penalty-miss

Diangana West Brom fee – Sky Sports -
https://www.skysports.com/football/news/11698/12061722/grady-diangana-aston-villa-and-fulham-enter-race-to-sign-west-brom-target-from-west-ham

Cooper pre Swansea (A) – Nottingham Post -
https://www.nottinghampost.com/sport/football/football-news/nottingham-forest-steve-cooper-swansea-6328691

Cooper post Swansea (A) – BBC Sport -
https://www.bbc.co.uk/sport/football/59529360

Forest 2015/16 season results – Soccerbase -
https://www.soccerbase.com/teams/team.sd?team_id=1845&team
Tabs=results

Cooper post Boro (A) – BBC Sport -
https://www.bbc.co.uk/sport/football/59715187

CHAPTER FOUR

Davis signs on loan – Nottingham Forest -
https://www.nottinghamforest.co.uk/news/2022/january/01/davis
-arrives-on-loan/

Forest pip QPR to Cook – Daily Mail -
https://www.dailymail.co.uk/sport/football/article-
10364331/Nottingham-Forest-set-pip-QPR-Steve-Cook-signing-
two-days.html

Cook signs on free – Nottingham Post -
https://www.nottinghampost.com/sport/football/football-
news/nottingham-forest-steve-cook-cooper-7026491

Cooper wanted Cook, Murphy didn't – The Athletic -
https://www.nytimes.com/athletic/4076657/2023/01/11/dane-
murphy-nottingham-forest/

Spence recall clause at Boro, Covid outbreak at Boro, Wilder
speaking to Cooper about recall, Wilder then committing to loan
deal – Nottingham Post -

https://www.nottinghampost.com/sport/football/transfer-news/middlesbrough-djed-spence-recall-forest-6435152

Osei-Tutu returns to Arsenal – Nottingham Forest - https://www.nottinghamforest.co.uk/news/2022/january/06/jordi-returns-to-arsenal/

Forest sign Laryea – BBC Sport - https://www.bbc.co.uk/sport/football/59907565

Martinelli says Spence is his toughest opponent – The Athletic - https://www.nytimes.com/athletic/3140984/2022/02/23/arsenals-gabriel-martinelli-my-game-in-my-words/?source=emp_shared_article

Derby docked 21 points – Goal - https://www.goal.com/en-gb/news/why-derby-deducted-21-points-can-rooney-keep-them-up-rams-championship-challenge-explained/bltd6f036768519e024

Derby embargo for not paying December wages – The Guardian - https://www.theguardian.com/football/2021/feb/25/derby-takeover-silence-and-mounting-debts-how-did-it-come-to-this

Lawrence car crash and punishment – BBC News - https://www.bbc.co.uk/news/uk-england-derbyshire-50041085

Brentford £18m bid for Johnson, believing bid was accepted, booking medical, Cooper and Murphy not being told, both fighting to keep Johnson – The Athletic - https://www.nytimes.com/athletic/4813613/2023/08/29/brennan-johnson-transfer-latest/

Assombalonga £15m sale – BBC Sport -
https://www.bbc.co.uk/sport/football/40633653

Promotion generating at least £170m in revenue – Consultancy.UK
- https://www.consultancy.uk/news/21572/promotion-to-premier-
league-worth-170-million

Carvalho to Olympiacos, plus his Forest fee – BBC Sport -
https://www.bbc.co.uk/sport/football/60157058

Taylor to Birmingham on loan – BBC Sport -
https://www.bbc.co.uk/sport/football/60152982

Grabban ankle injury – BBC Sport -
https://www.bbc.co.uk/sport/football/60260051

Panzo fee – Nottingham Post -
https://www.nottinghampost.com/sport/football/transfer-
news/breaking-nottingham-forest-transfers-panzo-6580830

Ely contract termination – Nottingham Forest via Twitter -
https://twitter.com/NFFC/status/1488246433618837504

Surridge fee, being O'Neill's top summer target for Stoke, set for
Cardiff before Forest swooped – Stoke Sentinel -
https://www.stokesentinel.co.uk/sport/football/transfer-
news/stoke-city-transfer-sam-surridge-6581088

Dräger to FC Luzern – BBC Sport -
https://www.bbc.co.uk/sport/football/60230178

Luke Thomas pre Forest-Leicester – Daily Mail -
https://www.dailymail.co.uk/sport/football/article-

10481949/Leicester-Luke-Thomas-winning-FA-Cup-Brendan-Rodgers-playing-England.html

Leicester derby day tweet – Twitter -
https://twitter.com/LCFC/status/1490226252963356672

Leicester fans smash up pub – Nottingham Post -
https://www.nottinghampost.com/news/local-news/violent-leicester-city-fans-smash-6611837

Worrall broken ribs – Nottingham Post -
https://www.nottinghampost.com/sport/football/football-news/nottingham-forest-joe-worrall-injury-6611341

Leicester fan punches Davis – The Athletic -
https://www.nytimes.com/athletic/3510900/2022/02/24/leicester-fan-sentenced-to-four-months-in-prison-for-assaulting-three-nottingham-forest-players/

Bournemouth-Forest postponed, Bournemouth injury crisis, Forest lodge EFL complaint, Bournemouth SAG pushed for postponement due to Main Stand damage – Sky Sports -
https://www.skysports.com/football/news/11095/12548377/nottingham-forest-complain-to-efl-over-bournemouth-postponement-caused-by-storm-eunice

Parker comments re postponement – Dorset Live -
https://www.dorset.live/sport/football/football-news/scott-parker-fixture-backlog-would-6712096

Cooper post Preston (A) – BBC Sport -
https://www.bbc.co.uk/sport/football/60383804

Forest leaving 97 seats free – BBC Sport - https://www.bbc.co.uk/news/uk-england-nottinghamshire-60812866

Klopp's Robin Hood comments – Sky Sports (via Twitter) - https://x.com/SkySportsNews/status/1504763906803314695?lang=en

CHAPTER FIVE

Grabban coaching Davis – Training Ground Guru (via YouTube) - https://www.youtube.com/watch?v=ssdnDbKpBWk

Grabban fee of £6m – BBC Sport - https://www.bbc.co.uk/sport/football/44745167

Luton (A) delay cos of Sky – Nottingham Post - https://www.nottinghampost.com/sport/football/football-news/sky-sports-luton-nottingham-forest-6958688

Cooper post Luton (A) – BBC Sport - https://www.bbc.co.uk/sport/football/61033688

EFL Awards 2022 – BBC Sport - https://www.bbc.co.uk/sport/football/61209416

Davis out for regular season, but available for play-offs – Birmingham Mail -

https://www.birminghammail.co.uk/sport/football/football-news/aston-villa-keinan-davis-injury-23720166

Frank watching Johnson at Fulham (A) – Sky Sports - https://www.skysports.com/football/news/11095/12598898/fulham-0-1-nottingham-forest-philip-zinckernagel-hits-winner-as-steve-coopers-side-maintain-charge

Murphy named Championship CEO of the Year – Nottingham Forest (via Twitter) - https://x.com/NFFC/status/1520030948905082881?lang=en

Grabban out for season – BBC Sport - https://www.bbc.co.uk/sport/football/61261341

Full Grabban Forest stats – Transfermarkt - https://www.transfermarkt.co.uk/lewis-grabban/leistungsdaten/spieler/35413

Cooper post Swansea (H) – BBC Sport - https://www.bbc.co.uk/sport/football/61198207

CHAPTER SIX

Coach getting a red sendoff for Bournemouth – Nottingham Post - https://www.nottinghampost.com/sport/sport-opinion/bournemouth-nottingham-forest-fans-promotion-7028636

Officials apologise to Cooper – The Guardian - https://www.theguardian.com/football/2022/may/03/bournemouth-nottingham-forest-championship-match-report

Cook's dad at Bournemouth – BBC Sport - https://www.bbc.co.uk/sport/football/61315558#:~:text=Nottingham%20Forest%20defender%20Steve%20Cook,promotion%20to%20the%20Premier%20League.

Heckingbottom post Sheffield United (A) – TeamTalk - https://www.teamtalk.com/sheffield-united/paul-heckingbottom-reaction-forest-gutted-despite-win

Robinson comments post Sheffield United (A) – Nottingham Post - https://www.nottinghampost.com/sport/football/football-news/nottingham-forest-sheffield-united-robinson-7089899

Spence's mum as part of the pitch invasion – Copa90 (via Twitter) - https://twitter.com/Copa90/status/1526891006926503937

Fan attacks Sharp – BBC News - https://www.bbc.co.uk/news/uk-england-nottinghamshire-61505835

McBurnie cleared – BBC News - https://www.bbc.co.uk/news/uk-england-nottinghamshire-63983666#:~:text=Nottingham%20Forest%20fan%20George%20Brinkley,assault%20by%20beating%20on%20Thursday.

Zoe Potts' fundraiser for Sharp – JustGiving - https://www.justgiving.com/crowdfunding/zoe-potts-3

Sharp responds to fundraiser – Nottingham Post - https://www.nottinghampost.com/sport/football/football-news/nottingham-forest-billy-sharp-charity-7240456

Samba's water bottle – Daily Mail - https://www.dailymail.co.uk/sport/football/article-10828269/Nottingham-Forest-keeper-Brice-Samba-taped-penalty-instructions-water-bottle.html

Barbeque and family comments – Nottingham Post/Garibaldi Red - https://www.nottinghampost.com/sport/football/football-news/nottingham-forest-steve-cooper-wembley-7118430

Don Goodman's comments re Forest support at Wembley – Nottingham Forest News - https://www.nottinghamforest.news/2022/05/30/don-goodman-shares-amazing-nottingham-forest-moment-at-wembley/

Daniel Mann's commentary, Cook's comments, Cooper's post-match teamtalk – Sky Sports (via YouTube) - https://www.youtube.com/watch?v=wsmRp3M_YYA

Spence tweet to Warnock – Twitter - https://x.com/DjedSpence/status/1530991112176934912?lang=en

Warnock tweet back to Spence mentioning PL/non-league comment – Twitter - https://x.com/warnockofficial/status/1531203695999868928?lang=en

Mark Dennison comments – Red Side of the Trent (via YouTube) - https://www.youtube.com/watch?v=_fkH8uN5ays

Cook's VAR comments – Nottingham Post -
https://www.nottinghampost.com/sport/football/football-news/nottingham-forest-steve-cook-promotion-7145792

Marinakis' comments at Market Square – BBC Sport -
https://www.bbc.co.uk/sport/football/61634515

CHAPTER SEVEN

City Ground infrastructure changes – Nottingham Post -
https://www.nottinghampost.com/sport/football/football-news/nottingham-forest-preseason-fixtures-notts-7289361

PL rules on away fans – The FSA - https://thefsa.org.uk/wp-content/uploads/2021/01/Away_Fans_Matter_PDF.pdf

Cooper wanting the training pitches improved – The Athletic -
https://www.nytimes.com/athletic/4107230/2023/01/20/nottingham-forest-season-transformed/

Murphy interview re loanees – Sirius XM (via The Athletic) -
https://www.nytimes.com/athletic/3490535/2022/06/01/nottingham-forest-keen-to-retain-loan-stars-after-premier-league-promotion-murphy/

Spence wanting Spurs in January – The Athletic -
https://www.nytimes.com/athletic/3434855/2022/07/20/djed-spence-tottenham-transfer/

Sheffield United's Lowe pricetag + January offer – Sheffield Star - https://www.thestar.co.uk/sport/football/sheffield-united/sheffield-united-send-nottingham-forest-a-warning-over-max-lowe-chase-3733488

Villa asking price for Davis – The Mirror - https://www.mirror.co.uk/sport/football/transfer-news/aston-villa-transfer-news-gerrard-27102064

Zinckernagel Olympiacos fee – Watford Observer - https://www.watfordobserver.co.uk/sport/20233073.zinckernagel-makes-permanent-move-watford-olympiacos/

Cooper close to new deal – The Telegraph - https://www.telegraph.co.uk/football/2022/06/16/nottingham-forest-manager-steve-cooper-close-signing-new-contract/

McKenna wins POTS – Nottingham Forest - https://www.nottinghamforest.co.uk/news/2022/june/13/mckenna-wins-uk-meds-player-of-the-season/

Cooper and Postecoglou on holiday – Celts Are Here - https://celtsarehere.com/ange-spotted-poolside-with-nottingham-forest-duo/

McKenna POTM at Wembley – Press and Journal - https://www.pressandjournal.co.uk/fp/sport/football/aberdeen-fc/6391977/exclusive-former-aberdeen-defender-scott-mckenna-says-1-75m-boost-payback-to-dons/#:~:text=Scott%20McKenna%20of%20Nottingham%20Forest,defeat%20of%20Huddersfield%20at%20Wembley.

Ten Hag running rule over Garner in pre-season – One Football - https://onefootball.com/en/news/man-utd-boss-ten-hag-keeps-forest-waiting-for-garner-decision-35277417

Study giving Forest a 32% chance of survival – The Athletic - https://www.nytimes.com/athletic/5566790/2024/06/20/steve-cooper-leicester-nottingham-forest/

Wolves wanting at least £20m for Forest target Gibbs-White – The Athletic - https://www.nytimes.com/athletic/3342291/2022/06/01/nottingham-forest-transfer-news-djed-spence/

Forest linked with Dovbyk – Sports Arena (via Nottingham Forest News) - https://www.nottinghamforest.news/2022/06/06/report-agent-confirms-nottingham-forest-talks-for-artem-dovbyk/

Awoniyi fee – TNT Sports - https://www.tntsports.co.uk/football/transfers/2022-2023/taiwo-awoniyi-nottingham-forest-sign-nigeria-international-for-club-record-fee-from-union-berlin_sto9005343/story.shtml

Forest wanting Cheick Doucoure – TeleFoot (via Nottingham Forest News) - https://www.nottinghamforest.news/2022/06/30/report-nottingham-forest-wanted-crystal-palace-bound-cheick-doucoure/

Forest wanting Sangaré, Forest being accused of distorting the market by other PL clubs – The Athletic - https://www.nytimes.com/athletic/3558295/2022/09/02/nottingham-forest-transfer-window/

Forest wanting Amadou Onana – Sacha Tavolieri (via Nottingham Forest News) -
https://www.nottinghamforest.news/2022/07/04/report-nottingham-forest-rejected-by-amadou-onana/

Onana Everton fee – BBC Sport -
https://www.bbc.co.uk/sport/football/62432408

Forest pre-season schedule – Nottingham Forest -
https://www.nottinghamforest.co.uk/news/2022/june/27/pre-season-schedule-announced/

Johnson four-year deal – Nottingham Forest -
https://www.nottinghamforest.co.uk/news/2022/july/01/johnson-signs-new-long-term-deal/

Steven Reid leaves Forest and Cooper wishing him well – Nottingham Forest -
https://www.nottinghamforest.co.uk/news/2022/july/08/steven-reid-leaves-forest/

Forest wanting Nick Pope – The Sun -
https://www.thesun.co.uk/sport/football/18784793/nottingham-forest-nick-pope-burnley-bid/

Forest wanting Henderson – The Guardian -
https://www.theguardian.com/football/2022/jun/15/nottingham-forest-manchester-united-dean-henderson-loan

Samba rejects deal and demands to leave – The Athletic -
https://theathletic.com/news/brice-samba-nottingham-forest-transfer/PkTD3Xzh8qtD/

Samba feeling he has unfinished business in France – L'Equipe (via Get French Football News) -
https://www.getfootballnewsfrance.com/2023/i-wont-close-the-door-lens-brice-samba-open-to-premier-league-move/

Samba fee of £4.3m – L'Equipe (via SportWitness) -
https://sportwitness.co.uk/player-little-bit-closer-nottingham-forest-exit-e5m-fee-clubs-basically-agreement/

Biancone £5m fee – The Athletic -
https://www.nytimes.com/athletic/4169754/2022/07/02/nottingham-forest-agree-5m-fee-for-giulian-biancone/

Niakhaté fee – BBC Sport -
https://www.bbc.co.uk/sport/football/62072070

Grabban rejects new deal – The Athletic -
https://theathletic.com/4169391/2022/07/08/lewis-grabban-turns-down-new-nottingham-forest-contract-offer/

Worrall named captain, Yates as vice – Nottingham Forest -
https://www.nottinghamforest.co.uk/news/2022/august/04/joe-worrall-named-nottingham-forest-captain/

Richards and Williams fees – The Guardian -
https://www.theguardian.com/football/2022/jul/07/nottingham-forest-agree-fees-neco-williams-liverpool-and-omar-richards-bayern-munich

Forest linked with Kabore – Nottingham Post -
https://www.nottinghampost.com/sport/football/transfer-news/nottingham-forest-manchester-city-kabore-7165697

Wayne and Terry Hennessy – BBC Sport - https://www.bbc.co.uk/sport/football/67005787#:~:text=Goalkeeper%20%2D%20Wayne%20Hennessey&text=However%2C%20you%20might%20not%20know,Nottingham%20Forest%20and%20Derby%20County.

Aguilera fee – Futbol Central America (via Nottingham Forest news) - https://www.nottinghamforest.news/2022/07/17/report-nottingham-forest-set-to-sign-brandon-aguilera/

O'Brien + Toffolo fee and deal nearly falling through – The Athletic - https://www.nytimes.com/athletic/4165652/2022/07/19/nottingham-forest-move-for-lewis-obrien-and-harry-toffolo-back-on-after-u-turn/

Forest name Richards on the bench v Hertha Berlin – Nottingham Forest (via Facebook) -

https://www.facebook.com/officialnffc/posts/-**TEAM-NEWS-HERTHA-BERLIN**-steve-cooper-names-his-side-ahead-of-tonights-pre-seaso/609095357251355/

Cooper quotes on Richards injury – The Athletic - https://www.nytimes.com/athletic/4165568/2022/07/20/nottingham-forest-new-signing-omar-richards-faces-injury-lay-off-after-suffering-hairline-leg-fracture/

Richards not having an X-ray during his medical, Forest going back to Bayern, choosing to pretend Richards wasn't injured – The Athletic -

https://www.nytimes.com/athletic/4693442/2023/07/17/nottingham-forest-omar-richards-injury/

Forest in talks with Lingard, £180k a week mooted – The Guardian -

https://www.theguardian.com/football/2022/jul/20/nottingham-forest-in-advanced-jesse-lingard-talks-west-ham

West Ham giving Lingard ultimatums and leaving him feeling disrespected, Cooper offering to go to his house, Marinakis offering to fly him to Greece – Steven Bartlett's Diary of a CEO podcast (via Hammers.News) - https://www.hammers.news/club-news/jesse-lingard-lifts-the-lid-on-the-real-reason-west-ham-move-negotiations-broke-down-before-he-chose-nottingham-forest/#:~:text=And%20he%20says%20West%20Ham,and%20issued%20him%20with%20ultimatums.&text=%E2%80%9CThings%20broke%20down%20at%20West,Diary%20of%20a%20CEO%20podcast.

Worrall comments on Lingard – Daily Express - https://www.express.co.uk/sport/football/1646691/joe-worrall-jesse-lingard-nottingham-forest-exclusive-interview

Lingard's real wages amidst £200k a week claims – The Telegraph - https://www.telegraph.co.uk/football/2022/07/21/jesse-lingard-sign-nottingham-forest-80000-per-week-deal/

West Ham offered more than Forest for Lingard – The Times - https://www.thetimes.com/sport/football/article/how-nottingham-forest-hijacked-deal-for-jesse-lingard-in-just-four-days-nvvlk3brd

Mangala fee – Nottingham Post - https://www.nottinghampost.com/sport/football/transfer-news/breaking-nottingham-forest-sign-mangala-7402160

Forest's £35m Gibbs-White bid rejected – The Guardian - https://www.theguardian.com/football/2022/aug/04/nottingham-forest-submit-improved-offer-for-wolves-winger-gibbs-white#:~:text=Wolves%20have%20rejected%20Nottingham%20Forest's,to%20do%20his%20best%20game%E2%80%9D.

Forest wanting Summerville – The Athletic - https://www.nytimes.com/athletic/3368826/2022/06/18/leeds-transfer-news-every-players-summer-move-and-contract-situation-explained/

Botman fee – BBC Sport - https://www.bbc.co.uk/sport/football/61974824

Colin Fray comments – Red Side of the Trent podcast (via YouTube) - https://www.youtube.com/watch?v=Feo-c-FVf2w

BOXT not paying what Marinakis wanted – Sportcal - https://www.sportcal.com/comment/why-have-nottingham-forest-started-the-season-without-a-shirt-sponsor/

Forest hire Charnley at Murphy's request – The Telegraph - https://www.telegraph.co.uk/football/2022/08/07/nottingham-forest-premier-league-survival-guide-newcastle/

Moreno rejects Forest – The Guardian - https://www.theguardian.com/football/2022/aug/08/nottingham-forest-close-to-signing-real-betis-defender-alex-moreno

Estupiñán rejects Forest for Brighton – The Athletic - https://www.nytimes.com/athletic/3513415/2022/08/16/brighton-transfer-pervis-estupinan/

Dennis fee of around £10m potentially rising to £20m – The Athletic - https://www.nytimes.com/athletic/4052261/2023/01/03/emmanuel-dennis-forest-transfer/

Freuler fee – The Guardian - https://www.theguardian.com/football/2022/aug/11/nottingham-forest-make-9m-remo-freuler-their-14th-summer-signing-football-atalanta-football#:~:text=Nottingham%20Forest%20have%20agreed%20a,Forest's%2014th%20incoming%20this%20summer.

Lolley's gripe – The Football Friends podcast (via Nottingham Post) - https://www.nottinghampost.com/sport/football/transfer-news/nottingham-forest-criticised-promotion-hero-9103177

Lolley fee, Cooper insiting it's nothing personal – The Athletic - https://www.nytimes.com/athletic/3428653/2022/07/18/joe-lolley-nottingham-forest/

Lolley stats – Transfermarkt - https://www.transfermarkt.co.uk/joe-lolley/leistungsdaten/spieler/287167

Forest wanting £15m for Lolley – The Sun (via Nottingham Post) - https://www.nottinghampost.com/sport/football/transfer-news/nottingham-forest-want-15-million-2932954

Gibbs-White fee, Cooper being annoyed he couldn't sign him on loan at Forest as he started too late – The Telegraph - https://www.telegraph.co.uk/football/2022/08/18/nottingham-forest-sign-morgan-gibbs-white-35m/

Gibbs-White rejecting contract offers – The Athletic - https://www.nytimes.com/athletic/3480311/2022/08/05/wolves-morgan-gibbs-white-nottingham-forest/

Everton last ditch bid for Gibbs-White, Cooper influence key – The Telegraph (via Twitter) - https://twitter.com/JPercyTelegraph/status/1560556809383038976

CHAPTER EIGHT

Hwang fee – L'Equipe (via Get French Football News) - https://www.getfootballnewsfrance.com/2022/nottingham-forest-set-to-sign-bordeauxs-hwang-ui-jo/

Lodi loan fee + option – Fabrizio Romano (via Twitter) - https://twitter.com/FabrizioRomano/status/1564177117658611712

Marinakis and Cooper courting Lodi, Lodi's World Cup intentions – The Athletic - https://www.nytimes.com/athletic/3546913/2022/08/30/forest-transfer-lodi-tactics-profile/

Boly fee – The Telegraph (via Twitter) - https://twitter.com/JPercyTelegraph/status/1564673901325606913

Bowler fee – The Athletic - https://www.nytimes.com/athletic/4060921/2023/01/05/josh-bowler-blackpool-forest-olympiacos-transfer-news/

Forest previous interest in Bowler – The Athletic - https://www.nytimes.com/athletic/3092565/2022/01/26/keeping-brennan-johnson-would-be-a-statement-of-intent-but-forest-have-a-plan-if-he-goes/

Chasing Batshuayi, Cooper being annoyed at contract talks being leaked, Marinakis Jnr having more of a say on transfers – The Athletic - https://www.nytimes.com/athletic/3558295/2022/09/02/nottingham-forest-transfer-window/

Cooper comments post Bournemouth (H) – BBC Sport - https://www.bbc.co.uk/sport/football/62697700

Forest break British record for most signings in one window – BBC Sport - https://www.bbc.co.uk/sport/football/62826452

FA postpone all football – The FA - https://www.thefa.com/news/2022/sep/09/statement-football-9-11-september-2022-20220909#:~:text=Her%20Majesty%20the%20Queen%20was,fixtures%20between%209%2D11%20September.

Crafton's NLD XI – Daily Mail - https://www.dailymail.co.uk/sport/football/article-5089853/Arsenal-v-Spurs-combined-XI-writers-pick-teams.html

Crafton QPR 2012 tweet – Twitter -
https://twitter.com/AdamCrafton_/status/1570870325147205632

Cooper on the brink post Leicester (A), Benítez, Nuno, Lage and Dyche in the frame – The Athletic -
https://www.nytimes.com/athletic/3657009/2022/10/05/forest-cooper-benitez-nuno-lage-dyche/

Murphy allegedly wanting Marsch – The Telegraph (via Twitter) -
https://twitter.com/JPercyTelegraph/status/1612510037687078912

Forest approach Benítez – The Times -
https://www.thetimes.com/sport/football/article/nottingham-forest-approach-rafa-ben-tez-as-pressure-rises-on-steve-cooper-btvm6hwd7

Cooper signs new deal – Nottingham Forest -
https://www.nottinghamforest.co.uk/news/2022/october/07/steve-cooper-signs-new-contract/

Giraldi hired, review into recruitment, Scott and Syrianios fired – The Telegraph -
https://www.telegraph.co.uk/football/2022/10/11/nottingham-forest-sack-recruitment-chiefs-150m-summer-spree/

Giraldi overseeing Richarlison and Doucouré signings – Daily Mail - https://www.dailymail.co.uk/sport/football/article-11283635/Nottingham-Forest-set-management-shake-new-sporting-director-Filippo-Giraldi.html

Murphy taking legal action over Forest re bonuses – The Athletic - https://www.nytimes.com/athletic/4076657/2023/01/11/dane-murphy-nottingham-forest/

Forest could replace Murphy with Charnley – The Telegraph - https://www.telegraph.co.uk/football/2022/10/04/nottingham-forest-owner-considers-sacking-chief-executive-head/

Gerrard comments on Cooper – BBC Sport - https://www.bbc.co.uk/sport/football/63159650

Forest's 'playtime' tweet, Neves seeing it and sharing, Wolves' subsequent tweet – BBC Sport - https://www.bbc.co.uk/sport/football/63281920

Tweet deleted after Forest official intervention – The Athletic - https://www.nytimes.com/athletic/3698551/2022/10/17/premier-league-drake-world-cup-ornstein/

CHAPTER NINE

Cooper disappointment post Arsenal (A) – BBC Sport - https://www.bbc.co.uk/sport/football/63362269

Biancone injury – Daily Mail - https://www.dailymail.co.uk/sport/football/article-11386581/Nottingham-Forest-defender-Giulian-Biancone-ruled-rest-season-knee-injury.html

Wissa penalty a VAR error – ESPN -
https://www.espn.co.uk/football/story/_/id/37634986/arsenal-goal-manchester-united-6-var-errors-premier-league

Lodi out of the Brazil squad – Be Soccer -
https://www.besoccer.com/new/lodi-s-move-doesn-t-work-out-he-will-miss-the-world-cup-1200816

Forest players picked for World Cup duty – Nottingham Forest -
https://www.nottinghamforest.co.uk/news/2022/november/10/five-reds-selected-for-world-cup/

Lingard's England ambition – Nottingham Post -
https://www.nottinghampost.com/sport/football/football-news/nottingham-forest-jesse-lingard-england-7584040

Cooper's quotes on the challenge at hand – The Athletic -
https://www.nytimes.com/athletic/4107230/2023/01/20/nottingham-forest-season-transformed/

Forest players given a break – Nottingham Post -
https://www.nottinghampost.com/sport/football/football-news/nottingham-forest-world-cup-break-7813674

Lingard documentary – Channel 4 -
https://www.channel4.com/programmes/the-jesse-lingard-story-untold

Lingard warm weather training with Welbeck, Lodi training in Brazil – Nottingham Post -
https://www.nottinghampost.com/sport/football/football-news/nottingham-forest-friendly-stoke-city-7856457

Lodi wins Goal of the Round – Nottingham Forest - https://www.nottinghamforest.co.uk/news/2022/december/01/lodi-wins-carabao-cup-goal-of-the-round/

Scarpa winning best player in Brazil award – Nottingham Forest News - https://www.nottinghamforest.news/2022/11/15/nottingham-forest-bound-star-gustavo-scarpa-claims-huge-accolade/

Cooper thought he was running rule over Scarpa's suitability for Olympiacos, coaching staff felt he wasn't PL suited – The Times - https://www.thetimes.co.uk/article/ea13e0b5-6a64-4be4-b357-acd35b3c3f28?shareToken=cfc629690a4ab406730333f0bc877866

Forest angry with Senegal – The Telegraph - https://www.telegraph.co.uk/world-cup/2022/12/09/nottingham-forest-furious-row-senegal/

O'Brien illness – The Athletic - https://www.nytimes.com/athletic/4336576/2023/03/23/dc-united-lewis-obrien/

Forest legends in Valencia, all red kit – Nottingham Forest - https://www.nottinghamforest.co.uk/news/2022/december/15/forest-to-wear-all-red-against-valencia/

Luke Edwards' comments – BBC Sport - https://www.bbc.co.uk/sport/live/football/63641454

CHAPTER TEN

Forest and UNHCR – Nottingham Forest -
https://www.nottinghamforest.co.uk/news/2022/december/22/forest-and-uk-for-unhcr-launch-charity-shirt-partnership/

Forest want Dennis out, Lingard injury, Forest targeting more signings – The Telegraph -
https://www.telegraph.co.uk/football/2023/01/02/exclusive-emmanuel-dennis-facing-nottingham-forest-axe-five/

FIFA laws complicating Dennis' future, interest in him from Saudi Arabia and America – The Athletic -
https://www.nytimes.com/athletic/4052261/2023/01/03/emmanuel-dennis-forest-transfer/

Rennes ask Forest not to play Badé – Le Telegramme (via Get French Football News) -
https://www.getfootballnewsfrance.com/2022/loic-bade-set-to-return-to-rennes-after-not-featuring-for-nottingham-forest/

Stuart Pearce wanting Che Adams for Forest in 2014 – The Athletic -
https://www.nytimes.com/athletic/4585804/2023/06/08/nottingham-forest-summer-transfers-2023/

Cooper comments post Southampton (A) – BBC Sport -
https://www.bbc.co.uk/sport/football/64106273

Cooper dispels Dennis rumours – Punch Newspaper -
https://punchng.com/forest-coach-cooper-dispels-dennis-exit-rumours/

Cooper comments post Blackpool (A) – BBC Sport - https://www.bbc.co.uk/sport/football/64167874

Murphy leaves by mutual consent – BBC Sport - https://www.bbc.co.uk/sport/articles/c72rq655ng30

Cooper comments post Wolves (H) – BBC Sport - https://www.bbc.co.uk/sport/football/64159376

Danilo fee – BBC Sport - https://www.bbc.co.uk/sport/football/64298998

Arsenal have bids rejected for Danilo – Metro - https://metro.co.uk/2022/12/14/arsenal-cool-interest-in-brazillian-star-danilo-for-two-major-reasons-17934547/#:~:text=Arsenal%20have%20cooled%20their%20interest,squad%20needed%20an%20extra%20midfielder.

Wood transfer clause – The Athletic - https://www.nytimes.com/athletic/4219262/2023/02/17/chris-wood-nottingham-forest-transfer/

Henderson out for four to five weeks – The Independent - https://www.independent.co.uk/sport/football/steve-cooper-nottingham-forest-dean-henderson-leicester-bournemouth-b2265372.html

Surridge applauded in the dressing room post Bournemouth – The Independent - https://www.independent.co.uk/sport/football/steve-cooper-nottingham-forest-sam-surridge-bournemouth-b2266733.html

Cooper utilising Miracle Men, organising regular team meals, calling his players – The Athletic - https://www.nytimes.com/athletic/4107230/2023/01/20/nottingham-forest-season-transformed/

Johnson Player of the Round – EFL - https://www.efl.com/news/2023/january/brennan-johnson-scoops-carabao-cup-player-of-the-round/#:~:text=Nottingham%20Forest's%20Brennan%20Johnson%20has,Blackburn%20Rovers%20in%20Round%20Four.

Cooper nominated for Manager of the Month, Arteta wins it – Premier League - https://www.premierleague.com/news/3043094

Felipe fee – Daily Mail - https://www.dailymail.co.uk/sport/football/article-11698537/Nottingham-Forest-complete-2m-deal-Atletico-Madrid-centre-Felipe.html

Shelvey signs on a free, Howe praises Shelvey – The Athletic - https://www.nytimes.com/athletic/4683409/2023/07/14/nottingham-forest-shelvey-wood/

Shelvey wages – The Telegraph - https://www.telegraph.co.uk/football/2023/01/29/nottingham-forest-verge-signing-jonjo-shelvey-25th-player/

PSG not wanting Navas to leave due to maintaining Donnarumma's standards, Marinakis suggesting it, Navas being keen and eyeing up the cup semi-final, deal seeming dead before being revived, PSG paying big part of wages, Henderson injury setback, United look to recall Henderson but he chose to stay, Henderson a key target – The Telegraph - https://www.telegraph.co.uk/football/2023/02/04/inside-story-how-nottingham-forest-signed-keylor-navas/

Henderson Player of the Round – Nottingham Forest - https://www.nottinghamforest.co.uk/news/2023/february/01/henderson-voted-carabao-cup-player-of-the-round/

Blackburn obligation to buy O'Brien if they were promoted – Lancashire Live - https://www.lancs.live/sport/football/transfer-news/obrien-blackburn-nottingham-forest-transfer-26587280

Blackburn statement re O'Brien – Lancashire Telegraph - https://www.lancashiretelegraph.co.uk/sport/23295451.blackburn-rovers-issue-club-statement-efl-reject-lewis-obrien-deal/

Cooper claims Blackburn let O'Brien down, Broughton comments – The Athletic - https://www.nytimes.com/athletic/4153642/2023/02/03/lewis-o-brien-blackburn-forest-transfer/

Cooper comments post United (A) – Sky Sports - https://www.skysports.com/football/news/11938/12799099/man-utd-2-0-nottingham-forest-agg-5-0-carabao-cup-goals-from-anthony-martial-and-fred-steer-red-devils-to-wembley-final#:~:text=Leading%203%2D0%20from%20the,seal%20a%202%2D0%20win.

O'Brien and Superstition – The Athletic -
https://www.nytimes.com/athletic/4336576/2023/03/23/dc-
united-lewis-obrien/

Bamford's flowers for Doughty – Yorkshire Evening Post -
https://www.yorkshireeveningpost.co.uk/sport/football/leeds-
united/leeds-united-man-reveals-reason-for-personal-nottingham-
forest-gesture-which-left-friends-in-tears-4015201

Navas Player of the Match v Leeds – Premier League -
https://www.premierleague.com/match/75128

Forest ask PL to include Cook after McKenna (six weeks) and Boly
(three months) get injured – Daily Mail -
https://www.dailymail.co.uk/sport/football/article-
11759527/Nottingham-Forest-turn-Steve-Cook-injuries-Willy-Boly-
Scott-McKenna.html

Cooper's comments post City (H) – Sky Sports -
https://www.skysports.com/football/news/11679/12811724/notting
ham-forest-1-1-man-city-chris-wood-scores-late-leveller-as-pep-
guardiolas-side-lose-ground-on-arsenal-in-title-race

CHAPTER ELEVEN

PL reject Cook appeal – The Athletic -
https://www.nytimes.com/athletic/4227752/2023/02/19/nottingha
m-forest-steve-cook-squad-appeal/

Cooper comments post West Ham (A) – BBC Sport - https://www.bbc.co.uk/sport/football/64686323

Conte explodes at Tottenham – The Guardian - https://www.theguardian.com/football/2023/mar/10/antonio-conte-tottenham-future-contract-richarlison-nottingham-forest#:~:text=We%20are%20trying%20to%20build,the%20board%20on%20numerous%20occasions.

Scarpa suffers crypto scam – The Guardian - https://www.theguardian.com/football/2023/mar/15/nottingham-forests-gustavo-scarpa-in-brazil-after-losing-1m-in-crypto-scam

Wood out for the season, Scarpa and Aurier injury concerns – BBC Sport - https://www.bbc.co.uk/sport/football/65124721

Blackburn O'Brien appeal rejected – BBC Sport - https://www.bbc.co.uk/sport/football/64816632

Cooper comments re Lopetegui – The Independent - https://www.independent.co.uk/sport/football/nottingham-forest-wolves-steve-cooper-julen-lopetegui-b2312421.html

Podence investigated for spitting, but cleared – BBC Sport - https://www.bbc.co.uk/sport/football/65681361

Cooper comments post Leeds (A) – Sky Sports - https://www.skysports.com/football/news/11095/12849261/leeds-2-1-nottingham-forest-luis-sinisterra-stunner-lifts-leeds-up-to-13th-in-premier-league

Vieira linked with Forest job – Daily Mail -
https://www.dailymail.co.uk/sport/football/article-11937571/Patrick-Vieira-emerges-leading-candidate-replace-Steve-Cooper-Nottingham-Forest.html

Marinakis speaks to Forest platers post Wolves, not happy with subs – Daily Mail -
https://www.dailymail.co.uk/sport/football/article-11930035/Steve-Cooper-great-coach-manage-Champions-League-club-hes-50.html

Cooper a 'dead man walking' after Leeds loss – The Athletic -
https://www.nytimes.com/athletic/5124157/2023/12/20/steve-cooper-nottingham-forest-exit/

Marinakis statement backing Cooper – Nottingham Forest -
https://www.nottinghamforest.co.uk/news/2023/april/05/statement-from-nottingham-forest-owner--evangelos-marinakis/

Forest sack Giraldi and hire Wilson – BBC Sport -
https://www.bbc.co.uk/sport/football/65249557

Rangers anger at Wilson – BBC Sport -
https://www.bbc.co.uk/sport/football/65258735

Giraldi speaks out – The Athletic -
https://www.nytimes.com/athletic/4609171/2023/06/19/filippo-giraldi-forest-watford/

VAR explanation for Maguire handball – ESPN -
https://www.espn.co.uk/football/story/_/id/37637961/harry-maguire-handball-west-ham-penalty-vs-arsenal

Niakhaté tweet – Twitter -
https://x.com/moussa_nkt/status/1647957962478977025

CHAPTER TWELVE

McKenna out for season – BBC Sport -
https://www.bbc.co.uk/sport/football/65378895

Shelvey banished + reasons why – The Telegraph -
https://www.telegraph.co.uk/football/2023/04/24/jonjo-shelvey-ordered-stay-home-angry-forest-substitute/

Shelvey offers John Legend £50k to a sing a song – Sky Sports (via TikTok) -
https://www.tiktok.com/@skysports/video/7213049072079473926?lang=en

Shelvey showing his highlights to random girl – Daily Mail -
https://www.dailymail.co.uk/sport/football/article-12262209/Woman-claims-Premier-League-footballer-highlights-night-out.html

Cooper post Brighton (H) – Nottingham Forest -
https://www.nottinghamforest.co.uk/news/2023/april/27/cooper-on-brighton-win--game-plan-and-looking-forward/

Henderson out for season – The Independent -
https://www.independent.co.uk/sport/football/dean-henderson-injury-man-utd-nottingham-forest-b2330729.html

Henderson sticking around regardless – Daily Mail -
https://www.dailymail.co.uk/sport/football/article-
12051669/Nottingham-Forest-boss-Cooper-says-hard-say-work-
Henderson-again.html

Cooper post Brentford (A) – BBC Sport -
https://www.bbc.co.uk/sport/football/65357222

Seb Hutchinson's commentary – Sky Sports -
https://www.skysports.com/watch/video/sports/football/1287674
5/nottingham-forest-4-3-southampton-premier-league-highlights

Awoniyi and Roy stat, Awoniyi comments post Chelsea (A) – BBC
Sport - https://www.bbc.com/sport/football/65506025

Arsenal 248 days stat – Opta (via Twitter) -
https://x.com/OptaJoe/status/1659991615853699083?lang=en

Marinakis comments post Arsenal (H) – BBC Sport -
https://www.bbc.co.uk/sport/articles/cn4e995g47vo

Cooper comments post Arsenal (H) – Sky Sports (via YouTube) -
https://www.youtube.com/watch?v=mcM2bC_cKVY

Niakhaté + Cooper interview – Nottingham Forest (via Twitter) -
https://x.com/nffc/status/1660236086151458817?s=46&t=n5digTa
oBoyfbCJSHT037w

Luke Edwards' tweet post Arsenal (H) – Twitter -
https://x.com/lukeedwardstele/status/1660006778459832321?s=46
&t=n5digTaoBoyfbCJSHT037w

Crafton tweet one – Twitter -
https://x.com/adamcrafton /status/1655674067595173894?s=46&t=n5digTaoBoyfbCJSHT037w

Crafton tweet two – Twitter -
https://x.com/AdamCrafton /status/1655674123454914592

Forest team post Arsenal (H) – Nottingham Forest (via YouTubeo
- https://www.youtube.com/watch?v=zUUHEqCcvQs

Awoniyi stat since Collymore – BBC Sport -
https://www.bbc.co.uk/sport/football/65661811

CHAPTER THIRTEEN

Cooper linked with Palace – Daily Mail -
https://www.dailymail.co.uk/sport/football/article-11887517/Crystal-Palace-Roy-Hodgson-short-term-solution-club-eye-Steve-Cooper.html

Leeds interest in Cooper, pre-season kit launch at Nottingham
Castle, Randall's comments on Worrall + Cooper's rage – The
Athletic -
https://www.nytimes.com/athletic/5124157/2023/12/20/steve-cooper-nottingham-forest-exit/

Steven Reid returns – Nottingham Forest -
https://www.nottinghamforest.co.uk/news/2023/july/03/reid-returns-to-forest-coaching-staff/

Forest spend 2022/23 being at least £150m, a focus on quality over quantity – The Athletic - https://www.nytimes.com/athletic/4585804/2023/06/08/nottingham-forest-summer-transfers-2023/

Randall assuring everyone PSR wasn't an issue – The Athletic - https://www.nytimes.com/athletic/5815371/2024/10/04/nicholas-randall-chairman-forest-explained/

Atletico bid around £43m for Johnson – 90min - https://www.90min.com/posts/premier-league-report-reveals-la-liga-giants-50m-bid-brennan-johnson

Atletico would need to sell before buying Johnson – The Athletic - https://www.nytimes.com/athletic/4813613/2023/08/29/brennan-johnson-transfer-latest/

Lodi clause expiring in March, Forest not willing to pay £26m – Marca (via SportWitness) - https://sportwitness.co.uk/nottingham-forest-want-coopers-side-set-reopen-negotiations-signing-club-keen-sell-player/

Lodi wanting Champions League football – GE Globo - https://ge.globo.com/pr/blogs/blog-da-nadja/post/2023/06/13/atletico-de-madrid-pede-alto-por-renan-lodi-e-dificulta-volta-ao-brasil-lateral-tem-desejo-de-retornar-ao-athletico.ghtml

Brazil position made untenable – The Athletic - https://www.nytimes.com/athletic/4631060/2023/06/26/gary-brazil-assessment/

Willian Forest U-turn – The Standard -
https://www.standard.co.uk/sport/football/willian-fulham-fc-transfer-b1094768.html

Forest adidas deal the biggest sponsorship deal in the club's history
– The Athletic -
https://www.nytimes.com/athletic/4394277/2023/04/10/chilwell-chelsea-deal-balogun-arsenal/

Forest bid for Sangaré – The Athletic -
https://www.nytimes.com/athletic/4685207/2023/07/12/ibrahim-sangare-nottingham-forest-transfer/

Sangaré needing convincing – ESPN (via Nottingham Forest News)
- https://www.nottinghamforest.news/2023/07/30/nottingham-forest-will-hold-talks-with-ibrahim-sangare-star-after-clash-with-psv-today/

Elanga fee – BBC Sport -
https://www.bbc.co.uk/sport/football/66301365

Elanga choosing Forest over Everton – The Guardian -
https://www.theguardian.com/football/2023/jul/25/nottingham-forest-sign-anthony-elanga-15m-manchester-united-everton

Henderson convinced he's going back to Forest, De Gea departure
making things difficult – Manchester Evening News -
https://www.manchestereveningnews.co.uk/sport/football/transfer-news/manchester-united-transfers-dean-henderson-27201333

Surridge fee – The Tennessean -
https://eu.tennessean.com/story/sports/nashvillesc/2023/07/14/na

shville-sc-new-player-sam-surridge-nottingham-forest-mls/70415540007/

Brentford £35m bid for Johnson rejected, Forest valuing at £50m – The Guardian - https://www.theguardian.com/football/2023/jul/28/nottingham-forest-brentford-brennan-johnson-35m-offer#:~:text=Brentford%20have%20tracked%20Johnson%20for,package%20to%20about%20%C2%A340m.

Full Brentford bid breakdown for Johnson, came via WhatsApp, Cooper explaining to Johnson he may be sold, Ojeda fee, Johnson signs for Spurs for £47.5m, Forest refusing to sell to Brentford – The Telegraph - https://www.telegraph.co.uk/football/2023/09/01/tottenham-transfer-brennan-johnson-joins-nottingham-forest/

United worried Henderson would fail a medical – The Sun - https://www.thesun.co.uk/sport/23384943/dean-henderson-man-utd-nottingham-forest-transfer-injury/

Turner fee – Daily Mail - https://www.dailymail.co.uk/sport/football/article-12388711/Arsenal-goalkeeper-Matt-Turner-completes-7m-Nottingham-Forest-four-year-deal.html

Arsenal's Turner fee – talkSPORT - https://talksport.com/football/1526955/arsenal-matt-turner-nottingham-forest-transfer/

Cooper tells Turner he's his number one, Forest hierarchy tell Vlachodimos he's number one – The Athletic - https://www.nytimes.com/athletic/5568031/2024/06/18/nottingham-forest-brice-samba-goalkeepers-transfer/

Cooper gives injury update and squad comment before Arsenal (A) – BBC Sport - https://www.bbc.co.uk/sport/articles/cyx9zknegnxo

Forest response to Nottingham tragedy, Cooper's comments, Wood and Worrall helping out, Yates donating, family in the director's box – The Athletic - https://www.nytimes.com/athletic/4772062/2023/08/17/ian-coates-nottingham-forest/

Awoniyi matches Collymore stat, Cooper's comments post Sheffield United (H) – BBC Sport - https://www.bbc.co.uk/sport/football/66470075

Richards' Instagram post – Instagram (via Nottingham Post) - https://www.nottinghampost.com/sport/football/football-news/omar-richards-issues-emotional-statement-8652565

Montiel allegations and Forest response – The Athletic - https://www.nytimes.com/athletic/4803504/2023/08/25/gonzalo-montiel-nottingham-forest-world-cup-argentina/

Cooper unaware of Andrey Santos' arrival – The Athletic - https://www.nytimes.com/athletic/5165753/2024/01/04/nottingham-forest-transfer-news/

Syrianos returns to Forest – The Athletic -
https://www.nytimes.com/athletic/4774426/2023/08/14/nottingh
am-forest-transfers-george-syrianos-recruitment/

Cooper comments post Man Utd (A) – Sky Sports -
https://www.skysports.com/football/news/11661/12945897/manch
ester-united-3-2-nottingham-forest-bruno-fernandes-scores-winner-
against-10-player-forest-who-had-led-by-two-goals

Forest lodge complaint over Attwell – The Telegraph -
https://www.telegraph.co.uk/football/2023/08/28/nottingham-
forest-complaint-over-referee-manchester-united/

Henderson's Palace fee, Forest exploring further loan moves for
him, Cooper wanting Tavares' pace, Omobamidele fee and
circumstances, Chalobah bid, Batshuayi chase, Origi loan fee – The
Athletic -
https://www.nytimes.com/athletic/4835013/2023/09/07/forest-
transfer-window-summer-2023/

Cooper's comments re Worrall, Worrall wanting to play – ITV -
https://www.itv.com/news/central/2023-08-31/family-comes-first-
football-comes-second-joe-worrall-grieves-hero-officer

Forest partner with Kaiyun Sports – Nottingham Forest -
https://www.nottinghamforest.co.uk/news/2023/august/30/forest
-announce-kaiyun-sports-as-front-of-shirt-partner/

Murillo fee, Tavarres being close – BBC Sport -
https://www.bbc.co.uk/sport/football/66676558

Leeds wanting Williams – The Telegraph - https://www.telegraph.co.uk/football/2023/11/03/steve-cooper-nottingham-forest-marinakis-yates-results/

Dominguez fee – Fabrizio Romano (via Twitter) - https://twitter.com/FabrizioRomano/status/1697643639978045802

Freuler fee for Bologna – Gazetta dello Sport (via Football Italia) - https://football-italia.net/bologna-and-nottingham-forest-finalise-dominguez-freuler-swap-deal-the-details/

Freuler comments on Cooper – Football Italia - https://football-italia.net/freuler-reveals-fall-out-with-nottingham-forest-coach-that-led-to-bologna-move/

Hudson-Odoi fee – The Telegraph - https://www.telegraph.co.uk/football/2023/09/01/transfer-deadline-day-2023-live-countdown-premier-league/

Forest beat Fulham to Hudson-Odoi signing – BBC Sport - https://www.bbc.co.uk/sport/football/66689010

Chelsea reject £70m offer for Hudson-Odoi from Bayern – Sky Sports - https://www.skysports.com/football/news/11668/12089273/callum-hudson-odoi-chelsea-reject-bayern-munich-bid-for-forward

Vlachodimos fee – Jornal de Notícas - https://www.jn.pt/3571545377/venda-de-vlachodimos-rendeu-cerca-de-cinco-milhoes-de-euros-ao-benfica/

Marinakis wanting a Greek international at Forest – Radar (via Nottingham Forest News) -
https://www.nottinghamforest.news/2023/09/13/report-shares-why-marinakis-really-wanted-nottingham-forest-to-sign-odysseas-vlachodimos/

Sangaré fee – Daily Mail -
https://www.dailymail.co.uk/sport/football/article-12472313/Nottingham-Forest-confirm-signing-Ibrahim-Sangare-PSV-30m-Ivorian-midfielder-Steve-Coopers-13th-summer-signings.html

Liverpool, PSG and Bayern chasing Sangaré – Goal -
https://www.goal.com/en-gb/news/liverpool-psg-bayern-ibrahim-sangare-nottingham-forest-bid-psv-rejected/blt9d6081117fc3b84a

Caicedo fee of £115m – Sky Sports -
https://www.skysports.com/football/news/11741/12939945/moises-caicedo-chelsea-sign-brighton-midfielder-for-british-record-fee-of-gbp115m

Cooper's superstitious towel – Hayters TV (via Twitter) -
https://twitter.com/HaytersTV/status/1698066408083476579?ref_src=twsrc%5Etfw%7Ctwcamp%5Etweetembed%7Ctwterm%5E1698066408083476579%7Ctwgr%5Ee3ce4a1e57a3904ecfce22ba673ace731130588%7Ctwcon%5Es1_&ref_url=https%3A%2F%2Ftribuna.com%2Fen%2Fnews%2Ffootball-2023-09-04-im-sweating-my-b-off-steve-cooper-reacts-to-schoolboy-error-he-made-against-chelsea%2F

CHAPTER FOURTEEN

Cooper's comments post Chelsea (A) – Nottingham Forest (via YouTube) - https://www.youtube.com/watch?v=WlJaQ5syRwg

Awoniyi matches African stat – Premier League (via Instagram) - https://www.instagram.com/premierleague/p/CwakefQIf-g/

Chelsea enquire for Awoniyi – The Athletic - https://www.nytimes.com/athletic/4835013/2023/09/07/forest-transfer-window-summer-2023/

Marinakis comments, Randall out and Cartledge in as chairman – Nottingham Forest - https://www.nottinghamforest.co.uk/news/2023/september/04/statement-from-owner--evangelos-marinakis/

Shelvey confusion, Forest initially announcing his departure as a loan before terminating his deal – The Guardian - https://www.theguardian.com/football/2024/jan/03/nottingham-forest-face-questions-over-jonjo-shelveys-confused-exit-from-club

Cooper comments post Burnley (H) – BBC Sport - https://www.bbc.co.uk/sport/football/66771266

Cooper comments post City (A) – BBC Sport - https://www.bbc.co.uk/sport/football/66828987

McKenna contract dispute before Man City game – The Telegraph - https://www.telegraph.co.uk/football/2023/12/07/steve-cooper-joe-worrall-nottingham-forest-captain/

Reason for McKenna contract dispute – The Telegraph -
https://www.telegraph.co.uk/football/2023/12/19/steve-cooper-sacked-nottingham-forest-manager-marinakis/

Cooper and Marinakis agreeing McKenna's priority wasn't Forest –
The Athletic -
https://www.nytimes.com/athletic/5124157/2023/12/20/steve-cooper-nottingham-forest-exit/

Cooper explains dropping Gibbs-White for Brentford (H) – Sky
Sports (via Nottingham Post) -
https://www.nottinghampost.com/sport/football/football-news/steve-cooper-explains-surprise-morgan-8795154

Cooper frustrated with so many deadline day arrivals, Worrall
reacting badly to being dropped and not attending Villa game –
The Telegraph -
https://www.telegraph.co.uk/football/2023/12/19/steve-cooper-sacked-nottingham-forest-manager-marinakis/

Cooper tells Turner he has faith in him after Brentford – The
Athletic -
https://www.nytimes.com/athletic/5024246/2023/11/03/turner-vlachodimos-forest-goalkeeper/

Awoniyi groin injury – Nottingham Post -
https://www.nottinghampost.com/sport/football/football-news/nottingham-forest-injury-news-awoniyi-8813860

Cooper comments post Palace (A) – BBC Sport -
https://www.bbc.co.uk/sport/football/66969156

Hudson-Odoi injury – Nottingham Post -
https://www.nottinghampost.com/sport/football/football-news/nottingham-forest-injury-hudson-odoi-8848246

Hudson-Odoi training away from main Chelsea group – The Telegraph -
https://www.telegraph.co.uk/football/2023/07/11/romelu-lukaku-miss-chelsea-return-inter-milan/

Yates and Kouyaté stats – Sofascore -
https://www.sofascore.com/football/match/luton-town-nottingham-forest/osxb#id:11352665

Boly needing to be subbed – The Athletic -
https://www.nytimes.com/athletic/4985540/2023/10/23/forest-luton-blame/

Wood injury – The Times (via Twitter) -
https://twitter.com/CharDuncker/status/1718623018950304243

Turner not playing until he was 14 – The Athletic -
https://www.nytimes.com/athletic/3342477/2022/05/31/matt-turner-usmnt-arsenal/

Cooper comments on goalkeeping situation – Nottingham Post -
https://www.nottinghampost.com/sport/football/football-news/nottingham-forest-cooper-turner-goalkeepers-8882412

CHAPTER FIFTEEN

Worrall row with Cooper, exiled with McKenna, Cooper and Marinakis ignoring each other's phone calls, players annoyed at team selection, Lopetegui wanting a bigger job, Marinakis unconvinced by Glasner – The Telegraph -
https://www.telegraph.co.uk/football/2023/12/19/steve-cooper-sacked-nottingham-forest-manager-marinakis/

Cooper comments post West Ham (A) – BBC Sport -
https://www.bbc.co.uk/sport/football/67325042

Forest players called up for November internationals – Nottingham Forest -
https://www.nottinghamforest.co.uk/news/2023/november/14/november-internationals--19-reds-called-up/

Awoniyi aggravates injury – BBC Sport -
https://www.bbc.co.uk/sport/football/67506385

Sangaré suffers malaria, loses weight as a result – The Athletic -
https://www.nytimes.com/athletic/5564710/2024/06/24/ibrahim-sangare-nottingham-forest-future/

Sangaré doing well statistically, being played in an advanced position – The Athletic -
https://www.nytimes.com/athletic/5113814/2023/12/06/steve-cooper-forest-fix/

Dunk sent off for personally abusive language – Daily Mail -
https://www.dailymail.co.uk/sport/football/article-12791287/Lewis-Dunk-shown-straight-RED-card-dissent-Anthony-

Taylor-Brightons-win-Nottingham-Forest-NOT-second-yellow-language-personally-abusive.html

Forest boardroom remaining calm, but Lopetegui respected – The Athletic -
https://www.nytimes.com/athletic/5089601/2023/11/26/steve-cooper-under-pressure/

Marinakis wanting a set-piece coach, Vio set to sign but move falls through, Marinakis wanting a return on his £250m investment since promotion and frustrated with results – The Telegraph -
https://www.telegraph.co.uk/football/2023/11/27/nottingham-forest-owner-evangelos-marinakis-steve-cooper/

Cooper vetoed Vio move hence it falling through, Cooper and Marinakis relationship fractious in last months, Cooper asks for Rusk, Cooper insists on saying goodbye to Marinakis personally – The Athletic -
https://www.nytimes.com/athletic/5124157/2023/12/20/steve-cooper-nottingham-forest-exit/

Cooper comments pre Everton (H) – BBC Sport -
https://www.bbc.co.uk/programmes/p0gwx5zs

Cooper comments post Everton (H), Awoniyi stat – BBC Sport -
https://www.bbc.co.uk/sport/football/67528612

Marinakis' AAA pass thrown in a hedge – Twitter -
https://twitter.com/dommanning/status/1732514357643255904

Cooper comments post Fulham (A) – BBC Sport
https://www.bbc.co.uk/sport/football/67562710

Cooper to get the Wolves game, but will be sacked if Forest lose, Marinakis concerned at direction, felt Cooper was being worn down, discontent among players, concern over tactics – Sky Sports - https://www.skysports.com/football/news/11095/13025044/steve-cooper-nottingham-forest-expected-to-sack-manager-if-they-lose-at-wolves

Cooper insists he wasn't saying goodbye to fans after Wolves (A), club sound out Glasner and Lopetegui – The Telegraph - https://www.telegraph.co.uk/football/2023/12/09/wolves-vs-nottingham-result-forest-steve-cooper-fans-chant/

Apology after commenting on Cooper's physical features – Twitter - https://x.com/FFTV_Forest_Ant/status/1736173171374489901

Forest hire Rusk – Daily Mail - https://www.dailymail.co.uk/sport/football/article-12862987/Nottingham-Forest-Simon-Rusk-specialist-set-piece-coach.html

Cooper comments post Tottenham (H) – Nottingham Post - https://www.nottinghampost.com/sport/football/football-news/nottingham-forest-steve-cooper-spurs-8978229

Forest sack Cooper – Nottingham Forest - https://www.nottinghamforest.co.uk/news/2023/december/19/Nottingham-Forest-confirm-departure-of-head-coach-Steve-Cooper/

Marinakis Jnr tweet – Twitter - https://x.com/mil7iadis/status/1737196397496078470/photo/1

Worrall waiting for Cooper – Daniel Taylor (via Twitter) -
https://x.com/DTathletic/status/1802320967298891862

Cooper says goodbye to terminally ill fan – The Athletic -
https://www.nytimes.com/athletic/5566790/2024/06/20/steve-
cooper-leicester-nottingham-forest/

Forest hire Nuno – Nottingham Forest -
https://www.nottinghamforest.co.uk/news/2023/december/20/fo
rest-appoint-nuno-espirito-santo-as-head-coach/

Cooper's Forest stats – Transfermaekt -
https://www.transfermarkt.co.uk/steve-
cooper/leistungsdatenDetail/trainer/37574/verein_id/703/datum_
zu/2021-09-21/datum_ab/2023-12-19

EPILOGUE

Nuno thanks Cooper – BBC Sport -
https://www.bbc.co.uk/sport/football/67767628

Mariankis thought process re new signings – The Telegraph -
https://www.telegraph.co.uk/football/2023/12/19/steve-cooper-
sacked-nottingham-forest-manager-marinakis/

Marinakis couldn't quite understand Cooper's popularity in bad times, stories being planted in the media, club social accounts not promoting Cooper, Cooper's closest advisors suggesting he resign after survival – The Athletic -

https://www.nytimes.com/athletic/5124157/2023/12/20/steve-cooper-nottingham-forest-exit/

Forest charged with breaching PSR – BBC Sport - https://www.bbc.co.uk/sport/football/67978537

Forest given points deduction – The Guardian - https://www.theguardian.com/football/2024/mar/18/nottingham-forest-docked-four-points-premier-league-financial-rules-breach-profitability-and-sustainability

Forest hire Clattenburg as referee analyst – Sky Sports - https://www.skysports.com/football/news/11727/13075734/mark-clattenburg-ex-premier-league-officials-referee-analyst-role-at-nottingham-forest-explained

Forest tweet after Everton (A) – Twitter - https://twitter.com/NFFC/status/1782056187652960764

Forest fined £750k for tweet – BBC Sport - https://www.bbc.co.uk/sport/football/articles/c33v274e7vdo

Neville comment, Forest sue, Sky apology – Daily Mail - https://www.dailymail.co.uk/sport/football/article-13604205/Sky-Sports-Nottingham-Forest-Gary-Neville-Premier-League.html

Clattenburg resigns – Sky Sports - https://www.skysports.com/football/news/11661/13128157/mark-clattenburg-resigns-from-nottingham-forest-role

Marinakis shares Key Match Incident panel findings – Daily Mail - https://www.dailymail.co.uk/sport/football/article-13412181/Gary-

Nevilles-comment-outrageous-NOT-Explosive-interview-Nottingham-Forest-owner-Evangelos-Marinakis.html

Wood comments on Nuno – New Zealand Herald - https://www.nzherald.co.nz/sport/all-whites-captain-chris-wood-reveals-his-staggering-future-ambition/VEK2WQOAU5BY5C2WJIIZU3OJ7Y/

Cartledge and Bradley – Nottinghamshire County Council - https://www.nottinghamshire.gov.uk/newsroom/news/nottinghamshire-county-council-and-nottingham-forest-fc-set-to-sign-up-to-a-new-partnership-agreement

Nuno pleads to stay at The City Ground – The Independent - https://www.independent.co.uk/sport/football/nuno-espirito-santo-nottingham-forest-premier-league-nottingham-city-council-luton-b2543632.html

Marinakis reveals expansion hopes for The City Ground – The Athletic - https://www.nytimes.com/athletic/5782559/2024/09/20/evangelos-marinakis-city-ground/

Cooper Palace's first choice, but didn't want to join midway through a season – Football Insider - https://www.footballinsider247.com/sources-crystal-palace-make-roy-hodgson-sack-decision-as-preferred-replacement-approached/

Sunderland, Burnley and Birmingham all keen on Cooper, Cooper not having to leave Nottinghamshire home as Leicester boss – The Athletic -

https://www.nytimes.com/athletic/5566790/2024/06/20/steve-cooper-leicester-nottingham-forest/

Leicester points deduction threat – Leicester City News - https://www.leicestercity.news/news/why-leicester-city-could-still-be-hit-with-a-points-deduction-this-season-despite-successful-appeal/

INDEX

Y

ABOUT THE AUTHOR

Since graduating from Southampton Solent University with a Sports Journalism degree, where he received a 2:1, Christian Brown has worked in a number of different content related roles, including as an Editor and a Content Manager. He has also worked on a freelance basis for several football focused websites, such as 90min and Nottingham Forest News. Christian is a Nottingham Forest season ticket holder and has been watching the Reds – home and away – since he was five. He is also one quarter of the Nottingham Forest podcast Red Side of the Trent. 'Just Can't Get Enough – The Steve Cooper Years' is his first book.